Dear Reader:

The book you are about to read is the latest bestseller from the St. Martin's True Crime Library, the imprint *The New York Times* calls "the leader in true crime!" The True Crime Library offers you fascinating accounts of the latest, most sensational crimes that have captured the national attention. St. Martin's is the publisher of John Glatt's riveting and horrifying SECRETS IN THE CELLAR, which shines a light on the man who shocked the world when it was revealed that he had kept his daughter locked in his hidden basement for 24 years. In the Edgar-nominated WRITTEN IN BLOOD, Diane Fanning looks at Michael Petersen, a Marine-turned-novelist found guilty of beating his wife to death and pushing her down the stairs of their home—only to reveal another similar death from his past. In the book you now hold, GOLDEN BOY, John Glatt returns to take an in-depth look at the life of a handsome, privileged young man, whose profound troubles led to an unspeakable act.

St. Martin's True Crime Library gives you the stories behind the headlines. Our authors take you right to the scene of the crime and into the minds of the most notorious murderers to show you what really makes them tick. St. Martin's True Crime Library paperbacks are better than the most terrifying thriller, because it's all true! The next time you want a crackling good read, make sure it's got the St. Martin's True Crime Library logo on the spine—you'll be up all night!

Charles E. Spicer, Jr.
Executive Editor, St. Martin's True Crime Library

ALSO BY JOHN GLATT

The Doomsday Mother
Golden Boy
The Perfect Father
The Family Next Door
My Sweet Angel
The Lost Girls
The Prince of Paradise
Love Her to Death
Lost and Found
Playing with Fire
Secrets in the Cellar
To Have and to Kill
Forgive Me, Father
The Doctor's Wife
One Deadly Night
Depraved
Cries in the Desert
For I Have Sinned
Evil Twins
Cradle of Death
Blind Passion
Deadly American Beauty
Never Leave Me
Twisted

Golden Boy

A Murder Among the Manhattan Elite

JOHN GLATT

St. Martin's Paperbacks

Published in the United States by St. Martin's Paperbacks, an imprint of St. Martin's Publishing Group.

GOLDEN BOY

For information, address St. Martin's Publishing Group, 120 Broadway, New York, NY 10271.

www.stmartins.com

ISBN: 978-1-250-08606-8

Our books may be purchased in bulk for promotional, educational, or business use. Please contact your local bookseller or the Macmillan Corporate and Premium Sales Department at 1-800-221-7945, ext. 5442, or by email at MacmillanSpecialMarkets@macmillan.com.

Printed in the United States of America

St. Martin's Press hardcover edition published 2021
St. Martin's Paperbacks edition / August 2022

10 9 8 7 6 5 4 3 2

For Peter Martin—the Pied Piper of public relations

CONTENTS

PROLOGUE

It was a routine Sunday afternoon for Thomas Gilbert Sr., the founder of a multimillion-dollar hedge fund and a longtime fixture on Wall Street. After playing two strenuous rounds of tennis at the River Club, he was relaxing in his bedroom watching a football game. Three days earlier, on New Year's Day 2015, the tall, athletic financier had quietly celebrated his seventieth birthday and showed no signs of slowing down.

Next door in the living room, his petite wife, Shelley, was chatting with friends on her laptop when the doorbell rang around 3:15 p.m. It was a surprise, as they weren't expecting anyone, and their doorman usually called to announce visitors.

Shelley opened the front door to find her son, Tommy, outside, wearing a hoodie and carrying a duffel bag. It was the first time she had seen him in five months; they had a difficult relationship, and he usually kept his distance. Shelley was delighted to see him, hoping it might be an encouraging sign of a better relationship between him and his father.

"He said it was real important," Shelley recalled. "He wanted to talk to Dad about business. I was thrilled."

As Tommy strolled into the apartment, he asked if his

younger sister, Bess, was there. Shelley told him she was at church.

Then he said he was hungry and asked his mother to go to the store and buy him a sandwich and a Coke. He told her to come back in an hour, so he would have enough time with his father. Unsure whether they should be left alone together, Shelley offered to make him a sandwich, but Tommy insisted she go.

As his sixty-five-year-old mother laced up her sneakers to leave, she looked up at Tommy and thought, *I don't like hoodies. They're a little creepy.*

Thomas Strong Gilbert Jr. was born into a world of wealth and privilege. He had an impeccable social pedigree, growing up in a mansion in Tuxedo Park, New York, before moving to a Manhattan apartment on Park Avenue and a town house on the Upper East Side.

He had the finest education money could buy, going to the Buckley School and then Deerfield Academy, where he shone at varsity football, basketball, and baseball. A straight A student, Tommy had an IQ of 140, was fluent in Mandarin Chinese, and excelled at higher mathematics.

"He is an excellent role model for our younger students," his Deerfield Academy college adviser wrote. "He will only get better as he continues to mature."

Known to everyone as Tommy, his movie star looks turned women's heads. Blond, blue-eyed, and six feet three inches tall, designer clothes framed his muscular body, carefully sculpted from daily workouts in the gym. He followed in his father's and grandfather's footsteps to attend Princeton University, where he majored in economics and graduated with honors.

Like a modern-day Jay Gatsby, he moved in the rarest of

social circles, the epitome of the rich, successful man-about-town. He was frequently seen in the society pages, squiring a beautiful socialite to a Manhattan black-tie event or attending a charity event in the Hamptons.

"He has the pedigree of this incredibly sophisticated person," explained a friend. "But the mind and the skin are two different things."

Underneath the carefully groomed façade was a socially anxious man with a long history of drug abuse and psychiatric illness.

After leaving Princeton, his much-anticipated career in high finance had failed to ignite. He told friends he was starting a hedge fund with his own secret algorithm, even registering the name Mameluke Capital with the Securities and Exchange Commission. But after twice failing the Chartered Financial Analyst Level II exam, essential for entrée to Wall Street, he had been reduced to a series of short-lived bartending jobs and giving surfing lessons to kids.

At the age of thirty, Tommy was still being supported by his father, who paid the rent for his Manhattan apartment as well as a generous $800 weekly allowance. He also paid for his sporty Jeep, expensive club memberships, and all other expenses.

At the end of 2014, Thomas Gilbert Sr., whose Wainscott Capital Partners hedge fund was itself struggling, had started cutting his son's weekly allowance, hoping to force him to get a real job.

On the morning of Tommy's visit that fateful Sunday, he had slashed it down to just $300 a week and knew his son would not be pleased.

After leaving her tony Beekman Place apartment building, Shelley Gilbert walked around the block. She felt uneasy, knowing her husband and son would be discussing the latest cut in Tommy's allowance. She wondered if it had been a bad idea to leave Tommy alone with his father, in case they argued.

So turning on her heel, she headed straight back to her apartment building, taking the elevator up to the eighth floor. Nervous about disturbing them, she first listened at the door, but could not hear anything. She paced up and down the hallway, trying to make up her mind what to do.

Finally, Shelley unlocked the door with her key and walked in. There was no sign of Tommy, although she'd only been gone a few minutes.

Then she went into the bedroom to find her husband lying dead on the floor. There was blood pooling from his head and a .40-caliber Glock clasped in his left hand over his chest.

"My first thought," she later recalled, "was 'Oh, Tommy, you are far sicker than we even knew.'"

PART 1

1

TO THE MANNER BORN

Thomas Gilbert Jr. could trace his illustrious family roots back ten generations to Robert Treat, the founder of Newark, New Jersey. Born in 1625 in Pitminster, England, Robert emigrated to America with his family at the age of fifteen, settling down in the newly established colony of Connecticut.

On Christmas Day 1647, the twenty-two-year-old Treat married Jane Tapp in Milford, Connecticut, who would go on to bear him eight children. He became a magistrate and served in the town militia. When the Connecticut and New Haven colonies unified in 1664, Treat, a deeply religious Puritan, led his followers on a pilgrimage to build a new religious settlement in New Jersey.

Two years later, he traded land by the Passaic River from the Hackensack Indians for gunpowder, guns, axes, swords, and beer. He then supervised the foundation of Newark, building two major thoroughfares, Broad and Market Streets, and dividing the new settlement into six-acre plots. Originally named New Ark, it was later shortened to Newark.

In 1672, Robert Treat moved his family back to Milford, Connecticut, leading the colony's militia in King Philip's War between the English colonists and the Narragansett tribe. It would be the Native Americans' final effort to stop the English colonist settlements of their lands.

Treat served on the governor's council from 1676 to 1708, before twice being elected the governor of Connecticut. He died on July 12, 1710. His great-grandson Robert Treat Paine would go on to sign the Declaration of Independence.

Almost two hundred years later, on October 8, 1904, Wilton Treat Rea, a direct descendent of Governor Treat through his youngest son, Joseph, was born in New York. At the age of six, he inherited $1,000 ($123,000 today) from his grandfather Charles H. Treat, who ran a plumbing business in Queens.

Wilton attended Flushing High School before going to Princeton, where he was a fine athlete and competed in the annual Caledonian Games. In March 1926, he was one of twenty seniors elected to Princeton's Phi Beta Kappa honorary scholastic fraternity. Three months later, he graduated Princeton magna cum laude with a BS degree in physics.

Rea began his career at the American Telephone and Telegraph Company's Department of Division and Development. Then in 1934, he joined Bell Telephone Labs, based in Holmdel, New Jersey, as an assistant vice president.

On August 25, 1934, Rea married Clare Hickey in Greenwich, Connecticut, and five years later, they had their first child, Suzanne. A son, William, followed in 1943, and six years later, Shelley was born.

During World War II, Wilton Rea served in the Marine Corps, developing radar systems. After his discharge, he returned to work for Bell Telephone Labs, receiving seventy-three patents in telegraphy, signaling, radar, and data transmission over the course of his illustrious career.

In the early 1950s, Rea was recruited by the U.S. Defense Department as an electronics consultant, where he pioneered early computer technology.

The Rea family lived in a splendid mansion on the exclusive Mine Brook Road in Bernardsville, New Jersey. Suzanne and Shelley Rea both attended the expensive Gill School for Girls, where their father was on the board of trustees.

Founded by Miss Elizabeth Gill in 1934, the Bernardsville school emphasized individuality, with small classes to provide a "rich school experience." As part of the curriculum, students spent at least two hours a day outdoors in the beautiful surrounding New Jersey countryside.

"It was lovely," remembered Shelley. "Lots of grazing and provincials out in the country. I loved growing up there."

In April 1957, the Gill School held a fashion show at the Somerset Hills Country Club, and ten-year-old Shelley Rea was one of the models. Two years later, she was pictured in *The Bernardsville News,* vying for the honor of being selected as the Gill School Carnival May Queen.

As one of New Jersey's most socially prominent families, the Reas' activities were closely followed in all the local newspapers.

"Bill Rea, son of Mr. and Mrs. Wilton T. Rea has a Summer job on a ranch in Chino, California," reported the *Plainfield Courier-News* on July 8, 1958. "He will be home to attend his sister's wedding Aug. 23."

Suzanne Rea's lavish wedding to H. Rowland Vermilye made the front page of the *Courier-News*. The ceremony was held in the Church of Saint John on the Mountain, Bernardsville, and Shelley was a bridesmaid.

"A reception was held in the Essex Hunt Club," read the report. "The bride is a descendant of Robert Treat, colonial governor of Connecticut."

Wilton Treat Rea's career in communications was soaring. In 1960, Bell Labs appointed him executive director, in charge of an ambitious project to build a new communication system for the military. But he was secretly struggling with depression, although he kept it well hidden from his family and business associates and never let it affect his work.

Two years later, he moved his family into Cannon Hill Farm, one of the oldest and most beautiful stately homes in Monmouth County, New Jersey. The early-American farmhouse in Holmdel Township dated back to the late 1600s. A larger wing with a spacious living room, dining room, hall, and kitchen was added in 1758.

The breathtaking white-clapboard house, with black shutters, was on the original farm, with rolling lawns, restored barns, and outbuildings. It boasted a meadow with a brook, as well as a modern swimming pool and poolside changing house.

In the early nineteenth century, Greek revival columns had been added on the porch and marble-faced mantels to the original fireplaces.

"The attractive and energetic Mrs. Rea," wrote the *Daily Record* newspaper, "has devoted much of her time and talent to renovating the newer wing of the old house."

The living room walls were covered with gold draperies, and ancient oriental rugs lined the floors. It was furnished with eighteenth-century English antiques, including Clare Rea's own handcrafted needlepoint chair seats.

But one particular family heirloom stood out.

"Notable among them is a small mahogany piece used as a desk by the Reas," the *Daily Record* reported. "This was once the dressing table of Robert Treat, who was one of Mr. Rea's ancestors."

In May 1965, the Reas opened Cannon Hill Farm up to the public for a hospital charity event. To mark the occasion, the *Asbury Park Press* ran a full-page feature entitled, LET'S VISIT: MR. AND MRS. WILTON T. REA.

"The restored early American home of Mr. and Mrs. Wilton T. Rea," began the piece, "is so beautifully done, without losing its authenticity, that it probably has surpassed even its original charm."

It then took readers on a tour of the house starting with the family sitting room, which included a small, paneled den "where Mr. Rea has a display of antique guns."

The centerpiece of the double-page feature was a large photo of a smiling Clare Rea by the fireplace, wearing a tailored skirt and jacket ensemble. A large portrait of King William III of England hung above her.

Readers were then taken up the back staircase to the bedrooms, cleverly concealed behind a door next to the fireplace.

"Daughter Shelley's room has a mahogany four poster bed," it reported, "white cover, delft blue wall to wall carpeting and blue and white flowered wallpaper. Her pink and white bath has rose paper."

On December 20, 1965, eighteen-year-old Shelley Rea made her debut at the annual Debutante Cotillion and Christmas Ball at the Waldorf Astoria. Wearing the traditional long white ball gown and white gloves, Shelley stood in the receiving line to make her bow and be officially welcomed into New York society.

Six months later, sixty-one-year-old Wilton Treat Rea was admitted into the Silver Hill psychiatric hospital in New Canaan, Connecticut, suffering from acute depression. Diagnosed as bipolar four years earlier, he had been in and out of psychiatric hospitals ever since.

"I remember my father seemed a lot quieter than he

usually was," recalled Shelley, "so I asked my mother if something was wrong at work. And she said, 'No, nothing.' But she had noticed it too and was concerned."

Rea entered the psychiatric hospital on May 14, and was placed in a single room on the sixth floor. He was confined to that floor and only allowed to leave with a member of staff to meet his psychiatrist for therapy.

At 4:00 p.m. on Thursday, June 2, Rea told a nurse that he was feeling fine. After she'd left his room, he sneaked downstairs to the fifth floor, which was unoccupied because of construction work. He then went into a bathroom, opened the window, and jumped out.

A ten-year-old girl saw him plunge eighty feet to his death. At 4:55 p.m., Wilton Treat Rea was pronounced dead at the scene.

His tragic suicide made front pages everywhere.

HOSPITAL PATIENT JUMPS TO DEATH FROM 5TH FLOOR was the headline in the *Greenwich Time*.

"This was a most unfortunate accident," Silver Hill Hospital director William J. Donnelly told a reporter.

Four days after his death, Wilton Treat Rea was buried at the Church of Saint John on the Mountain, with two members of his Princeton class of 1926 attending.

Shelley Rea was devastated, after seeing her father struggling with mental illness for so long. And his tragic death would have a lasting effect on her and her mother as they soldiered on to the next chapter of their lives.

"It was very brutal," Shelley remembered, "and you have to deal with it the best you can."

After her husband's suicide, Clare Rea sold Cannon Hill Farm and moved into River House, an exclusive art deco–style co-op apartment building on East Fifty-Second Street near Sutton Place. Built in the 1930s on the banks of the East River, River House was intended for the crème de la crème of New York society.

"The assumption was that at River House one had a community made up entirely of people who were socially beyond reproach," wrote historian Michael Henry Adams. "Becoming a shareholder at River House, conferred automatic eligibility on one for River Club membership too."

Occupying five levels at the base of River House, the River Club has been called "New York Society's favorite family club."

The River Club boasted two tennis courts, three squash courts, a pool, and a gym. But its crown jewel was the majestic ballroom, with its blue glass and silver leaf panels.

Shelley and her mother would frequently entertain friends at their palatial apartment, which would be written up in the society columns.

Soon after they moved to Manhattan, Shelley was sent to the prestigious Ethel Walker private boarding school for girls in Simsbury, Connecticut. She then went to Hollins College, now a university in Roanoke, Virginia, which boasted the motto: "Women who are going places start at Hollins."

After graduating with a BA in economics, Shelley entered the business world, landing a job at New Court Securities Corporation. The investment bank specialized in handling American investments for the European-based Rothschild banking family. With all her New York society connections, Shelley was a valuable asset to the company. Over the next few years, she would work her way up to vice president, running the corporate underwriting department.

* * *

Around 1980, Shelley Rea attended a charity benefit party in Manhattan, where she struck up a conversation with a tall, handsome Wall Streeter named Thomas Gilbert. They discussed their careers in finance and at the end of the night swapped phone numbers.

When he called the following Tuesday to ask her out on a date, Shelley couldn't quite place him, but agreed to go anyway.

"We went to a discothèque called the Hippopotamus for drinks," she fondly remembered. "Three-quarters of the way through, I wanted to give him a shake and say, 'Where have you been all these years?'"

2

"A CERTAIN GATSBY-ESQUE QUALITY"

William and Jennie Goldberg were children of Russian emigrants who had arrived in America in the late nineteenth century. They soon changed their last name to Gilbert and went on to have fourteen children, including Thomas Strong Gilbert's father, Abner.

Abner Ira Gilbert was born in New York City on June 1, 1905. Growing up into a hardworking and ambitious young man, Abner was accepted by Brown University in Rhode Island. As a handsome six-foot-one-inch sophomore, Abner was a fine tennis player and won one of Brown's most coveted tennis awards.

He graduated in 1926, joining a garment company called Roth Fabrics Inc. as a textile salesman. At the age of thirty-four, he got engaged to Mabelle Strong Harris, who came from one of Poughkeepsie's best families.

They married in January 1940 and went to live on West Eighty-Sixth Street on Manhattan's fashionable Upper West Side.

During World War II, Abner served in the U.S. Army and after his discharge went to work for his uncle H. Walter Gilbert, whose Cutting Room Appliances (CRA) Corporation had become the world's leading manufacturer of cloth-spreading machines.

H. Walter had made a fortune inventing industrial machines, which had revolutionized the textile industry. He and his wife, Greta, were also part of the fashionable New York and Palm Beach social set, where they wintered each year.

Now in his late fifties and ready to retire, H. Walter mentored his nephew with a view to him taking over his business one day. He appointed Abner chairman and CEO of the company, and over the next few years, they would jointly invent several lucrative textile machines.

H. Walter and Greta retired to Palm Beach in the late 1940s, and Abner went on to run the company for the next two decades. H. Walter Gilbert died in April 1951 in a Palm Beach hospital at the age of sixty-one.

On February 8, 1942, Abner and Mabelle Gilbert had a son they named George Seymour Beckwith Gilbert. On January 1, 1945, Thomas Strong Gilbert was born.

Thomas grew up in a life of luxury, in a smart Park Avenue apartment. His first memory was having his photograph taken in Central Park, safely strapped into his stroller to prevent him falling out.

"According to my mother," he would later explain, "I was a rather large and active baby."

Abner Gilbert, affectionately known as Papa, gave his sons a top-tier education, sending Tom, as he was then known, to the elite Buckley School on Manhattan's Upper East Side. After graduating in 1958, he went to Phillips Academy in Andover, Massachusetts. One of his proudest memories was being awarded the Butler-Thwing Academic Award in his freshman year for the highest entering academic achievements. At Andover, he made the honor roll four terms running, excelling at soccer, squash, and tennis.

By his late teens, Tom Gilbert stood six feet six inches tall, with a winning charm that endeared him to everyone. He had an offbeat sense of humor and was affectionately known to his friends as "Gilbo" or "Trunk."

When he graduated in 1962, his senior photograph presented a well-groomed, exceptionally handsome young man, wearing a classic Ivy League jacket and tie, sporting a sharp preppy haircut.

Tom Gilbert followed his older brother, Beckwith, known to the family as Beck, to Princeton, where he joined the legendary Colonial Club. Founded in 1891, the Colonial was immortalized by F. Scott Fitzgerald, who referred to it as the "flamboyant Colonial" in his novel *This Side of Paradise.*

Tom fitted right into the Colonial Club with his refined country gentleman style, often mixing corduroy trousers with saddle shoes.

"He had a certain Gatsby-esque quality," remembered Lanny Jones, a fellow member of the Colonial. "He was refined in his manner . . . the beau ideal of a college student."

Tom was also an outstanding athlete, playing varsity squash, tennis, and soccer.

"We both played on the same soccer team in our freshman year," said Jones. "He was quite a good midfielder."

Tom's best friend and roommate was Lew Polk Rutherfurd, who would soon marry Jackie Kennedy's half sister Janet Auchincloss. At Princeton, the two were inseparable, sharing many rowdy adventures.

Late one Saturday night in their sophomore year, Tom bet Rutherfurd "the outrageous sum of twenty dollars" that he could run naked from their dormitory to the Firestone Library and back.

"I rather unceremoniously streaked out of the dorm as Lew attempted to keep up with me," wrote Gilbert in his class of 1966 reunion book. "I must confess that I don't ever remember running that fast either before or afterwards in my life."

Halfway to the library, Rutherfurd stopped to round up people to watch the naked Gilbert on his way back to the dorm.

"I was pleasantly surprised to be the center of attention," recalled Gilbert, "as a small, civilized group, and several cars with headlights glaring, appeared on the scene as I came streaking back. I didn't stop to notice if the group included any ex-girlfriends, proctors, or professors. I can say with the greatest certitude that I learned a lot at Princeton."

Apart from the occasional high jinks, Tom Gilbert was an excellent student. He chose public and international affairs as his major, writing a thesis on the constitutional philosophy of the renowned nineteenth-century U.S. Supreme Court Justice Benjamin R. Curtis.

In his senior year, Gilbert was a member of the Jamesburg Reformatory Program, helping juvenile delinquents in one of New Jersey's most infamous detention centers.

In 1966, Tom Gilbert graduated Princeton with a BA. "Business or law wait in an undecided future for Tom," read his entry in the Princeton yearbook, listing his smart Park Avenue address. He then went on to Harvard Business School, achieving an MBA in finance and general management.

Tom Gilbert soon found work on Wall Street as a financial consultant to the investment banking house of Allen & Company. His career took off as he worked for the global asset management company White Weld & Co. and Reynolds Securities, a long-established brokerage firm.

For the next few years, he lived "a carefree existence" with an apartment in New York and a house in Bridgehampton. By the time he met Shelley Rea at a Manhattan dance party in 1980, he was ready to settle down and start a family.

In early 1981, a few months after their first date, Tom Gilbert proposed marriage to Shelley Rea and she accepted. He would later describe it as a "momentous event."

They married on Saturday, September 26, 1981, at the iconic Saint Bartholomew's Episcopal church in midtown Manhattan. The following day, the *New York Times* Style section reported the wedding under the headline SHELLEY REA HAS BRIDAL with a picture of the bride.

The newlyweds settled down in Tower Road Hill, Tuxedo Park, New York, forty miles north of Manhattan.

"I decided the proper move was to buy a house," explained Tom. "I thus purchased a small mansion . . . in Tuxedo Park."

In June 1982, Shelley proposed Tom for legacy membership of the exclusive River Club. From then on, the River Club would become a central part of their lives.

Tom played tennis and squash, competing in matches all over the world. He also played the eight-hundred-year-old racket game of court tennis. Unlike the modern game, court tennis uses handmade balls with a cork core, which play entirely differently. Tuxedo Park boasted one of only ten courts in the United States. One of Tom Gilbert's proudest achievements was playing "rather effectively" with a 102-degree fever in the Tiffany Cup national court tennis tournament in Newport, Rhode Island.

Over the next few years, they lovingly renovated their home, commuting into Manhattan for their respective high-power jobs in finance. Settled down in their beautiful mansion upstate, Tom and Shelley knew they were ready to start a family.

3

WORLD'S GREATEST DAD

On July 13, 1984, Tom Gilbert was in the delivery room to witness the birth of his son, Thomas Strong Gilbert Jr. Later, Tom would humorously describe the birth in his fellow Princeton class of 1966 reunion book.

"The greatest spectator sport," he wrote, "was participating with Shelley using . . . the Le Mas [sic] technique while she deftly delivered Tommy."

From an early age, the Gilberts' son stood out with a keen intelligence and a thirst to learn. He had a fascination with numbers before he could talk, and from the beginning, according to his mother, would set himself goals to accomplish.

In April 1984, Tom Gilbert had joined Loeb Partners Corporation, one of Wall Street's last independent investment banking firms, eventually working his way up to managing director. He loved undertaking "difficult financing challenges" and raising capital for his clients.

Shelley was still working for New Court Securities, which had recently been renamed Rothschild Inc. But in 1985, she retired from her job to become a full-time mother for Tommy.

Tom Sr. loved playing with his little son and taught him to play baseball outside on the lawn of their Tuxedo Park home.

"They had a great time together," recalled Shelley. "They

spent hours wrestling each other on the floor or watching sports on television."

A strikingly handsome little boy, Tommy had bright blue eyes and long, curly blond hair. In one of his mother's favorite photographs, an infant Tommy stands in a rustic field in a baggy woolen sweater with a wide grin. He looks like an angel.

In 1989, Tom Gilbert moved his family from Tuxedo Park into a large apartment in a luxury building on East Eightieth Street. It was just seven blocks north of the Buckley School, where Tom Sr. was now on the alumni board. He arranged for Tommy to take an ERB (Educational Records Bureau) test for admission to Buckley's nursery school.

Tommy and five other boys sat the test in a classroom, while their parents were interviewed in another room. With an almost perfect score, Tommy was welcomed into the beginners class.

Founded in 1913 by Professor B. Lord Buckley, the Buckley School had a well-earned reputation for excellence. With its Latin motto, "Honor et Veritas" (Honor and Truth), it had educated some of New York's richest and most privileged boys. Tuition costs ran $30,000 a year.

"The school strives to educate the whole boy," read the Buckley manifesto. "Foster a lifelong love of learning and develop personal integrity and respect for others."

Parents were expected to participate in hallowed events like the Mother-Son Heritage Lunch and the Father-Son Overnight camping trip to Lakeville, Connecticut. Every September, Tom would accompany his son on the camping trips, playing baseball and eating dinner over a campfire.

* * *

Little Tommy Gilbert fitted right into Buckley, forging friendships that would last for years. Bart Hayes (not his real name) was in the same class as Tommy and would remain close to him right through to the ninth grade.

"We were good friends," said Hayes. "He was a little bit quiet but certainly had a goofy sense of humor. He was fun."

A few months after Tommy started at Buckley, Shelley Gilbert gave birth to a baby girl, Bess. Once again, Tom Sr. penned an amusing account of her birth.

"I remember going into the delivery room with Bess on the way," he wrote, "and being somewhat panic stricken because the doctor was on another floor, hobnobbing with one of the more attractive night nurses. He did arrive in time to put on his delivery jacket before Bess was born. Shelley does not believe in wasting her time."

At the time, Tom's career on Wall Street was taking off, and he had an excellent reputation as a tough negotiator who always sealed the deal.

A workaholic, Tom rose at 4:30 a.m. and was always in motion. When he came home from work, he enjoyed quality time with Shelley and the children. The Gilberts would eat "family dinner" together and discuss their day. Shelley kept "a watchful eye for burnout," always trying to keep the dinner conversation light so her husband could relax after a long day's work.

"Life was hectic in those days," she recalled.

In the summer of 1991, Tom Gilbert attended the twenty-fifth reunion of his Princeton class of 1966. In his reunion book biography, he described Shelley as "wife and mother, and 'The Boss' of Gilbert, Gilbert, Gilbert and Gilbert & Company."

Next to it was a photograph of his six-year-old son, Tommy, and the baby, Bess.

Though Tom Sr.'s career kept the patriarch busy, the Gilberts seemed like the perfect American family, and Tom Sr. had an offbeat, quirky sense of humor, which his son would play off.

Once, he wagered to eat his hat if his little daughter accomplished some task. After she did it successfully, he gamely posed for a photograph with Tommy and Bess, pouring pepper on his hat before eating it.

On New Year's Day 1993, Tom Gilbert celebrated his forty-eighth birthday, and Tommy presented him with a "World's Greatest Dad" statuette. Tom loved it, and it became one of his most prized possessions.

The extra-tall financier was also delighted to receive a pair of blue jeans that actually fit.

"He was showing us his new jeans," recalls Shelley, "and Tommy took one look at them and thought a second. Then he put Bess inside one leg and himself in the other."

Tommy was a well-adjusted, happy little boy who got on well with his parents.

One summer, Tom sent his young son to the NASA space camp in Huntsville, Alabama, where he spent five days learning to be an astronaut. Activities included a simulated space shuttle mission, lectures, and movies about space exploration. It made such an impression on Tommy that for years he would tell friends that he wanted to be a NASA astronaut when he grew up.

His father could be somewhat overbearing, though, with his high expectations. He was proud of his only son and wanted him to follow in his footsteps on the path to excellence—and he would push hard for Tommy to get there.

4

THE MAIDSTONE CLUB

In early 1993, the Gilberts moved to a Park Avenue apartment, just two blocks from Central Park and only a short walk to the Buckley School.

Tom Gilbert also rented a place on the fashionable South Fork of Long Island for the season. The Gilberts had been accepted into the ultraexclusive Maidstone Club in East Hampton, considered to be the most prestigious, elite, and difficult club in the Hamptons to join.

They had been sponsored by no fewer than six Maidstone Club members, including Tom's elder brother, G. S. Beckwith Gilbert.

Founded in 1891 as a tennis and bathing club for wealthy summer residents, Maidstone is famous for its renowned eighteen-hole golf course. The Maidstone Club quickly became *the* summer retreat of New York's most socially prominent families, including Jacqueline Kennedy's father, John "Black Jack" Bouvier III.

"Because of its extraordinary assets and aura of exclusivity," wrote *Hamptons* magazine, "the club has been the envy of the East End's socially ambitious for decades."

The Gilberts were granted a family membership and came to view the club as their home away from home.

"We loved it," said Shelley. "Loved our life out there and had wonderful friendships."

Many of Tommy's friends at Buckley had parents who were Maidstone members, so he had lots of playmates.

The next summer, the Gilberts were back in their rental but determined to buy a place of their own. They eventually settled on a stunning 1930s cottage on the über-private Georgica Association Road in Wainscott, on the east end of Long Island.

The sprawling thirty-eight-thousand-square-foot, five-bedroom, four-bathroom home enjoyed magnificent views of the sunset, and from the deck, guests could see the ocean over farm fields. The house had a library, a large kitchen, and a living room boasting a fireplace. The property came with more than two and a half acres of land, including a swimming pool.

The home was part of the rarified Georgica Association, and the Gilberts automatically became members, entitling them to all association amenities. These included a private beach, ocean beach club, four tennis courts, and sailing on Georgica Pond.

Known as "the Settlement" to residents, the Georgica Association was founded in the late nineteenth century by banker William H. S. Wood, who bought 40 acres of land and sold off lots to his rich circle of friends. It became so popular that Wood bought more land, until it grew to its present 137 acres.

Today, there are only thirty-five homes in the private enclave, and it is rare for one to come on the market, as they are passed down from generation to generation.

"For anyone who knows the Hamptons," wrote Michael Braverman in a 2017 feature for *Hamptons,* "Georgica evokes history and charisma, character and a complexity—a mystique, if you will, that goes beyond geography."

On November 2, 1994, Tom Gilbert officially closed on 8 Georgica Association Road, paying $920,000 for the property. Shelley immediately took charge of renovating it. And for the next two decades, the gorgeous house would become the central part of their idyllic summers.

"God has really blessed us to have a house that we loved so much," said Shelley. "I never got over the fact, at the end of our road . . . was the beach."

These were transformative times for ten-year-old Tommy Gilbert. He adored the beach and learned to surf, which would become a lifelong passion. He was a strong swimmer and later became a Hamptons lifeguard four summers running.

Under his father's tutelage, he also became a skillful tennis player, competing in and winning many of the children's tennis tournaments at the Maidstone Club.

A photograph from those early days shows a smiling Tommy Gilbert at the Georgica Association beach with his parents, little sister, and Trigger, their beloved pet wheaten terrier. They look every inch the perfect American family, and little Tommy appears to have the world at his feet.

As Tommy progressed through the Buckley Lower and Middle Schools, he excelled at sports and was known as a team player. He was captain of the football team and a starting running back. Although he was naturally quiet, a good friend fondly remembers him as "socially affable."

But others said he could also be a "verbose and cocky" daredevil, who loved taking risks without ever considering the consequences. He would deliberately flaunt Buckley rules by "making jokes" in class and landing in trouble.

It was on the Buckley football team that Tommy first met Peter Smith Jr., who was a couple of years older. His father, Peter Smith Sr., was a Lazard Frères bank investment banker who rode the weekend jitney bus from Manhattan to the Hamptons with Tom Gilbert. His mother played tennis at the Maidstone Club with Shelley.

Chris Oliver (not his real name), who was in the academic year between Tommy and Peter Smith, knew both families well.

"[Tommy's] father was a very quiet, nice, friendly guy," said Oliver, "and very much like Tommy in a way. Not ostentatious at all. Not flashy. Just a good wholesome American family."

Tom and Shelley Gilbert ran what another friend described as a "1950s-style home," and Tommy and his sister were expected to do daily chores.

"We all depended on each other," said Shelley. "We were a happy, normal family."

While Tommy was in middle school, Shelley spent the summers supervising extensive renovations on the new Georgica Association house. She added a roof deck with sweeping views and extended the first and second floors.

Tom Gilbert would spend the week in Manhattan, where he was getting a new company, Knowledge Delivery Systems Inc., off the ground. The company provided online teacher education in over thirty-six states, as well as full online MBAs.

He appointed himself chairman and CEO, and his brother, Beck, had agreed to invest $700,000 in the company. By now, Beck had become a highly successful leveraged-buyout investor and philanthropist, running his company from Greenwich, Connecticut.

As he entered his teens, Tommy seemed a model Buckley pupil—although he had already learned to fake good behavior. He was a straight A student, a champion athlete, and a student council member. One classmate would later describe him as "a golden boy."

His parents were proud of his progress and had high hopes for his future.

"He was very bright," said his mother, "and he worked extremely hard to maximize his abilities. [He was] a good athlete and very focused on his sports."

But deep inside Tommy Gilbert's head, seeds of anxiety and paranoia were taking root. He started developing irrational fears of his father and some of his classmates. He experienced social anxiety and was becoming increasingly insecure.

Years later, Tommy would tell a psychiatrist that in the sixth grade something strange happened to his brain during a bus ride with a friend. He would describe it as the first time he experienced any mental problems and had no idea why.

"I didn't feel like myself," he explained. "This hadn't happened before. It was alarming because I immediately lost social skills. Luckily, my friend was listening to music at the time, so I didn't have to speak with him."

He also started having dreams about his father sadistically harassing him—and vice versa. In a recurring one, he would be kicking his father and shouting at him to stop upsetting him.

In another one, he'd be eating potato chips when his father

suddenly snatched them out of his hand and started yelling at him for no reason.

Up to that point, Tommy told the psychiatrist, he had adored his father and they had shared a great relationship. Then something changed.

Suddenly, Tommy Gilbert's relationship with his father started becoming more and more fraught. Tom Sr. would press his son to play tennis or take a certain course at school, but Tommy would refuse and get angry. He felt his father was overbearing and pushy, and Tommy stubbornly resisted him.

"They were both alpha males," explained Shelley. "Tommy didn't want to be told what to do."

One example of this was in the seventh grade when Tom wanted his son to go on a soccer trip to Stockholm to learn one of his favorite sports. Without consulting Tommy first, Tom Sr. called the Buckley coach, Per von Scheele, asking if Tommy could go to Sweden. But Von Scheele ruled him ineligible, as he was not on the soccer team. When Tommy found out, he felt humiliated and angry at his father for interfering in his life.

Tommy Gilbert was in the same class at Buckley as Nick McDonell, who would later write the bestseller *Twelve,* based on his own days at Buckley. The book was a thinly veiled exposé of sex and drugs among Manhattan's rich prep school boys and girls.

By the seventh grade, Tommy had started drinking and smoking marijuana with his friends. Later, he would boast to a girlfriend that he had actually lived a much wilder life at Buckley than McDonell ever had.

Therefore, he was furious when his father called the Buckley principal after that year's father-son camping weekend because Tom had heard rumors of the boys smoking marijuana. When Tommy found out, he was livid, afraid that he would lose all his friends, who would think he'd ratted them out.

In ninth grade, Tommy began committing minor acts of vandalism and bullying some of his classmates. He was already almost six feet tall and could be physically intimidating. After school, he and his friends would hang out outside the Spence School on East Ninety-First Street to meet girls and smoke cigarettes on the Metropolitan Museum of Art's lawn.

Tommy was part of a tight clique of half a dozen Buckley classmates who would party together on Friday and Saturday nights.

"It was usually at my spot," said Bart Hayes. "And we would pick one of our houses for the weekend and just hang out. We had girls over, play music, and try to get laid but fail. We'd smuggle beer up and a little weed every once in a while, but nothing too chaotic."

They all spent their long summer vacations in the Hamptons, hanging out together for impromptu parties.

"Tommy had a place in the Hamptons, and we were members at Maidstone," said Hayes, "so I'd see him throughout the summer as well."

One weekend, Tommy was invited to a birthday party in fashionable Locust Valley, Nassau County. He brought along some fireworks to liven things up. But when he set them off, they were far louder than anyone had expected, and the birthday boy's parents were furious. They demanded to know who had brought the fireworks and were told it was Tommy

Gilbert. Then they angrily confronted Tom Sr. and Shelley about how dangerous it could have been.

"Tommy's parents refused to believe it," a party attendee told *Vanity Fair* reporter Benjamin Wallace. "They said, 'No. We asked him—he said no. We don't think it happened.' So there was a tendency, when Tommy would do something extreme, for them to underplay it."

In June 2000, Tommy Gilbert graduated from Buckley and won an award for his excellent grades. He had been accepted at the prestigious Deerfield Academy in Massachusetts for tenth grade.

Before leaving for the boarding school, he summered in the Hamptons, working as a busboy at Maya's in East Hampton. His mother hoped that this was a sign that Tommy was improving.

"It was wonderful," said Shelley. "He was able to bike there [and] occasionally he would bring me home dessert, and we'd sit in the kitchen and talk."

A Buckley classmate had asked if he could stay at the Wainscott house for a few days that summer. Tommy didn't like him but felt unable to refuse, as the boy was at the hub of his social circle and it would have looked bad to snub him.

Ultimately, the boy spent four days at the Georgica Association house as Tommy gritted his teeth. It was a pivotal moment for the teenager, who became convinced that he had "caught depression" from this classmate.

"This was an annoying experience for me," he told a psychiatrist, "and triggered whatever depression/anxiety mechanism I was genetically disposed to."

Later, he would blame the boy for being the catalyst that caused his crippling mental downfall.

5

DEERFIELD

In the fall of 2000, Tommy Gilbert started his sophomore year at Deerfield Academy in western Massachusetts. Founded in 1797, Deerfield is one of the oldest secondary schools in the United States. Highly selective and coeducational, it has 650 pupils from all over the world with annual boarding fees of $54,000. Deerfield lays great emphasis on athletic prowess, and Tommy would shine in that regard, competing on its basketball, baseball, football, and cross-country teams against boarding and private schools from all over New England.

On the academic side, he joined the Algebra 2 accelerated course in advanced mathematics, but after two weeks decided he didn't like it, switching over to precalculus and easily making up his missed classwork.

He also started studying Chinese, which came naturally to him. His teacher, Xiaofeng Kelly, noticed Tommy's passion for the course.

"He is focused and curious about the language and culture," wrote Kelly. "He absolutely excels."

Each night at 10:30 p.m., Tommy would call his parents from his room in the Scaife dormitory to proudly update them on his studies and latest sporting achievements.

"It was wonderful," said his mother, who always looked forward to the call.

He also signed up for a confirmation class after dropping out of one at Buckley a year earlier. Tommy's parents and sister attended his confirmation ceremony at an Episcopal church in Deerfield.

"We went to a lovely ceremony," said Shelley. "I was surprised and pleased."

Tim Loh was his senior proctor at Scaife House and roomed three doors down. Two years older, he supervised Tommy during his sophomore year, and they became close.

"I really, really enjoyed Tommy," recalled Loh. "It was a pleasure to be his proctor."

Loh remembers Tommy being popular and sociable, although somewhat quiet. He was already so good looking that many female classmates vied for his attention.

"He was the definition of what girls like," said Loh, "but he was slightly shy and really, really mild mannered. I cannot recall Tommy having a single girlfriend, although the girls would practically throw themselves at him."

During his three years at Deerfield, Tommy's best friend was Alberto "Tito" Mejia, whose parents, Alberto Sr. and Peggy, were prominent socialites in Manhattan, Southampton, and Palm Beach. Tito had attended Buckley with Tommy, and by the time they started Deerfield, they were inseparable.

"I was pretty close to the two of them," said Loh. "It was always Tito who did the talking, and Tommy just smiled and was always three steps behind him. He was a tall presence behind Tito, kind of dwarfing him almost."

After a rocky start academically, Tommy Gilbert made the honor roll for the winter term, becoming a star of his class debating team.

"Congratulations," wrote his English teacher Suzanne

Hannay in his year-end report. "You are one of the select group of students who made the honor roll list. Your hard work, your dedication to excellence and your enthusiasm for learning were appropriately rewarded."

He was also all over Deerfield's 2001 *Pocumtuck* yearbook, featured in photos of the cross-country, basketball, baseball, and football teams.

But despite his outward success, on the yearbook's page speculating what Scaife pupils would be doing in twenty years, Tommy's entry read: "Living in a van down by the river."

In his junior year, Tommy transferred to the Doubleday dorm with a new roommate named Bob. They were assigned the infamous room 206, known as "the small double." It was so cramped that Tommy couldn't imagine how the two of them could get all their "essential stuff" inside.

They finally managed to do so thanks to "highly creative stacking" and utilizing every inch of space, although there was no room for Bob's guitar.

By October, Tommy became convinced Bob was "contaminated." He tried to avoid him, but sharing such close quarters made this impossible. Later, Tommy would describe the rest of that year as "severely traumatic."

Tommy's concentration started to suffer as he became obsessed that Bob was contaminating him. It was the first time his irrational fears affected his schoolwork.

"He faltered somewhat," noted his Deerfield adviser in his semester report. "Tiredness also took its toll. We discussed all this at length and I am sure that he will return from this welcome Christmas break, refreshed, recharged, reorganized and all ready to resume 'battle.'"

* * *

When Tommy Gilbert returned to Deerfield in January 2002, he did indeed seem reenergized and back on track. He joined the school's Big Brother / Big Sister program and was assigned an eight-year-old fatherless boy from Deerfield Township. Every Friday night, the boy came to the campus for Tommy's companionship and mentoring. They soon bonded, and Tommy loved his visits.

Outgoing when he wanted to be, Tommy was appointed as a tour guide for the admissions office. He enjoyed shepherding prospective students and their parents around the campus.

"[Tommy] is an excellent ambassador for Deerfield," wrote his college adviser, Nicholas Albertson.

Tommy was a star in all three of his varsity sports, and his proud parents often visited on Saturday afternoons to see him in action. Tom Sr. especially loved to watch his son compete against other schools before adjourning to the dorm to deliver his analysis of the game.

In his junior year, Tommy again made the honor roll, and his end-of-semester report was glowing.

"Tommy has a positive upbeat attitude," it read, "a terrific sense of humor, a calm unflappable manner, growing confidence and a sound sense of self."

During summer vacation, Tommy Gilbert traveled to China for Deerfield's monthlong study abroad program, polishing his Chinese language skills at the Beijing Normal High School.

On his return, he encamped in the Hamptons and signed on as a lifeguard in East Hampton. Over the next four summers working there, he would make several dramatic rescues.

It was around this time, however, that his parents first noticed a difference in Tommy. He was less easygoing and more aloof, continually washing his hands. Then he started "losing" clothing because it had become contaminated.

"He didn't seem to be himself," recalled his mother. "Tom thought something was wrong, I thought it was just fatigue. But as the summer wore on, I realized something was amiss."

When they tried to persuade Tommy to see a doctor and get tested in a hospital, he absolutely refused, becoming angry at the suggestion.

Tommy's close friends also noticed a change in his mannerisms as he became less social and more insecure.

"Things got weird for Tommy," said Bart Hayes. "His speech pattern was the giveaway. It was sort of like an 'aaaahhh' and then a rapid fire of two or three words and then the 'aaaahhh.' He was always stopping and starting a new sentence."

Another Buckley friend, Chris Oliver spent the summer in the Hamptons with Tommy and wondered if something was wrong.

"I remember surfing with him," said Oliver, "and getting a sense that he wasn't on the golden child path completely. There were a couple of hiccups."

By his own admission, Tommy felt like a loser. He later told a psychiatrist that he deliberately alienated his Deerfield friends because he felt he was an outsider. He began avoiding anyone from the Buckley School.

"The minute he would see Buckley kids at Deerfield, he would run away," said Hayes, who went to another school and heard it in gossip from his Deerfield friends. "It was a very strange thing that he would have completely disassociated with anyone who had gone to Buckley."

* * *

But the pressure to fit in was only rising. College now loomed on the horizon, and Tom Sr. wanted his son to follow in the family tradition at Princeton.

In his official application to Princeton University, Tommy candidly addressed the severe depression that had dogged him over the last couple of years. He claimed, however, to have conquered it.

"Many people go through a difficult adolescent period," he wrote, "when they are not sure of themselves or what they believe in. I am glad to have come out of this period with a set of beliefs and standards by which I can always act."

But the truth was that Tommy's contamination fears were now consuming him. He believed some friends were trying to steal his soul, and he had developed a set of rituals to protect himself. These included secretly giving someone the finger from inside his pocket, turning his head away and spitting, or humming tunes under his breath.

After graduating Deerfield with honors in May 2003, Tommy became convinced that everything he had worn there had become contaminated by insects or bugs.

"It was very upsetting to him," said his mother. "Even our clothing became contaminated if we brushed up against him."

That summer, nineteen-year-old Tommy Gilbert stayed in the Hamptons, frequenting the Maidstone Club. He worked as a lifeguard, surfed, and played tennis.

One night at the Maidstone Club, he was introduced to a young girl named Lila Chase, whose grandfather had originally proposed the Gilberts for club membership. She was immediately struck by his charm and good looks.

"He might as well have been a movie star," said Lila,

whose uncle is comedy icon Chevy Chase. "He was so handsome and nice [but] I was eighteen and it was just like a fleeting thing."

It would be another four years before they would meet again at the Maidstone Club under entirely different circumstances—and find love.

6

PRINCETON BREAKDOWN

Tommy Gilbert had no problem getting into Princeton University after several glowing letters of recommendation from his Deerfield teachers. His long family history with the university did not hurt either. He would major in economics and his wealthy uncle Beck had generously offered to pay for his tuition and Tom had taken him up on it.

The plan was for his parents to drive him to Princeton from the Hamptons and then help him settle in. But at the last minute, Tommy suddenly told his father not to come, saying he wanted time alone with his mother. Tom Sr. insisted on going anyway, even though his relationship with Tommy was becoming increasingly difficult.

As they drove past JFK International Airport, Tommy became very upset and threw a tantrum in the car.

"My dad made me pull over for gas near JFK," he would later write, "which at the time was severely contaminated. This led to all my new clothes being contaminated."

He finally arrived at Princeton in tears, calling it "one of the single most traumatic experiences of my life."

From then on, Tommy would avoid JFK airport like the plague.

* * *

Soon after he arrived, Tommy became convinced that his old Deerfield roommate Bob was back and contaminating the Princeton campus, even though he was not a student there. Tommy told his parents he wanted to transfer to Duke for a fresh start, but Tom Sr. persuaded him to stay.

His freshman year was a psychological nightmare for Tommy. To survive campus contamination, he developed a new set of rituals, like wearing different outfits on different parts of the campus and changing three or four times a day. He often threw clothes away and expected his parents to replace them.

Despite these internal struggles, Tommy was accepted into the Charter Club, which dates back to 1913. One of the wildest fraternities, Charter is famous for its rowdy parties and initiation nights.

He soon threw himself into the Princeton drug scene, which revolved around the eating clubs. Marijuana, LSD, and cocaine were easily available, and Tommy indulged in them all. He also began injecting himself with anabolic steroids so he could perform better at varsity football.

"The culture there was very druggy," said a close friend, whose brother attended Princeton with Tommy. "Those eating clubs are like country clubs for rich kids. Their parents pay a fortune so they can be just bathing in alcohol and drugs."

In his freshman year, Tommy Gilbert was placed on academic disciplinary probation after drugs and paraphernalia were found in his car. He was also caught with software for hacking into other students' computers.

Tommy then flew to Charleston, South Carolina, for an

extended surfing vacation. He would later tell a psychiatrist that he was fleeing his father. He checked into a hotel and started spending his days surfing and getting high, with his parents footing the bill.

Tom Sr. was so concerned about his son's suspension from Princeton that he reached out to child psychiatrist Dr. Theodore Shapiro for help. Dr. Shapiro met with Tom and Shelley Gilbert separately, where they each outlined Tommy's "adolescent crisis."

Tom Gilbert told the doctor his son had started becoming "frequently irritable" at the age of fourteen and had gone downhill ever since. He was particularly upset that Tommy had recently called him an asshole. He referred to himself as the odd man out in the Gilbert family, complaining that his wife and son often ganged up on him. In his notes after the session, Dr. Shapiro described Tom Sr., who seemed threatened by Shelley and Tommy's close relationship, as "a somewhat peculiar man."

In her session with Dr. Shapiro, Shelley Gilbert was very protective of Tommy and appeared in total denial that he had any mental problems.

"She insisted that there was nothing wrong with him," Dr. Shapiro would later testify, "and that he was functioning just fine."

Dr. Shapiro then referred the Gilberts to a Charleston psychiatrist named Dr. Kevin Spicer, who agreed to treat their son.

On October 15, 2004, Tommy Gilbert had his first session with Dr. Spicer, complaining that people were contaminating him and stealing his personality.

"They're killing my thoughts," he told Dr. Spicer. "I can't deal with that. I know it sounds crazy."

Dr. Spicer diagnosed Tommy Gilbert with a depressive disorder and possible psychosis.

Four days later, Dr. Spicer saw Tommy again, prescribing him six milligrams of the antipsychotic drug Risperdal. He then called Mr. and Mrs. Gilbert and told them their son should be hospitalized immediately. There is no indication that the Gilberts ever followed up on this, knowing Tommy would refuse inpatient treatment.

Over the next few months, Tommy Gilbert saw Dr. Spicer regularly. He fell into a routine of taking cabs to his therapy sessions before hitting the beach to go surfing.

On October 19, Dr. Spicer upped his dose of Risperdal, noting that Tommy had "a well circumscribed ego-delusional system regarding contagion."

By the first week of November, Tommy's fears of contamination had worsened, but he adamantly refused Dr. Spicer's request to list in order exactly what he was afraid of.

"Paranoia remains evident," the doctor wrote in his report. "He's unwilling to write anything down, due to perceived fears of telling them I'm fighting their ass."

On November 29, Tommy had a full-blown panic attack in Dr. Spicer's office. He burst into tears, complaining that he hadn't had any social interaction with anyone for weeks, except the doctor and cabdrivers.

"I feel kind of out of control at the moment and scared," he sobbed.

The next day, Tommy suffered another panic attack and went to a hospital emergency room. At their next session, Dr. Spicer prescribed him more Risperdal, which Tommy refused to take because of the side effects. Later, he would confide that the high doses of Risperdal had made him start growing male breasts (gynecomastia), and some of the other prescribed drugs had turned him into a zombie.

In mid-December, Dr. Spicer diagnosed Tommy Gilbert with possible schizophrenia, putting him on Zoloft and another antipsychotic called Geodon.

The dictionary definition of schizophrenia is a long-term mental disorder involving a breakdown in the relation between thought, emotion, and behavior. It leads to faulty perception, inappropriate actions and feelings, and a withdrawal from reality and personal relationships into fantasy and delusion.

After his diagnosis, Dr. Spicer had several lengthy telephone conversations with Tom Sr. and Shelley Gilbert about their son's possible schizophrenia.

"Both Tom and Shelley Gilbert were frustrated to hear this," noted Dr. Spicer, "and resistant to the concept."

A few days later, Beck Gilbert joined his brother and sister-in-law for a fifty-minute call to Dr. Spicer. They discussed how mental illness ran in both sides of Tommy's family, as his paternal grandmother, Mabelle, had been diagnosed as psychotic, and maternal grandfather, Wilton Rea, was bipolar and a victim of suicide.

"Mr. Beck Gilbert was very interested in the degree of infectious history evident in Tommy's situation," Dr. Spicer later wrote in his report.

Despite their alarming conversations with Dr. Spicer, there is no indication that the Gilberts took any further action at that time to ensure Tommy got the treatment he so desperately needed.

Tommy Gilbert spent the holidays alone in Charleston as his condition became more alarming. On February 18, 2005, he told Dr. Spicer that he was "struggling" and planned to go to New York and buy a gun. The doctor made a note about the gun and wrote, "He is clearly a very disturbed young man."

A few days later, Tommy called 911 after being overwhelmed by suicidal thoughts. He was rushed to the emergency room, where a doctor wanted to admit him for observation. But Tommy refused any treatment and walked out of the ER.

At the beginning of March, Dr. Spicer had Tommy admitted to the Medical University of South Carolina hospital. He had not slept for four days and was "struggling with frustration and fear."

The hospital gave him some medication to help him sleep. But after one night, he discharged himself against medical advice, complaining that he didn't like the other patient in his room.

His mother had flown to Charleston to try to help him, but by the time she arrived, he had walked out of the hospital. Tommy told her that the other patient in his room had upset him, so he had to leave.

"And I'm sure that freaked Tommy out," said Shelley, who spent a few days with her son before flying home.

Dr. Spicer recommended that Tommy undergo inpatient psychiatric treatment at McLean Hospital in Belmont, Massachusetts. His parents agreed and sent him the necessary paperwork to fill out. But although he promised to check himself in, he never did.

Dr. Spicer then wanted to forcibly commit Tommy to a psychiatric hospital, but the Gilberts were against it. In most states, including South Carolina, hospitals can only hold involuntary patients legally for seventy-two hours. Once the hold was lifted, they knew Tommy would immediately discharge himself.

"It's bad enough having a mentally ill child on your hands," explained Shelley. "It is worse to have an angry mentally ill child."

* * *

At the beginning of April, Tommy Gilbert flew to Hawaii for a surfing vacation, telling his parents it would be therapeutic. The plan was for him to continue his psychotherapy sessions with Dr. Spicer over the telephone, but he never bothered to pick up the phone for his scheduled appointments.

Over the next year, Tommy Gilbert surfed his way around the world at his parents' expense. He hit the waves in South America, Africa, and Brazil before returning to the United States and spending time in the Deep South, where he worked construction.

Under pressure from his family, Tommy finally moved back to Charleston for more therapy with Dr. Spicer.

But his father was determined that Tommy should go back to Princeton and graduate, still optimistic that his son would get his life together and make his mark in the financial world.

7

OUT OF CONTROL

In the fall of 2006, twenty-two-year-old Tommy Gilbert resumed his studies at Princeton, to the delight of his parents. He also began seeing Princeton-based psychiatrist Dr. Les Linet, who immediately diagnosed Tommy with a variety of mental problems. These included attention deficit disorder, hyperactivity, obsessive-compulsive disorder (OCD), Tourette syndrome, and possible Lyme disease. He was prescribed Lexapro, Klonopin, and Risperdal.

Dr. Linet wrote to the university authorities, requesting that Tommy be allocated a single-accommodation room, as he was suffering from mental illness. It cited the 1990 Americans with Disabilities Act. However, ever manipulative, Tommy asked the doctor to clarify that his disability would not prevent him from playing football.

Tommy Gilbert soon made the Princeton varsity football team, using anabolic steroids as a performance enhancer. And he was welcomed back by the Charter Club, where the drugs still flowed freely.

On Sunday, May 6, 2007, Tommy Gilbert went on a three-day drug binge, snorting cocaine and ingesting "a massive amount" of hallucinatory mushrooms. The following Tuesday afternoon, he called 911, telling the emergency dispatcher that he was overdosing on cocaine.

The Princeton First Aid & Rescue Squad sent an ambulance to Tommy's university-owned apartment at 162 North Stanworth Drive and alerted police.

Three Princeton police officers arrived to find Tommy sprawled out on his living room floor, wearing only boxer shorts. He told the officers his heart was pounding because he had snorted four grams of cocaine and eaten ten grams of psychedelic mushrooms. He said he had been unconscious since Sunday.

"Gilbert had dilated pupils," wrote Officer Ronald Wohlschleg in his report. "Appeared very nervous and jittery."

While the EMS workers were treating him, the officer saw a large quantity of drugs and paraphernalia lying on a small table.

"Gilbert started displaying signs of being agitated," wrote Wohlschleg, "trying to walk and raising his voice."

He was then taken to the emergency room at the University Medical Center in Princeton, and police seized almost a dozen small plastic bags containing different varieties of mushrooms, marijuana, and six red caplet pills. They also took two rolled-up twenty-dollar bills, two rolled-up one-dollar bills, a Hamilton Beach grinder covered in white powder, a metal cigarette case, and a mirror covered in cocaine.

Officer Wohlschleg went to the ER to arrest Tommy Gilbert, where he found him lying on a stretcher, about to be admitted for a drug overdose.

"The nurses and I tried to speak with Gilbert," the officer later reported, "but he was just staring at the ceiling with a blank look on his face and would not speak."

Tommy Gilbert was then arrested for being under the influence of drugs and possession of cocaine, psilocybin mushrooms, marijuana, and drug paraphernalia.

The next afternoon, he was placed in restraints by medical staff after becoming uncooperative. Then he viciously attacked fifty-three-year-old nurse Susan Kollar, head-butting her to the floor as she attempted to administer emergency first aid.

Two police officers went to the hospital to arrest Gilbert, but by the time they arrived, he had been discharged. They then went to his apartment and brought him back to headquarters, where he was charged with aggravated assault. He was fingerprinted, photographed, and ordered to appear at Princeton Boro Municipal Court the following week.

On June 14, Tommy Gilbert agreed to probation and supervisory treatment, under the Mercer County pretrial intervention program. Fifteen months later, in September 2009, all charges were dismissed after he successfully completed the program.

One day after his court appearance, Tommy Gilbert flew to Beijing for a two-month Mandarin Chinese course at the Boomerang Institute. Later, he would boast of dropping a dose of LSD on the long flight over.

On his résumé, he would describe the visit as "total immersion" in the Chinese language as he traveled all over the country and "effectively adapted to the Chinese culture."

While there, he had an affair with a Chinese mother who had a young son. When she asked Tommy to bring her and her son back to America, he refused, and later, he told a friend that it had ended badly.

But for years afterward, Tommy treasured her photograph, which he kept in his wallet.

8

LILA CHASE

Tommy Gilbert's always difficult relationship with his parents had improved when he spent the Labor Day weekend with them in the Hamptons. It was a welcome weekend away from Princeton, and Tommy surfed and enjoyed the nightlife.

One night at the Maidstone Club, he bumped into Lila Chase, who was there with her cousin Sarah. It was the first time their paths had crossed in four years, as they moved in different social circles.

"We both had our eye on Tommy just because he was so handsome," Lila recalled. "We were thrown in with this group of Maidstone types that go out to bars."

When Tommy's group left for Murf's Backstreet Tavern in Sag Harbor, Lila and Sarah tagged along. The noisy bar was packed, and Lila attempted to make conversation over beers with Tommy, who said little. Lila put it down to Tommy being cool with women, but would soon realize that was not the case.

"He's insecure and horribly shy," said Lila, "and probably because he was on a lot of drugs."

After Murf's closed, Lila invited everyone back to the house her parents were renting, where she had an uneasy conversation with the socially awkward Tommy before he left to go home.

The next day, he invited her to the Maidstone Club's annual cocktail party. He told her to come over to his parents' house in Wainscott for dinner beforehand, as they were out that night.

When she arrived, Tommy suggested Chinese takeout from a nearby restaurant. He picked up the phone and began speaking in Chinese, which totally threw Lila, who thought he was mocking them.

When she confronted him about it, he started laughing hysterically. He explained that he spoke fluent Mandarin and had just returned from China.

Throughout the long weekend, Lila kept running into Tommy Gilbert at the Maidstone Club. Slowly, he started opening up to her, and they found a rapport.

Before leaving for Manhattan that Monday, Tommy told Lila that he wanted to see her again. She gave him her phone number, telling him to call in a week's time, as she still wasn't sure about him.

That week, Lila, who managed an equestrian barn for a top dressage competitor, made some discreet inquiries about Tommy Gilbert. A friend who was at Princeton with him warned her to be careful, as he did a lot of drugs.

The following week, Tommy asked Lila out on a date. She agreed on the understanding that she could bring a friend.

For their first date, Lila and her friend met Tommy for dinner at a Japanese restaurant in midtown Manhattan. After the friend left, Tommy invited Lila back to his parents' beautifully furnished town house on East Sixty-First Street.

It was a romantic night, and Tommy relaxed, opening up about himself and his plans for the future. He felt safe with Lila, who kept the conversation going and instinctively knew how to draw him out of his shell.

"He told me a lot about himself," recalled Lila, "and it became clear to me that he'd not had any real girlfriends. I had thought that he was a Casanova because of his looks."

Over the next few weeks, they regularly met for dinners and got to know each other. One night, Tommy invited her out to the Hamptons for the weekend to stay at his parents' Georgica Association house. It was a great success, and Lila met Tom Sr. and Shelley Gilbert, who were delighted that Tommy's condition seemed better and he had a respectable girlfriend to give him more stability.

Now that he was dating Lila, Tommy seemed happier than he had been for years and far less paranoid.

"You had to peel away a few layers," Lila explained. "He was wickedly funny [with] a very dry sense of humor. People would say he was so quiet, but when he was comfortable, he would talk a lot."

As Tommy became more comfortable in the relationship, he opened up about his fears of contamination, which he was trying to overcome at Princeton. For the first time in his life, he felt he could truly be himself and not have to put on an act.

Lila in turn told Tommy about her lifelong battle with depression and her suicide attempt at nineteen, which she had overcome to launch a successful career in international dressage.

She wanted to be totally honest with Tommy if they were going to have a real relationship, and this mutual openness took them to a new level.

"He was so loving and okay with that," recalled Lila. "He said, 'I love you more.'"

* * *

Tommy and Lila soon fell into a routine. He would spend the week at Princeton and the weekends with Lila. They tooled around the Hamptons in his beloved Jeep Wrangler, with his pet dog, Tucker, in the back.

Tommy also taught her to surf, and they would swim past the breakers together in search of that special wave. After a long day at the beach, they would share romantic dinners at La Fondita Mexican restaurant in Amagansett.

"It was our special thing," she explained. "I felt like we were the only people in the world."

As Lila got to know him better, she realized Tommy smoked a lot of marijuana. Lila, who had no experience of narcotics, once asked Tommy if he did them on weekends. He laughed and said he did them every day.

"And I said, 'Really, are you high all the time?'" she recalled. "And he said, 'Yeah, pretty much.'"

Lila then asked if he felt drugs were a problem in his life, but Tommy said they were not and that they helped him.

He even smoked at his parents' Wainscott house, although Lila was unsure if they were aware of it. She suspected that even if they were, they would not have done anything.

"[His parents] were always nervous to deal with him head-on," she observed. "And in fairness to them, I don't think he made it easy."

She also introduced Tommy to her family, who thought he was charming, and thoroughly approved of the relationship.

"He was beloved by everyone in my life," said Lila. "I would bring him to a party and [introduce] him as my boyfriend. They'd say, 'Oh my god, you've hit the jackpot.'"

Tommy Gilbert was still undergoing therapy from his Princeton psychiatrist, Dr. Les Linet. At one session at the beginning of December 2006, Tommy said he was scared of spending the holidays at his parents' home. He complained that his father had refused to throw out his Deerfield clothes, so the entire house and his father were contaminated.

He also told the psychiatrist that *Saturday Night Live* sketches were making fun of him, and he was thinking of hiring an entertainment lawyer to sue NBC. He also felt that *New York Times* articles and various blogs were targeting him.

Tommy began running some of these ideations past Lila Chase, whose Uncle Chevy had starred in the original *Saturday Night Live*. She told him that it was all in his head. So he started using Lila as his litmus test as to what was real and what was not. He would ask her about something he'd read, and they'd turn it into a joke.

"I would say, 'Nope, that's totally nuts,' and he would laugh," she explained. "I think he would halfway believe me most of the time."

In early January 2008, Tommy Gilbert flew to Jamaica for a surfing vacation. He forgot his medication, and by the time Lila arrived for the last four days, he was in a terrible state and seemed paranoid of everything.

"It was awful," she remembered. "The whole thing was weird."

Lila took charge, insisting he get more psychiatric help when they got back to America. Tommy grudgingly agreed and started seeing Dr. Michael Sacks, the professor of psychiatry at the Weill Cornell Medical College.

For the next six years, Tommy would be treated by Dr. Sacks, seeing him once or twice a week. The psychiatrist made varying diagnoses of Tommy's mental problems, including severe compulsive, depressive, paranoid, and delusional disorders. He would prescribe Tommy a cocktail of narcoleptics, including Lexapro, Risperdal, Latuda, and Klonopin.

But Tommy never stayed on any of them, complaining that they affected his sexual performance.

At one early session, Tommy told Dr. Sacks that he would look into the mirror and see his father's face. He feared that Tom Sr. was stealing his soul and he was turning into him.

"He had an ideation that his father had some kind of wizard-like influence on everything bad that happened to him," said Lila. "And that grew and grew and grew."

Tommy also feared that people were trying to kill him, saying he felt like a deer in headlights. He thought they were using magnets to steal his spirit and considered buying a CO_2 detector for protection.

He frequently discussed his parents' relationship, telling Dr. Sacks that his mother took a back seat to his more dominant father. He blamed Tom Sr. for jinxing him and making him fail exams.

After hearing this, Dr. Sacks said Tommy was using his father as a scapegoat for anything going wrong in his life. Later, Tommy told Lila about that session and agreed that Dr. Sacks had been right.

"I thought that was something of a breakthrough," said Lila, "that he said it out loud . . . but this was at a time when he was much healthier."

9

CLEANING UP

By spring 2008, Tommy Gilbert was scoring drugs on the internet's dark web in increasing quantities. He was kicked off the Princeton varsity football team after testing positive for anabolic steroids.

Lila Chase was worried about her boyfriend's drug usage, as well as his burgeoning obsession with Red Hot Chili Peppers' guitarist John Frusciante, a longtime heroin addict. Lila's aunt had once dated the troubled rock star, and Tommy continually questioned her about heroin and whether it had improved Frusciante's musicianship.

Drugs became such a big issue in their relationship that, after finding narcotics in her car, Lila finally gave him an ultimatum to choose between drugs or her. After she read him the riot act at his parents' house, Tommy sheepishly produced a big bag of cocaine, boasting it was worth thousands of dollars. Then he flushed it all down the toilet as she watched.

"And that's when I knew," she said, "that I really, really cared for him."

After Tommy cleaned up his act, his relationship with Lila blossomed. He moved into her parents' house in Bronxville,

New York, where he would live for the next several years. Lila's father, Edward Thornton Chase, was a Harvard-educated criminal lawyer, and her mother, Joan Gregory, also practiced law. They soon accepted Tommy as part of their family.

He started commuting back and forth between Princeton and Bronxville and, for a while, seemed to be getting his life together.

"It was an unspoken contract," explained Lila, "that if he was to live with us, he would be on the straight and narrow in terms of being clean and getting help."

Soon after moving in, Tommy invited Lila to meet his new psychiatrist, Dr. Sacks. She agreed. He went in first for a forty-five-minute session, and Lila followed.

Tommy told the doctor that he smoked marijuana daily and took psychedelics, but claimed to have given up cocaine. He said he had moved into Lila's house because he was "very uncomfortable" living with his own parents.

Lila also gave Tommy a complete makeover. She brought him to her favorite designer discount store in Yonkers and picked out a new wardrobe for him. And she taught him little tricks like buying a T-shirt one size too small, to make his arms look bigger.

"He had no idea how to dress when I met him," she explained.

During the summer break, they spent time apart. Tommy went on several surfing vacations, catching up with his old friends from Buckley. He seemed happier than he had been for years.

"They were good times," said Chris Oliver. "He was always down and game to go surfing."

On one occasion, Bart Hayes was in the Hamptons with

an old friend from Deerfield. They ran into Tommy, who immediately apologized for being so weird at Deerfield. The two of them went off to talk for a few minutes, before Hayes's friend came back looking shell-shocked.

"And my buddy was like, 'That was the strangest conversation I've ever had,'" said Hayes. "'He had a really aggressive manic energy.' I said, 'That's okay, it's Tommy.'"

Tommy also took a bartending course and would demonstrate his new cocktails for his mother, who was delighted he was broadening his horizons. He was especially looking forward to the final lesson of the course, where he would work a shift at a real bar and be graded. But on the night of the test, he came back early, and Shelley asked what was wrong. Tommy just shrugged, saying it didn't work out.

Later, he would tell Dr. Sacks that he became so paranoid of the customers that he had run out of the bar.

Tommy and Lila Chase's relationship was deepening. It was the first serious relationship for both of them, and they were in love. Marriage seemed in the cards, and they had already started planning for a future together.

Lila found Tommy very supportive and patient as he helped her overcome her insecurities.

"He validated me and my intelligence," she explained, "and my worth in a way that I hadn't had before."

They loved going out for dinner and a Broadway play. On November 4, 2008, they were attending a performance of *The Sound of Music,* when the performers stopped the show to announce Barack Obama had won the presidency.

"It was very special," remembered Lila. "We had both voted for Obama."

Tommy loved driving Lila into Manhattan to go and see

an independent or foreign movie at the Angelika Film Center in the West Village.

"And I remember realizing how much he loved me," she said, "when I noticed a pattern of him watching me watching the movie and smiling. He was happy because I was, and I felt the same way."

They also stayed home watching their favorite television shows like *The Office, Arrested Development,* and *Curb Your Enthusiasm.*

That Thanksgiving, Lila spent the holidays with the Gilbert family in Wainscott. She was impressed by how well Tommy now appeared to be getting on with them, although he made a special effort to do so while she was around.

"He loved his parents," she said. "I remember him saying on the phone to his father, 'I love you.' He actually verbalized love on the phone."

Lila always got on well with Tom Sr. but saw how he was Tommy's opposite in temperament. Mr. Gilbert was always cheerful and positive and would be up for anything, whereas Tommy was far quieter and often seemed embarrassed by his father.

One time, Tom Sr.'s tooth had fallen out, and he triumphantly showed it to everyone at the dinner table. Tommy was disgusted and told his father off for being so gross.

Every winter from January to April, Lila relocated to Wellington, Florida, for the Winter Equestrian Festival. Known as the horse capital of America, the world's best dressage riders arrive each year to compete for millions of dollars in prize money. It's a firm fixture on the winter society circuit, attracting a select group of Olympians and the equestrian daughters of Mike Bloomberg, Bruce Springsteen, and Bill Gates.

As well as being a trainer, Lila also managed one of the world's leading dressage riders, Ashley Holzer. She was in charge of million-dollar horses, and it was a highly demanding job.

Tommy Gilbert would drive her to Florida in his Jeep, staying for a few days in her rented condo before heading back to Princeton. One year, she was hospitalized with pneumonia and put on an IV drip. She called Tommy, who said he was coming down immediately.

"And he drove twenty-five hours," she said. "He just got in his car and drove to see me in the hospital."

For his senior year at Princeton, Tommy Gilbert rented a house near the Princeton campus. He was now working on a sixty-four-page thesis entitled "The Word Effect: Effects of the Word Content in the Financial Times on Firms' Earnings in the U.K."

"He seemed kind of gentle but insecure," said a Princeton classmate. "He always seemed ambivalent . . . abnormally calm. He wasn't even anxious about his thesis."

Concerned that his prospective son-in-law wasn't taking his future seriously enough, Lila's father, Edward Thornton Chase, gave Tommy a pep talk to try to motivate him.

"My father said, 'My daughter loves you and she needs you,'" said Lila. "'You can do it. Work on yourself. Get yourself together [and] you're so capable to get a good job.'"

In a late April 2009 therapy session, Tommy told Dr. Michael Sacks that Lila's family was pressuring him into marriage. He also said that he "felt rejected" by them.

Nevertheless, the pep talk did make an impression on Tommy, who compiled a résumé for summer internships as graduation approached.

"Job Objective," he wrote. "Summer position in a global

investment management firm, with fast track learning opportunity that leverages current developing skills in global stock picking and ability to source and assess Asian investment opportunities (conversational in Chinese)."

He claimed to be currently managing a "global long/short hedge fund," listing a number of Chinese companies he represented. As for his previous experience, he listed four summers as a lifeguard in East Hampton, citing more than twenty ocean rescues and thirty additional saves.

But that spring, Tommy and Lila's relationship changed. Tommy was back on drugs and asked Lila to keep his cocaine and dole it to him whenever he asked for it. She refused, saying that she didn't want to be around drugs, as they could jeopardize her career.

Their relationship was becoming more platonic and less physical, as Lila worried about Tommy's drug taking and distanced herself. Although marriage was no longer in the cards, they remained close.

"We weren't [in] a sexual relationship for that long," Lila explained. "And we really morphed into becoming best friends. It wasn't sexual but it was very intimate. Although we weren't together as boyfriend and girlfriend, he still lived at my house like he was our family."

Lila now encouraged Tommy to get closer to his father, after seeing the growing tension between them. At her suggestion, they started meeting once a week for dinner at the Topaz Thai restaurant on West Fifty-Sixth Street.

"I thought if I could make his father less of this . . . magical entity," said Lila, "he would just see him as a person."

10

"HE'S GOING TO RUN A HEDGE FUND"

In June 2009, Tommy Gilbert finally graduated Princeton with a degree in economics, two years later than he should have done. His parents and younger sister, Bess, were there for his graduation ceremony.

"He's going to run a hedge fund," Tom Sr. proudly announced when asked what Tommy planned to do with his BA degree.

The Gilbert family posed for photographs under the spreading elm trees outside Princeton's renowned Nassau Hall. They looked like the embodiment of success, going through a rite of passage on a very special day.

Wearing his graduation gown, Tommy has a wry smile of accomplishment and must have been relieved that his Princeton days were finally over.

After his graduation, Tommy and Lila rented an apartment in Riverdale, New York. Tommy started a summer internship at Dawson-Herman Capital Management Inc., but was soon fired for playing video games instead of working.

"It was too much for him," explained Lila, "to work in an

office environment where he thought people were stealing his ideas, looking at his computer, and plotting against him."

They only spent a couple of months in Riverdale before moving back with her parents to save money.

Tommy then started trying to get an incubator hedge fund off the ground. He named it the Bayberry High Growth Fund. His father was very supportive, giving advice and helping him prepare a profile and presentation for possible investors.

"He wanted to have his own hedge fund," said Lila. "He wanted to get investors [and] he presented pretty well."

But Tommy's stock-picking methods were something of a cheat. He would take a consensus of recommendations from various financial investing services like the Motley Fool, portraying their market tips as his own analysis. He also employed the Elliott wave method, which analyzes financial market cycles to forecast trends by identifying extremes in investor psychology, like highs and lows in share prices.

Against all his natural instincts, Tommy embarked on a charm offensive to find investors. Lila would often accompany Tommy to cocktail soireés in the Hamptons to network and try to persuade wealthy friends to invest in his Bayberry fund. It was listed on the Princeton alumni directory Tiger-Net, with Tommy as manager.

"We made a point of trying to be social," said Lila. "Princeton is coming to an end, and he needs to get on to the next thing. And this is how it's done in these circles. You hang out where the rich guys are, because those are the hedge fund guys that are making the money. And you bring your girlfriend."

On July 13, 2009, Tommy Gilbert turned twenty-five, officially too old to use the Maidstone Club under the Gilberts' family membership. So his parents arranged junior club privileges at $3,000 a year, as well as a further $600 for dining room fees and expensive sessions with the club golf pros.

"We wanted him to have access to the club," explained Shelley, "because he has friends there, and we thought that tennis would be good for him."

In December, Tommy Gilbert escorted the daughter of a family friend to the debutante ball at the Waldorf Astoria. He drove to Queens to rent a tuxedo and put it on at Lila's parents' house to everyone's amusement.

"It was goddamn awful," she remembered, "so we were all kind of laughing."

A neighbor arrived to borrow some sugar, and a tuxedoed Tommy suddenly decided to play butler, answering the door with a bow and declaring, "Your sugar, madam."

"It was very funny," said Lila. "For someone who's always so quiet, when he had the opportunity, he could be hilarious."

In early 2010, Thomas Gilbert Sr. turned sixty-five and took his career in a new direction. He cofounded Syzygy Therapeutics Management, a private equity fund focusing on identifying newly developed biotech drugs with potential billion-dollar markets.

He also downsized, leaving the house on East Sixty-First Street to rent a two-bedroom apartment on Beekman Place, in Manhattan's fashionable Turtle Bay, for $6,000 a month. Like everyone else, the Gilberts had been hit by the 2008 recession and were now trying to save money.

In January, Tommy and Lila moved to Florida for the Winter Equestrian Festival, renting a condo in Wellington with another couple. Lila worked long hours, leaving Tommy alone most of the time. He spent his days surfing and getting high, instead of working on his hedge fund.

"I grew increasingly frustrated," said Lila. "I'm working all day and coming home to [Tommy], who's done nothing. Then he started doing drugs again . . . and it just didn't work anymore."

In mid-April, Tommy's childhood best friend, Alberto "Tito" Mejia, tragically drowned during a spring break trip to Antigua. He and a group of friends had spent Friday night drinking in a bar and then returned to their rooms at the chic Mill Reef Club. The next morning, Tito had disappeared, and a few hours later, divers pulled his body from the ocean.

Tommy Gilbert was still in Florida when he heard the news and was devastated.

Soon after they returned from Florida, Lila was offered a job in Europe, and she and Tommy decided she should take it. He drove her to the airport to say goodbye. They would remain close, Skyping each other daily.

After Lila left, Tommy Gilbert moved back in with his parents, as he had nowhere else to live. He summered in the Hamptons, frequenting the Maidstone Club, where he won a mixed doubles tennis tournament. He halfheartedly tried to network with possible investors for his Bayberry fund, but his main priority was surfing. His father frequently tried to offer advice on getting his fund off the ground, but Tommy ignored it, angry that he would try to interfere.

The first week of September, as Hurricane Earl powered toward the East Coast, Tommy Gilbert drove to Montauk in search of the perfect wave. He hit the beach at sunrise, and as he zipped up his wet suit, he was interviewed by *New York Times* reporter Joseph Berger, who was doing a story on the hurricane.

"The approach of a hurricane seems to bring out a touch of recklessness in some people," wrote Berger in his article. Describing himself as a twenty-six-year-old Manhattan stock trader, Tommy told Berger that he had not seen twelve-foot-high waves since the previous year's Hurricane Bill.

"You rarely get surf this good on the East Coast," Tommy said, "especially with these long waves that come from a ways away."

In April 2011, Tom Gilbert left Syzygy Therapeutics to launch his own hedge fund, Wainscott Capital Partners. To get it off the ground, he used $500,000 of his own money, as well as investments from various friends.

The hedge fund, named after the Hamptons town where he owned a home, would specialize in biotechnology and health care stocks, with a $500,000 minimum for investors. In his company overview, Tom Gilbert wrote that Wainscott Capital Partners would invest in worldwide public equity markets.

"It primarily invests in value stock of companies," it stated. "The fund employs fundamental analysis to create its portfolio."

Tom Gilbert had big plans for Wainscott Capital, hoping to grow it to a billion-dollar fund. He strategized with a hedge fund consultant and worked twelve-hour days and the occasional weekend from his office in his Beekman Place apartment. Although he still played golf, tennis, and squash as much as possible, he would never take another vacation.

Tom Sr. included his son in his new venture, listing him as a market strategist on Wainscott's new website and marketing materials. He wanted Tommy to analyze biotech market trends and send him regular reports via email.

He wrote a detailed five-page job description for the key

role he saw Tommy playing in Wainscott Capital. He hoped it would also bring them closer together.

"Please take a look at the attached," Tom wrote in a cover letter. "I hope you will find it helpful in laying out a clear structure for success, and that you can enthusiastically jump aboard. Please bury the hatchet permanently, warm regards, Dad."

PART 2

11

"A QUICK ROMANCE"

In mid-May, Tommy Gilbert began weekly therapy sessions with Dr. Susan Evans, a professor of psychology at Weill Cornell. He had been referred by Dr. Michael Sacks, as his mental condition had begun to deteriorate once again. Tommy was now less worried about contamination than social embarrassment.

"He was very interested in making friends," wrote Dr. Evans in an early therapy report. "He feared that people would see he's anxious and think he's a loser."

Tommy told Dr. Evans that he was interested in acting, so she advised him to take acting lessons, but concentrate on getting a job.

Concerned about his son's lack of drive and ambition, Tom Gilbert decided to reach out to Dr. Evans. He had started keeping a computer diary, jotting down to-do notes on how to help his errant son, who appeared to have little interest in working for Wainscott Capital.

"Susan Evans," he wrote. "What can we do to be helpful to Tommy, and to her? What kind of feedback (for her ears only) from us would be of value? We are a resource that is not being used."

He then listed in order what Tommy needed to do to get his life back on track:

- Ability to take responsibility and not blame others
- Willingness to work hard and focus on details
- What does [Dr. Evans] see as the timeline for Tommy, short term, longer term?

In September 2011, Tommy Gilbert ran into his old Buckley schoolmate Peter Smith Jr. on East Hampton beach. Smith was zipping up his wet suit to go surfing, when Tommy asked to join him. It was the first time they had seen each other in years.

As they paddled out into the water, they couldn't have looked more different. Tall and muscular, Tommy towered over Smith, who only came up to his shoulders.

While they sat with the other surfers waiting for waves, they discussed their lives after Buckley. Socially well connected and radiating confidence, Smith had a law degree and was trying to get a shop-local e-commerce start-up off the ground. Tommy spoke of his plans for a hedge fund, saying he was back living with his parents and hated it.

"He told me that he didn't get along with his father," said Smith. "He was overbearing and mean to him [and] he wanted to get out of there."

Smith sympathized, saying he was looking for a roommate, as he had an extra room in his Williamsburg apartment. He invited Tommy to move in.

"It was kind of a quick romance," recalled Smith. "[I said], 'Dads can be tough. Why don't you come and live with me, it will probably [make] a world of difference in the relationship.'"

Tommy said he was interested but would have to ask his father first.

A week later, Tommy Gilbert moved into a small back room in Peter Smith's row house apartment on North Seventh Street and Bedford Avenue, Brooklyn. They split the $2,800 monthly rent; Tom Sr. had agreed to pay Tommy's half.

Peter Smith now made it his mission to help Tommy, who was two years his junior. Shy and socially awkward with no close friends, Tommy was insecure in any social situation. Peter Smith was the total opposite, always gregarious, and provided Tommy an entrée into his fashionable set, taking on the role of wingman. If anyone called Tommy strange, Smith would jump to his defense. He made a point of including him on surf trips, beach parties, musical backyard jams, and a weekly Monday night drum circle in Sagaponack.

Over the next few weeks, Tommy's confidence grew, as he hung out with the higher echelons of the Hamptons' in crowd.

"Peter really brought him into our circle," said Chris Oliver, whom Tommy had replaced in the Williamsburg apartment. "He's kind of quiet and had been painted with a certain brush, but now that he's in the gang he's great. And he was doing great."

As part of "the pack," Tommy partied in fashionable Williamsburg, played tennis and squash, and weekended in the Hamptons. He was now living the life he had always felt he deserved.

"At that point, Tommy was probably the happiest he's ever been," said Peter Smith.

But no one ever knew what mood Tommy would be in, as he was so "socially quirky," though many found this endearing initially.

"There were times when Tommy was incredibly engaged," Smith explained. "He was playing music. He was laughing and being part of the group. There were other times where he was quiet and withdrawn."

When he felt like it, Tommy could be the life of the party, once donning a fake mustache, which stayed on for a whole weekend. He had a bizarre sense of humor and became known for his charming, off-the-wall remarks.

"He was coming out of his shell a little more," said Oliver. "But we just didn't know how far out that would go."

Exceptionally good-looking with long, blond hair and piercing blue eyes, Tommy was a magnet for the beautiful girls who flocked around Peter Smith's crowd. At parties, they would vie for his attention, coming over to make conversation. But after fifteen minutes of him standing there stone-faced, they moved on.

"He didn't do very well with [women]," said Bart Hayes, "despite sitting on third base in the looks department."

The one girl he did pay attention to was Lizzy Fraser, a young blond Barnard graduate with a reputation for hard partying. Three years earlier, the Gawker gossip site had dubbed the beautiful socialite as "the ghost of Edie Sedgwick reincarnate: model, Columbia undergrad, Warholophile and photographer."

The daughter of renowned architect Arthur William Lovat Fraser and his wife, Linda, Lizzy was well known on the Hamptons' social circuit for frequently carrying a water bottle full of vodka.

"Lizzy was a girl who if you were in our social circle you probably hooked up with at some point," said Hayes. "She's a very fun girl and she loves to have a good time."

* * *

Tommy remained in touch with Lila Chase, who was now back in New York. He regularly updated her about his glamorous new social life, which did not impress her. She worried it was not helping his always fragile mental health.

"I think Peter thought the fun environment, models, maybe some drugs and parties would be good for Tommy," said Lila. "But he wasn't qualified to take care of Tommy or understand what he needed."

Indeed, as they grew closer, Tommy began to feel threatened by Peter Smith, who had the social and financial success he so craved. He became jealous of his new best friend, who was living the life that he felt he was denied because of his psychological inadequacies.

"Peter was very confident and the dominant guy in their life," said Hayes. "Like Peter threw the parties, Tommy would scream into his pillow."

Peter Smith was a regular at Dorrian's Red Hand bar, an Upper East Side institution. Through his connections, Smith, whose band occasionally played music in the back room, found Tommy a job as a barman/bouncer.

Dorrian's made front-page news in August 1986 in the infamous case known as the Preppy Murder. Nineteen-year-old socialite Robert Chambers and his girlfriend, Jennifer Levin, had left the bar at 4:00 a.m. after a heavy night's drinking. They walked into Central Park, and at dawn, eighteen-year-old Levin's body was found by a cyclist, her clothing torn and showing obvious signs of a struggle.

Chambers later told police that he had accidentally killed her during rough sex. But he could not explain why he had abandoned her body in Central Park before going home to his parents' apartment.

After a sensational three-month trial, Chambers accepted a plea deal during jury deliberations, admitting to first-degree murder in exchange for a sentence of five to fifteen years. He went on to serve the full fifteen years because of prison violations, including assaulting a guard and drug possession.

Tommy never felt comfortable working behind the busy bar at Dorrian's. He soon quit, finding it too high pressure as he was unable to handle the necessary small talk with customers.

Instead, he turned his attentions to developing a new hedge fund he named Mameluke Capital Fund. The Mamelukes were slaves who had seized control of the Egyptian sultanate in 1250 before ruling for almost three centuries. They remained a powerful force until being massacred by Mehmet Ali in 1811.

Tommy asked Peter Smith to help him raise money with investors and started boasting about his new hedge fund at social gatherings. With his impeccable Ivy League credentials and Princeton degree, people gave him a second look, but his sales pitch was pitiful.

Chris Oliver, who was now working in finance, was initially interested in investing in Mameluke.

"Tommy was pretty deep into it," he recalled. "A part of it was pretty harebrained, but this is a Princeton guy who was quiet, and a lot of times that produces some great minds."

But Tommy's halting speech patterns and lack of strategy did not inspire confidence.

"It wasn't like you saw the determination in his eye and

he went for it," said Oliver. "It was more like, 'Oh, I'm starting a hedge fund.'"

He also approached Bart Hayes, who was equally unimpressed by Tommy's vague pitch.

"I don't know anything about hedge funds," he said, "but I know what people sound like when they're actually doing things and when they're just talking shit."

In January 2012, Peter Smith invited Tommy and a group of their friends on his annual surfing trip to the Dominican Republic. They all stayed in separate cabins at the luxurious Dominican Tree House Village in Samana, where rope bridges and paths connect to secluded lagoons and pools.

Throughout the trip, Tommy seemed restless and uneasy around Smith and the others. One night, they all went out to the resort owner's house to play music and drink. Tommy seemed unusually quiet and then "weirded" everyone out by suddenly leaving.

A couple of days later at a beach party, Tommy once again took off by himself into the night. This time, Peter Smith went after him.

"He was speaking to an underaged girl in an alleyway," Smith remembered. "She looked like she could be a prostitute."

Back at the resort, Smith went to Tommy's cabin to confront him, as the manager did not allow prostitutes in the resort. Tommy angrily denied the allegation, slamming the door on him.

The next day, they had a big argument, and Tommy accused Smith of pursuing Lizzy Fraser behind his back. Although Smith had had a brief fling with Lizzy six years earlier, he was no longer interested.

Soon after returning to Williamsburg, Tommy suddenly announced that he was moving out of the apartment. He said he wanted to travel the world and could no longer afford the rent.

Tommy moved back in with his parents, but that did not work out, as his father constantly badgered him to concentrate on his hedge fund. Several months later, when his room at the Williamsburg apartment became vacant again, Peter Smith allowed him to move back in.

Since leaving, Tommy had developed his own set of friends on the periphery of Smith's social circle, often hanging out with them. Almost every night, he was out at various events, occasionally making the society pages. He was frequently seen with a beautiful young blond actress named Monika Plocienniczak, who had a minor part in the 2011 action movie *Tower Heist,* starring Eddie Murphy and Ben Stiller. Often dressed in a tuxedo and bow tie, with a carefully groomed beard and long, blond hair tucked in a fashionable man bun, Tommy was the epitome of a high society man-about-town.

But soon after moving back into Peter Smith's apartment, Tommy's old fears started resurfacing. He told Lila Chase that he was getting a lock on his door because he thought Smith was hacking into his computer.

Once again, Lila gave him a reality check, saying these new fears were totally irrational and mirrored his old ones about his father.

"This is your brain playing tricks on you," she told him. "You've got to talk to your doctor about it."

During his weekly sessions with Dr. Susan Evans, he did talk about how he thought certain people were hacking into his phone to sabotage his hedge fund. He also told the psychologist that he was thinking about buying a gun.

"Something's going on," he told Dr. Evans, who dutifully noted it down but never took any further action.

In early 2012, Tom Gilbert quietly put the Wainscott house up for sale, as he needed more seed money for his hedge fund. He had also discovered that Billy Babinski, who operated a nearby farm stand, was building a barn that would obscure the view from his deck and dramatically cut the value of the house.

On Wednesday, March 7, Tom and Shelley Gilbert turned up at an East Hampton planning meeting to stop the barn being built. Wearing a country-casual, loose-fitting V-neck sweater and corduroy pants, Tom came well prepared, setting up an easel in front of the planning board with a photo presentation for an alternative barn site.

"This is shaping up to be a zero-sum game," he declared, "where there's a winner and there's a loser. So what we're really saying is that this should be a win-win."

He began by complimenting the Babinski family for their "wonderful" homegrown produce, including sweet corn, strawberries, tomatoes, and peppers. Using flowery language, Gilbert then cited an obscure eighth-century English law called Droit du Seigneur. It gave the lord of the manor absolute rights over his serfs, including their wives' sexual favors. Members of the committee looked puzzled as to how this applied to the barn situation.

Gilbert asserted that the U.S. Constitution protected owner's rights. One of the main reasons he had bought his house, he said, were the sweeping views of the overlooking fields, which the proposed barn would ruin. He appealed to the committee to approve his alternative barn site and protect his rights.

"And we do want to encourage the economy," he told the meeting. "So let's come up with a solution collectively that makes everybody look good. I'm a big believer in win, win, win."

Billy Babinski then spoke, complaining that the Gilberts' alternative plan wouldn't allow his food delivery wagons enough room to turn.

"There's very good reasons for this barn," he declared. "I didn't just simply take out the survey and throw a dart and, 'Oh no! It's in front of Mr. Gilbert's!'"

He told the board that he made his living off the land and his proposed barn was inoffensive.

"It's not, 'We're winning, we're losing,'" he said. "It's my livelihood."

An attorney then addressed the planning board in support of the barn. He revealed that the Gilbert house was actually on the market "for not an inconsiderable amount of money."

Taken by surprise, Tom Gilbert replied that the proposed Babinski barn would slash the value of his property by millions of dollars.

"We have been out here for seventeen years and we love the area," he explained. "But we have for personal reasons put it on the market . . . but we will still be out here."

Shelley Gilbert then invited all the planning board members to come and stand on her deck so they could see for themselves the damage the barn would do.

The battle over the Babinski barn soon became hot gossip in the Hamptons, pitting a wealthy Manhattan-based family against a prominent local farmer.

At its next meeting in April, the East Hampton planning board ruled against the Gilberts, voting 5–1 to greenlight the Babinski barn.

"Shelley Gilbert," reported *The East Hampton Star,* "sitting in the audience with her attorney, left the hall dejected. 'I don't understand. Community should be about compromise,' she said, stepping out into the early spring night."

Six weeks later, the Gilberts sued Billy Babinski, the East Hampton planning board, and the town's architectural review board in the New York State Supreme Court, and all construction work was halted.

"It would be easy to cast the Gilberts as villains," wrote Paul A. Johnson on the Curbed Hamptons website. "Unfortunately, before the matter could even go before the Town Board for a public hearing, the Gilberts filed suit in New York State Supreme Court bringing everything to a screeching halt. Now the barn sits, about 80% done, while the legal proceedings delay its completion."

Tom and Shelley Gilbert ultimately lost their suit, and the Babinski barn was built—resulting in 8 Georgica Association Road being taken off the market. It would be the beginning of several years of uneasy relations with their Hamptons neighbors, exacerbated by their son's unruly behavior.

12

"TO THE MOST BEAUTIFUL GIRL I'VE EVER MET"

Meanwhile, Tommy Gilbert was under increased pressure to succeed, as his dreams of starting a hedge fund failed to materialize. His Buckley and Deerfield friends were all on their way to successful careers, but Tommy wasn't even out of the starting gate. Although he constantly talked up his new Mameluke hedge fund, he knew he was falling behind everyone. Tom Sr. was still trying to involve him in Wainscott Capital, but Tommy had zero interest in working for his father.

"He seemed like a guy that was a failure to launch," one of Tommy's Buckley friends told *Vanity Fair*. "He enjoyed a lifestyle that he could not afford."

At a session with his longtime psychiatrist Dr. Michael Sacks, Tommy spoke about the pressures he felt to make it on Wall Street. When the doctor asked what success meant to him, Tommy replied, "Power, stature, beautiful women, and philanthropy."

His growing frustrations made him even more resentful of Peter Smith, whom he appeared to blame for his failures. Tommy was now convinced that Smith had hacked into his computer and stolen his secret hedge fund algorithm, which he believed would be his key to riches.

He was now so self-conscious about what people thought of him that he fled a Princeton weekend reunion before it had even started, afraid of having to explain himself to his former classmates.

At the Williamsburg apartment, he became passive-aggressive, venting his growing anger through small things, like not doing his household chores or being late with the rent. "He wasn't pulling his weight," recalled Smith, "doing dishes or cleaning up after himself."

He also made everyone uncomfortable with his loud, contentious rows on the phone with his father, followed by slamming doors in fits of anger. This was a scary new Tommy that Peter Smith had never seen before.

When Smith finally confronted Tommy, he became "very aggressive." He accused his benefactor of "trying to mess with him" by hacking into his bank account and stealing things from his room.

Chris Oliver had also noticed Tommy's weird behavior, putting it down to the pills he was taking that made his hands shake.

"Something radical shifted," said Oliver, "and his behavior got pretty erratic and odd. I was hearing a lot of this through Peter. And he's like, 'Dude! Tommy's kind of flipping out at me on certain stuff.'"

Many of their friends laughed it off and thought Smith was exaggerating.

"I wasn't hugely concerned," said Oliver. "But Peter kept bringing it up like, 'This is crazy.'"

Then Tommy suddenly informed Lila Chase in a telephone call that they couldn't have any further communication, without giving her any explanation.

"He actually called me to say he loved me," she said. "I was his best friend but we couldn't talk anymore. I remember I said, 'That's ridiculous. That doesn't make any sense.'"

* * *

One Sunday night, Lizzy Fraser was out drinking with her friend Annabelle Summers (not her real name) at the trendy Surf Lodge in Montauk. When they found themselves without a ride back to the Hamptons, Lizzy suggested calling Tommy Gilbert, well aware he had a crush on her. As soon as he got her call, he dropped everything to come to her rescue.

"We had been drinking all weekend," recalled Annabelle. "Then Tommy came in from East Hampton, where he had been playing tennis. It was the first time I ever met him."

As soon as they got in his green Jeep, Annabelle fell asleep in the back. Tommy took Lizzy for dinner in East Hampton before driving them back to his parents' house to spend the night.

By this time, Lizzy had passed out, so Tommy carried her upstairs into his bedroom, directing Annabelle to the guest room.

"And his mom was still up," said Annabelle. "He just carried Lizzy like deadweight right past her. I was so embarrassed at her seeing me like this."

The next morning, Annabelle woke up hungry. Tommy and Lizzy were still asleep in his bedroom, so she went down into the kitchen for something to eat.

When Shelley Gilbert walked in, Annabelle introduced herself, thanking her for letting her stay the night.

"She's like, 'Oh, you guys must have had a really good Sunday night,'" said Annabelle. "'Help yourself to a yogurt.' I couldn't tell if she was pissed or perturbed."

Tommy and Lizzy Fraser began dating. Annabelle Summers was a confidante to both of them and often stayed over at the Fraser house, as she had become Lizzy's designated driver.

Lizzy's parents seemed to approve of Tommy, who had the perfect society pedigree of Buckley, Deerfield, and Princeton. He was totally smitten. In a rare display of emotion, he even wrote Lizzy a love letter, although he never summoned up the nerve to give it to her.

> To the most beautiful girl I've ever met—your brilliance, charm and spirit are unparalleled.
>   Love, Tommy

Peter Smith had also started a relationship, dating a girl named Laurel Cummings. Over the next several months, Tommy often socialized with them, attending many black-tie charity events together. A clean-shaven Tommy was photographed with various young socialites at the New York Philharmonic Young New Yorkers Summer Party, the Greensward Seventh Annual Evening in the Garden, and the First Young Professionals Event.

Lila Chase, who was no longer in touch with Tommy, would often see him in the society pages and notice how uncomfortable he always looked.

"Given where he came from," she said, "I wasn't shocked to see him in the society pages. That was the kind of thing that would make him anxious, and you can see that he sweated through his shirt."

That summer, Tommy suggested that Laurel move into the Williamsburg apartment, saying he'd look for a new place to live. He had become something of a third wheel in the relationship and felt Laurel had taken his place.

"I didn't want Tommy to feel kicked out," said Peter Smith. "So I told him he could take a couple of weeks."

Tommy seemed to be doing well, settling into an easy daily routine, playing tennis, working out at the gym, and doing mixed martial arts. He was also injecting anabolic steroids, drinking, and smoking marijuana.

Then in late July, Tommy suddenly refused to move out of the apartment, and tensions escalated.

"He had some kind of physical altercation with Peter," said Oliver. "He was creeping around the house, and it was all downhill from there."

At the end of August, Tommy finally agreed to move out. Despite the bitter argument, he still continued to socialize with Peter Smith and his friends.

That August, Wainscott Capital Partners reported steady growth. The *Hedge Fund Alert* announced that Tom Gilbert's new fund had $5 million under management. Over the next fifteen months, its funds would swell to $7.3 million, an excellent return for investors. It was still a comparatively small hedge fund, but Tom Gilbert was confident it would eventually hit the billion-dollar mark.

"For the next ten years we really have the wind at our back," he told the hedge fund website FINalternatives.

Still working from home, Tom Gilbert negotiated several lucrative deals with investment banker Ralph Isham, his longtime tennis partner at the River and Maidstone Clubs.

In the fall of 2012, Tom Gilbert reached out to a leading equity research analyst named Dr. Raghuram Selvaraju, who specialized in health care companies. Gilbert invited him to dinner to discuss refocusing his fund strategy into health care.

The dinner was a success, and Gilbert subsequently hired Dr. Selvaraju as a consultant, appointing him Wainscott's co–portfolio manager and health care strategist. He told Dr. Selvaraju that his son, Tommy, would be adding his expertise to the hedge fund.

"[He] indicated to me," said Dr. Selvaraju, "that Tommy would be providing us with market color and technical analysis, [and] he was good at these kinds of things."

During the eighteen months he worked for Wainscott Capital, Dr. Selvaraju only saw Tommy at a handful of meetings with potential investors, where he never said a word.

At around the same time, Tom Gilbert sponsored his son to become a legacy member of the River Club, paying his $6,000-a-year membership fees and other charges. Tommy became a River Club regular, making full use of the tennis courts, where he was often successfully partnered with his father in doubles matches. It was the only time they saw each other, and their games were often strained, with the undercurrent of Tom wanting his son to become more involved in his hedge fund.

Tommy was still secretly dating Lizzy Fraser, as well as seeing various women on a casual basis. One night, he invited a woman, whom he had known since she was a child, on a date to a club in Brooklyn. When they arrived, Tommy apologized for not having any cash, expecting her to pay the cover charge. When she decided to end the date and go home, Tommy insisted on driving her back to her parents' apartment in uptown Manhattan. On the way there, he asked her to spend the night with him, but she refused. Then he drove straight past her parents' street, and she asked what he was doing.

"You're going to sleep over," he informed her before locking the car doors.

"We [were stopped at] one of those long lights and he put the car in park," she later told the *New York Post*. "I knew the child locks go off in park because my sister had the same car. So I opened the door and ran out."

This predatory behavior was perhaps a symptom of his stagnating mental condition.

Tommy also occasionally dated a rich young socialite named Jen, who told her friend Arianna Li about a hand-some, rich surfer guy she was seeing. One night, Jen invited Arianna to go to a Hamptons bar with them.

"She said he was from this good New York family," said Arianna. "That he went to Princeton and owned a hedge fund."

Tommy and Jen arrived at Arianna's house early to pick her up. She was surprised at the "beat-up Jeep" Tommy was driving, wondering why a hedge fund owner wouldn't have something nicer.

At the bar, Tommy bought her a drink, taking his money out of a cheap Velcro wallet. He then started boasting about his hedge fund and how well it was doing.

"It was so obvious that something was off," said Arianna. "It just didn't add up."

Then Tommy suggested they move on to the Surf Lodge in Montauk, and Arianna reluctantly went, as she didn't have any transport.

"They ended up getting totally wasted," said Arianna. "I felt like I was a prisoner. It was an absolute disaster."

13

THE CLOSET AFFAIR

Now in his late twenties, Tommy Gilbert had no visible means of supporting himself. He was still completely reliant on his parents, who gave him almost $74,000 in 2012, as well as paying his rent, expensive club memberships, and car expenses. Shelley Gilbert was particularly generous, transferring money into his Citibank account whenever he requested it.

On Thursday, January 3, 2013, she emailed him asking what night he could come over for dinner to celebrate his father's sixty-eighth birthday.

"Maybe Sunday night," Tommy replied. "Also could I have 200 for a party I went to on New Year's."

"Sunday night will be great," Shelley wrote back. "I will try to figure out something yummy!!!"

In early March, they helped him move into a new basement studio at 155 East Eighty-Eighth Street and Lexington Avenue, putting down a deposit and paying the $1,750-a-month rent.

"Hope you are settling into your new digs," emailed his mother.

A week later, the River Club paired Tommy with another member for a tennis match, referring to him as Thomas

Gilbert. Furious, Tommy told the club organizer to differentiate between him and his father in the future.

"Could you refer to me as Thomas Gilbert Jr.," he wrote, "just to clarify."

But soon afterward, Tommy was incensed to accidentally receive an email from the River Club meant for his father.

"Tommy, so sorry to confuse you with your dad," wrote the club secretary.

At the end of March, Tommy flew to Palm Beach, Florida, charging the air tickets to his parents' account without consulting them. This prompted his mother to ask him to be thriftier in the future, as they were watching their expenses.

"Hi, Palm Beach sounded like fun," she emailed him. "In the future, for any flights you take let Dad know before the flight so you can use frequent flier miles instead of paying real money. This will save us money which we are always eager to do. Xoxoxox."

Although Tommy Gilbert had settled into his new Upper East Side apartment and was out almost every night, he was depressed at the lack of progress with his hedge fund. At a psychotherapy session in April, he told Dr. Susan Evans that he was suicidal and had gone on the internet searching for guns. She was so concerned that she alerted Dr. Sacks, who immediately summoned Tommy to a meeting.

"We talked about it," said Dr. Sacks. "He said he had [done] it out of curiosity. He denied having any suicidal . . . or any homicidal ideation."

Dr. Sacks took him at his word. He did not feel Tommy's actions met the requirements of the recently passed New York SAFE (Secure Ammunition and Firearms Enforcement) Act, which stops the dangerously mentally ill from buying firearms.

* * *

Over the next few months, Tom Gilbert made a concerted effort to repair his strained relationship with Tommy and get him involved in his growing hedge fund. He invited him along for his regular Tuesday tennis nights at the River Club, followed by dinner. Tommy was agreeable, emailing his father back that it would be fun, as "it tends to be a good match."

When his father sought his advice on current trends in the biotech market, Tommy advised buying.

Encouraged by the response, Tom Sr. asked his son to start accompanying him to meetings with potential investors.

"I would like you also to become more involved in portfolio selection and some monitoring," he emailed on May 2. "I would like to discuss same with you at leisure. Perhaps this afternoon at 2:30 at 410 Park. Let me know, Much love, Dad."

To prepare Tommy for one important meeting, he sent him a list of non-health-care stocks he had recently sold, asking for his thoughts. Tommy didn't bother to reply or turn up at the investor meeting.

At the beginning of June, Tom Gilbert was busy working on a lucrative deal for Wainscott Capital with a water company and invited his son to participate.

"We would love to have you join forces," he emailed Tommy. "It's an extremely interesting deal."

Receiving no reply, his father followed up, asking for Tommy's thoughts on the "impact of the global slowdown," "deflation vs inflation," and his prognosis on the technical market. Once again, there was no reply.

In mid-June, he informed Tommy that he wanted him to attend strategy meetings with him and his new fund adviser, Dr. Raghuram Selvaraju, followed by dinner afterward.

He also asked him to drop his Princeton Club membership, as he rarely used it and his annual dues of $464 were coming up.

"I would prefer not to pay for this club," Tom emailed his son, "given all your other clubs, and relative lack of use."

After ignoring several more invitations to investor meetings and strategy sessions, Tommy told his mother to have his father stop texting him.

"I will stop texting you, as you requested to Mom," Tom Sr. replied, "but please respond to my emails on a timely basis going forward. Is that OK with you? Much love, Dad."

Tommy occasionally attended investor meetings as part of the Wainscott team but never played an active role. Tom Sr. was becoming so worried about Tommy's nonperformance for Wainscott, which he was paying him for, that he vented in his computer journal.

"Tommy—20 hours of technical work overdue," he wrote. "No market calls. Question of consistency. Trading account. See his biz plan. Mom to talk to him."

The first week of July, Tommy Gilbert did attend a business meeting but became incensed about his father moving chairs into the conference room. Tom immediately apologized, saying he hadn't realized it would disturb his son's work environment.

"You however should realize," he wrote Tommy in an email, "that this was totally inadvertent on my part and that I love you very much and would do nothing ever to hurt you. Much love, Dad."

That summer, Peter Smith Jr. and his business partner Zach Terzis relocated to the Hamptons with a small team of programmers to launch an e-commerce website called MadeClose.com. Peter Smith Sr. was allowing his son the use of one of two houses he owned in Sagaponack, but he laid down strict ground rules that there be no parties or girl-friends to distract from their work.

The house was directly across Sagg Main Street from the Smith family's historic 350-year-old house, listed on the National Register of Historic Places. Just a short walk from the beach, the former inn dated back to the first English settlement in Southampton Town. Over the years, it had been meticulously restored by Peter Smith Sr., who entertained friends there like Oliver Stone, Candice Bergen, and the late artist Larry Rivers.

Every year, the Smiths hosted a lavish summer party at the house, inviting hundreds of the Hamptons' heaviest hitters.

For the next few months, Peter Smith Jr. and his eight-member team knuckled down to work across the street. Also in attendance was Rocket, Smith's very frisky, ninety-pound designer-breed Labradane.

Soon Tommy Gilbert began showing up for business meetings and meals, trying to ingratiate himself into the group. Smith strongly discouraged him, explaining that it was strictly work and they were far too busy to socialize.

"I got the sense that Tommy was jealous that we were doing something," said Smith. "He told people that he worked for our company [because] he wanted to be part of the team."

In mid-July, Tommy threw himself a twenty-ninth birthday party at his parents' Wainscott house and asked Shelley to sleep elsewhere that night.

"I'm having a party this sat [*sic*], does that work?" he told his mother. "It might go late so if there is anyway [*sic*] you guys could stay with friends that night I'd greatly appreciate it."

More than fifty people came to the party, and Tommy was in unusually good spirits. He was the perfect host and made sure the drinks and drugs were flowing.

"Tommy could be the most charming person," said Peter Smith, "getting along with everybody and laughing."

In July, Lizzy Fraser broke up with Tommy Gilbert. He was devastated and called Annabelle Summers for advice on how to get their relationship back on track.

"He was telling me how he and Lizzy had had a fight and he wasn't sure what to do," she recalled. "I said, 'You know Lizzy drinks and that kind of throws her off. I'm sure she'll apologize and you guys will talk.' He even texted me afterwards to thank me for the advice."

Tommy now became obsessed that Lizzy was seeing other men. He knew she often hung out at the Surf Lodge in Montauk with a group of Manhattan bankers, who had taken a summer share at nearby Hither Hills beach. So he started staking out their house, looking for Lizzy.

One weekend toward the end of July, Tommy suddenly appeared there without explanation. Everyone assumed that he had been invited.

"Tommy just showed up," remembered Alyson Crowe (not her real name), who had rented the house with friends. "We always thought he was so strange because he never really said anything, just sitting there listening and watching."

At first, people wondered if he was just socially awkward or stoned. If anyone tried to engage him in conversation, he'd just stare blankly and mumble something incomprehensible. That seemed strange for someone with such an impeccable pedigree and education.

"He was a very good-looking guy," said Alyson, "and at first we thought, 'Maybe he's just shy. He doesn't know any of us.' But we're all like, 'Did he actually graduate from Princeton? He can't form sentences.'"

The next weekend, Tommy was back at the house like he

belonged there. When someone asked what he did, Tommy said he ran a hedge fund. But when questioned about whether he employed long/short investment strategy, Tommy had no clue what they were talking about.

"Then he realized," said Alyson, "that we were a house full of bankers and not just other rich kids. So when we would ask him questions about it, he shut down."

There were a lot of drugs in the house, and Tommy was always there for a line of cocaine or a beer. Then he would spend hours just sitting by himself in the corner with a thin smile on his face.

"He never really added much to the conversation," said Annabelle. "But he would laugh, so no one had a problem with him at first."

But Tommy soon started making people feel uncomfortable, as he always seemed to be lurking around aimlessly.

A couple of weeks later, Tommy was back at the Montauk house with Lizzy Fraser and Annabelle Summers for a party. During the evening, Lizzy disappeared, and Tommy eventually found her in a bedroom making out with a guy.

He ran downstairs, asking Annabelle what she thought Lizzy was up to.

"He was super jealous," Annabelle recalled. "It was then we all realized that he was obsessed with Lizzy."

At the following weekend's party, Tommy hid in a closet in a basement bedroom, trying to catch Lizzy with another man. A couple came in to have sex and heard something moving in the closet. They carried on regardless, but after finishing, the man went to the bathroom and caught Tommy sneaking out of the closet with a guilty look on his face.

"That was the final straw," said Alyson. "He was definitely not allowed back after that."

For the rest of the summer "the Closet Affair," as it became known, became a running joke in the house.

But even this did not stop Tommy from turning up at the Surf Lodge as if nothing had happened. He'd position himself near the table where everyone sat, just listening and drinking beer on the group tab.

"He was always alone, and it really started bothering us," said Alyson. "Our guess was that he was trying to pick up tidbits about Lizzy, because he was so obsessed with her."

Tommy's behavior was becoming more and more outlandish and unpredictable. The word had gone out on the Hamptons grapevine to avoid him.

14

"YOU'RE A LOSER"

At the beginning of August, Tommy took his parents' Mustang for a road trip without permission. When his mother discovered it gone, she reached out to Tommy.

"Hey," Tommy emailed back a couple of days later. "Just got back from DC yesterday, was playing golf. I will drop the Mustang. Can I have 450 for the trip if possible, stayed in a hotel overnight."

Because his parents were renting out 8 Georgica Association Road at $40,000 a month for much of the summer for the extra money, Tommy had nowhere to stay in the Hamptons. So he started sneaking into Peter Smith's basement to sleep, often bringing girls with him.

Several times, Smith caught him and warned him to stop, as it was supposed to be strictly business and no partying.

"I told him we're not allowed to have anyone here," recalled Smith. "There are rules [and] we're not trying to mess it up."

Tommy said he understood but continued creeping into the basement anyway, much to everyone's annoyance. Finally, Peter Smith cut Tommy off, telling friends not to invite him to any more social gatherings.

* * *

One Sunday in September, Peter Smith organized a small poker night, asking guests not to tell Tommy. He heard about it anyway through the Hamptons grapevine, turning up with Lizzy Fraser and her friend Lauren Davenport.

During the evening, Smith's pet dog, Rocket, accidentally knocked over a wineglass and broke it. To rein him in, Smith grabbed him by the scruff of the neck and pulled him away.

Then Tommy started "freaking out on" Smith, a party attendee later told *Vanity Fair,* accusing him of violently abusing the dog. But Smith thought the issue went deeper than that.

"It was a Lizzy issue for him," Smith later testified. "He thought I was going after his girl. He identified some reason to be angry with me and he was going for it."

For the next few minutes, everyone watched Tommy scream at Smith, calling him a "scumbag" and "the most violent person" he'd ever met.

Suddenly, Smith had had enough and turned the tables.

"You're a loser," he told Tommy. And as Lizzy Fraser and the rest of the party looked on aghast, Smith threw Tommy out of his father's house.

After his public humiliation, Tommy Gilbert seethed with anger. Being called a loser in front of his friends had really struck a nerve. It was something he feared being more than anything else, and he swore revenge on his former friend.

The next morning, he began telling friends that Peter Smith was cruelly mistreating Rocket.

"He became obsessed with the notion that Peter was

dangerous for this dog," said Oliver, who had originally given Rocket to Smith as a present. "That's when it started to get a little creepy."

A week later, Tommy Gilbert returned to the house when Peter Smith was out. Zach Terzis told him to go away, as they were working, but Tommy just ignored him and went up the stairs.

"[Zach] called me in a panic," said Smith, "and said Tommy had showed up at our house and said he had to get something from my room."

While they were on the phone, Tommy stole the flagpole from the porch outside Smith's bedroom. He carried it downstairs and then left.

The next day, he returned with the flagpole and hurled it through the kitchen door window before running away. Two nights later, Tommy threw a full can of Hawaiian Punch through the windshield of a car parked in the Smith driveway.

When Peter Smith Sr. heard about the incident, he reported it to the Southampton Town Police, and Tommy was brought in for questioning. Ultimately, Peter Smith's father declined to press charges, as he had known the Gilberts for years and didn't want to ruin their son's life.

Later, Tom Gilbert sent a check to his old friend to cover all the damage that Tommy had caused.

A few days after the flagpole incident, Tommy Gilbert called Peter Smith Jr., claiming it was just a harmless prank. Smith disagreed and told him that his crazy behavior was worrying everyone.

"And then he told me that I should be worried," Smith would later testify, "because he was coming for me."

For months, Smith had been telling friends about Tommy's increasingly bizarre behavior, but everyone had thought he was exaggerating.

"I thought, Peter's just being an asshole," said Bart Hayes. "Peter was like, 'You don't understand, guys, he's fucking crazy!' And we're all kind of rolling our eyes like, 'All right, dude.'"

Chris Oliver advised Smith to talk to Tommy's parents, but he said he had already done so, and they weren't receptive to hearing anything bad about their son.

"Peter was scared," said Oliver. "No one really believed him."

On Wednesday, October 2, after renewed pressure from his father to become more involved in Wainscott Capital, Tommy terminated their relationship in a bizarre email.

> Dear Dad,
> I can't even begin to explain what an incredible father you've been! Throughout my entire life you have been totally supportive of me. The level of attention and support I've received from you is totally remarkable. I've been lucky to have you as a father and owe you a great deal. Therefore I hope you understand that we should part ways right now! At this point, the best gift you could continue giving me as a father is my own space and freedom from you. I think it is common for children to drift away from their parents as they age and I wouldn't worry about it. If you ever miss me and want to reach out, know that I will always be there with you! I can't begin to tell you how wonderful you've

been in my entire life. I'm going to stay with
friends this summer, and if I see you around
we should politely say hi and continue walking.
The more you respect my space, the more I will
appreciate you! This gesture is currently the
best thing you could do for me. I wish you all
the best and love you.

Love,
Tommy

After receiving the letter, Tom Gilbert cut and pasted it
into his computer diary before introspectively analyzing
their relationship over the years. They were "opposites," he
wrote, but what repels also attracts. One example was him
being an entrepreneur, while Tommy feared the business environment.

"He is a great team player," Tom noted, "[and] can imi-
tate the exact proper motions, positions, etc. of a great first
baseman. [He] played high level sports through his problems
at Deerfield."

He then went back to their earliest days in Tuxedo Park,
when he had taught his infant son to play catch. He noted that
Tommy had "a great arm" but had developed "an intractable
throwing problem," after he himself had injured his shoulder and could no longer take a proper windup.

He correlated this to Tommy's present problems in business, finding that if his son totally immersed himself in a
wealth management program, instead of just "skimming the
surface," he would be able to do anything.

But he admitted that he was not helping Tommy by providing unlimited financial support.

"Not having to make a living," he wrote. "I am not doing
him any favors by letting him know that he can . . . be in
the in crowd, without doing all the 70 hours of work away

from such entertainment. With his connections, and clubs, he could get into a wealth management program."

Tommy's letter marked a new low in their relationship, and Tom must have been very hurt by it. From then on, he would avoid direct contact with his son, using Shelley as a go-between to try to influence him when he felt it necessary.

15

"WHAT A NIGHTMARE"

Tommy was now veering dangerously out of control. The day after he severed his relationship with his father, he turned his attention to getting even with Peter Smith.

On Friday, October 4, they were both due to attend the screening of a short movie called *And After All,* coproduced by their old Buckley schoolmate Jack Bryan. It starred socialite Annabelle Dexter-Jones, and Tommy, Lizzy Fraser, and Peter Smith all appeared in it as extras.

That afternoon, Tommy started calling Smith's cell phone incessantly. Getting no answer, he went to the Williamsburg row house they had once shared and began ringing the doorbell.

Smith came down and stepped outside, carefully locking the door behind him. Tommy suddenly appeared out of the shadows, saying they needed to talk and he needed to see if Rocket was okay. Smith said he didn't have time, as he was in a rush to make the screening.

Tommy told Smith he was still his best friend and they should make up, so things could go back like before. He also wanted to know why the police were "harassing" him after the flagpole incident.

"He said, 'I need your help,'" Smith recalled. "'I'm starting to forget things.'"

When the diminutive Smith turned around, he saw Tommy towering over him with his fist raised.

"He swung at me [and] missed," said Smith. "But as I ducked, he grabbed the back of my head with both hands and he kneed me in the face about eighteen to twenty times."

At this point, a bystander ran over and grabbed Tommy to stop him. Tommy immediately jumped up and started pointing at Smith, who had blood pouring from his nose, shouting, "He attacked me! He attacked me!"

As Tommy ran off down Bedford Avenue, Smith called the police, who soon arrived and wrote out a report. A few minutes later, Tommy was picked up near McCarren Park. He was taken to a nearby police station, arrested and booked, and given a desk appearance ticket to appear at a criminal court for arraignment at a later date.

Peter Smith suffered a broken nose and concussion. He took a selfie of his bloodied face, texting it to their friends at the screening.

Later that night, Chris Oliver went to see Smith, who was still in shock.

"His nose was messed up, and he'd been hit really hard," said Oliver. "Tommy's a powerful, strong guy, and that was a real thing. Okay, this had gotten bad."

Oliver called Tommy to try to make some sense of what had happened.

"I said, 'Why did you hit our friend?'" he recalled. "And he just went on about the dog. It was crazy what he was saying."

Suddenly, Tommy became angry, demanding to know whose side Oliver was on.

"He was all fired up," said Oliver. "But I told Tommy, 'Look, man, what's the deal? Are you okay?' I was just trying to mend the wound before it got out of control."

Jack Bryan, whose movie screening they were all supposed to attend that night, also called Tommy to find out what had happened. Tommy claimed it was just a misunderstanding and he didn't want his friendship with Peter to end like this.

Then Bryan asked him about throwing the flagpole through the window of the Smith house in the Hamptons.

"I asked him if he did [that]," said Bryan. "And he was like, 'No! No! No!' He was really aggressive and it was like rapid fire, but also he was clearly searching his mind for an answer. And his being defensive and cagey scared me."

Then Tommy told his old Buckley friend to mind his business.

"He got really mad at me," said Bryan. "This is not a person that wants my help . . . and that was the last time I talked to Tommy."

By all accounts, Tommy failed to grasp the gravity of what he had done. The next day, he texted Smith's business partner Zach Terzis to see if he wanted to hang out, acting as if nothing had happened.

The unprovoked attack on Peter Smith scared everyone in their tightly knit social circle, who finally realized that Smith had been right all along about Tommy's strange behavior. From then on, everyone avoided him like the plague.

"That was a real turning point in everybody's association with Tommy," one of their circle told *Vanity Fair*. "I don't know a lot of people who hung out with him after that."

* * *

Lila Chase heard about Tommy's assault on Peter Smith from her father. She was shocked, as she'd never seen a hint of violence during their three-year relationship.

"My father sat me down and said, 'Sweetie, I think Tommy's really ill,'" Lila recalled. "'He's in serious trouble, and he beat up Peter Smith very badly.'"

Then Lila called Tommy. It was the first time they had talked in months. She told him that he was in serious trouble and needed to get help.

Tommy claimed it was all a big misunderstanding, totally denying beating up Peter Smith and breaking his nose.

"It wasn't even like he made an excuse," she said. "His version [was] kind of a different reality."

Soon after the attack, Peter Smith Jr. called Tom Gilbert, saying his son was dangerous and should be committed to a mental hospital. Gilbert later summarized the call in his computer diary.

"Call from Peter," he wrote. "Peter says Tommy . . . is trying to kill him. Peter thinks Tommy [has lost] touch with reality and his life is in danger. Peter wants Tommy committed."

Smith also said he planned to get a restraining order against Tommy and wanted to know his new address.

But instead of confronting his son directly, Tom asked Shelley to do so.

Tom Gilbert was extremely concerned about Tommy's arrest, musing in his computer diary about whether his son should use an insanity defense. He noted that it could mean more time in a mental institution than jail. He debated "criminal strategy," writing that no one would ever believe that Smith had thrown the first punch.

He also consulted his brother, Beck, who did not approve

of Tommy not having a job while enjoying a playboy life-style. After they spoke, Tom paraphrased his older brother's thoughts on the matter and the best way to handle Tommy.

"He has always been [an] extremely selfish, con artist," he wrote. "This is an outgrowth of his personality. He is milking us, and then something worse will happen in the future."

Beck had said that Tommy needed to understand that he couldn't keep manipulating the family to his own advantage.

"We can't continue to bail him out," Tom wrote. "He has to look in the mirror, and become less self-centered."

He also outlined Beck's strategy for fighting a criminal assault case at trial by painting Peter Smith as "the bad guy" with a history of fights and drug abuse. Beck speculated that the issue might just go away, as Smith would not want to be cross-examined on the stand as a hostile witness.

"Most importantly," Tom wrote, "[is] how to make Tommy realize that he has [to be] responsible for his action[s], stop milking others with his complete lack of disregard."

As chairman emeritus of the board of the Harvard Medical School, Beck Gilbert used his connections there to hire defense attorney Alex Spiro. The ambitious thirty-year-old was uniquely qualified to defend Tommy Gilbert, as he had a strong background in psychiatry.

Spiro was a biopsychology major at Tufts University before working at McLean Hospital, one of the leading psychiatric hospitals and affiliated with Harvard Medical School. During his five years there, he developed an education program for children with Asperger's syndrome.

He did a complete career U-turn in 2005 and was accepted by Harvard Law School, where he first came to the notice of Beck Gilbert. After graduating from Harvard, Spiro briefly worked for the CIA before joining the Manhattan district attorney's office as a prosecutor.

In early 2013, he became a defense attorney for the top New York law firm of Brafman & Associates, who specialized in high-profile clients. And a few months later, Beck Gilbert hired Spiro to defend his nephew, paying him $7,000 up front and a $25,000 total retainer.

Spiro immediately went into action. The Brooklyn district attorney's office soon dismissed the assault charge, after Tommy agreed to anger management counseling. Spiro then had the case sealed by a Kings County judge, and Tom Gilbert breathed a sigh of relief that they had avoided an embarrassing trial.

When Dr. Michael Sacks heard that Tommy Gilbert had turned violent, he was alarmed.

"That got me very concerned," said Dr. Sacks. "It was the first time, to my knowledge, that he had acted in a very physical way against somebody he felt was persecuting him."

Six months earlier, after learning Tommy was looking for guns on the internet, he had felt it had not met the requirement of the New York SAFE Act. Now he decided it did and reported him. Tommy Gilbert would be added to a list of criminals and mentally ill people who were banned from legally buying firearms.

At their next therapy session, Dr. Sacks asked Tommy about the attack. Tommy refused to discuss it and dismissed it as nothing. The doctor did not take any steps to have Tommy hospitalized as he could have done.

In his computer diary, Tom Gilbert mused about what needed to happen to prevent another violent attack in the future.

"What a nightmare," he wrote. "Tommy must go back on medication. Should get committed or fundamentally change his spots. Will be a long siege."

He also planned to do extensive research on a variety of drugs to help his son's paranoia, fearing there might be more violence.

"After two weeks he will attack Peter Smith again," he wrote. "Needs to show substantial improvement in two weeks or put him away."

16

"SAVING TOMMY GILBERT"

Tommy was floundering after being ostracized by his circle of friends that fall. He was seeing a string of psychiatrists, describing symptoms of anxiety and paranoia. He had recently been diagnosed with hypogonadism, a condition where the body doesn't produce enough testosterone for male growth and development during puberty. It is either congenital or caused by an injury later in life. Tommy was prescribed testosterone to treat the condition.

Since his attack on Peter Smith, Tommy's paranoid ideations had worsened, and he struggled to survive in the real world. He now feared his father was trying to control him by limiting his money. That was hardly true, as Tommy was still receiving up to $10,000 a month from his parents in addition to his rent payments. His mother made that point by once sending Tommy a handwritten list of expenses he'd run up during a single two-week period, including travel, Jeep maintenance, towing charges, and $600 of charges from Amazon.

He largely avoided his father, although they occasionally crossed paths at the various clubs they had in common. Tommy suspected that this was no accident and warned Tom Sr. to keep his distance.

"Good seeing you today," he emailed his father in October,

"but part of keeping space means not showing up to events that you know I'm going to attend. The more you do this, the more distance I will keep from you. Please don't follow me and don't do that again."

Tom Sr. now relied on Shelley to try to get their son to start pulling his weight, as he was still receiving a stipend from Wainscott Capital despite not producing anything.

"Tommy," she wrote him in late October, "I just put the money into your account but what needs to be addressed is your workload for the money you are earning. There are many things you are very excellent at that you could be doing for Wainscott Capital and if you accomplished more for the fund you could possibly increase your earnings. Let me know what you think."

Three and a half years after launch, Wainscott Capital only had $7.3 million under management, a paltry sum in the billion-dollar world of hedge funds. The Georgica Association Road house was back on the market, and Tom Gilbert was about to take a $4 million equity loan against its value to boost his company.

At the end of October, Tommy fell asleep in the men's locker room at the Maidstone Club. The locker room attendant, Michael Capozzola, came over to ask if he wanted anything, addressing him as "Tom." Insulted at not being called "Mr. Gilbert," Tommy flew into a rage.

When Capozzola tried to calm him down, asking how he had disrespected him, Tommy threatened to kill him and then stormed out. Tom and Shelley Gilbert were officially informed of their son's bad behavior, which would be added to the agenda at the next Maidstone Club board meeting the following spring.

The incident soon became the talk of the Maidstone Club, with various embellished versions circling the Hamptons for weeks.

"I heard about it because people like to gossip," said Chris Oliver. "But Tommy was kind of going crazy."

Tom Gilbert was deeply embarrassed and called Capozzola to apologize on Tommy's behalf.

"We had a good sympathetic chat [and] mended some fences," Gilbert later noted in his computer diary. "I need to tip him $100 at year end (more?) I also need to mend fences with Eden, Golf Committee, and with Wainscott yacht racing."

At the beginning of November, Tommy Gilbert decided to beef up his security, as he determined his home was under threat. He bought several No Trespassing signs and installed a lock on his upstairs bedroom door. He also purchased a safe for his valuables.

Then, without consulting his parents, he ordered an expensive ADT security system for the Wainscott house. When Tom Gilbert found out, he ordered ADT to cease work immediately. But his son overrode him.

"You have my permission to continue with this order," Tommy emailed the ADT representative. "Unfortunately my parents are unwell and have a history of harassing people working for them. I apologize for their behavior [and] will get in touch about the exact installation date this week."

Tommy invited Lila Chase over to see his new Upper East Side apartment. She had been worried about him. When she arrived, he was wearing a smart suit but looked miserable.

"And I said, 'You're in a suit,'" she recalled. "'You're a businessman, just like you always wanted.' He said, 'No, I'm just in a suit.' And he looked broken."

When she asked to see the apartment, Tommy at first refused to allow her inside. Finally, he relented after she reminded him that was why she was there.

"And the apartment was weird," she said. "The TV was on the floor. He'd cut out sheets of black paper and covered the windows with it. It was a weird situation."

Lila was so concerned that she offered to drive him to New York–Presbyterian Hospital to see Dr. Sacks.

"I said, 'I'll sit with you. I will not let them hospitalize you. You're not a danger to yourself or others. They can't [commit you], but we just need to evaluate and make a plan.'"

But Tommy refused, saying he was late to a tennis game at the Union Club.

That winter, Tommy Gilbert drowned his sorrows by hitting the glamorous Manhattan social circuit. In mid-November, he made the prestigious *New York Social Diary,* photographed with Ann Morrison Calvert at an Audubon Young Members of New York silent auction. He was now sporting a full beard and wore a black suit and striped tie. He had visibly aged in the last few months but was still strikingly handsome.

"Guests enjoyed cocktails, nibbled on pizza and danced to the rug cutting tunes of DJ Luther Riggs," read the accompanying story. "An expansive silent auction spread including everything from Polo Lessons in Greenwich, CT to a piece of art by Faust was up for bids."

As the year drew to a close, Tom Gilbert was working behind the scenes with Alex Spiro to try to persuade Tommy to start taking his medication. Spiro had become more than just an attorney to Tommy, who looked up to him. And his father used Spiro to communicate with Tommy, who now was avoiding all contact with him.

In a computer diary entry, "All About Saving Tommy

Gilbert," Tom Sr. viewed Spiro as his last chance to rescue his wayward son.

"Alex may be the hero that gets Tommy to get back on meds," wrote Gilbert. "This is essential for the psychiatrists who have the power to commit Tommy if he doesn't improve rapidly. That would be a game stopper for Tommy. (Alex can tell him that—not me)."

While Tommy was avoiding all contact with his father, he continued to use his mother like a cash machine, demanding money almost daily. In the space of one week, he wanted $250 for clothes, $250 for his gym, and $800 for his stock-picking service.

"Need the money please if you can put it in," he emailed his mother at the end of November. "Also have more doctors [*sic*] appointments."

He would also have her run errands for him while he surfed in the Hamptons.

"Found a better garage for the car," he emailed her. "It's on 49th between 1st and York and 350 a month. If you have a sec today can you pick up the car . . . and bring it to the [new] one? Will give you the info on who to talk to there."

Days later he requested $400 for "wetsuit stuff," and Shelley dutifully transferred $1,150 into his Citibank account.

17

ANNA ROTHSCHILD

The week before Christmas, Tommy Gilbert met an attractive blond publicist named Anna Rothschild at a birthday party. A fixture on the New York and London social set, twice-divorced Anna ran her own public relations company and organized society events.

She told Tommy he could easily be a model, offering to arrange headshots for his portfolio. Tommy was very interested.

"He came on to me with a vengeance," she recalled. "He asked me for my number, and I gave him my card."

The next day, he asked Anna out on a date. She immediately accepted, flattered that such a handsome, eligible young man, nineteen years her junior, would be interested in her.

"I just thought, why isn't he dating a twenty-five-year-old model?" she said. "But if he wants to go out with me, so be it. I'm not going to fight."

The relationship soon turned physical, and Tommy began staying over at Anna's apartment, which was only a couple of blocks away from his. She brought him along as her date for her round of Christmas parties, although he hardly said a word and never drank.

At one party, a mutual friend took Anna aside, warning

that Tommy was dangerous and one day they were going to find her chopped up into little pieces.

"And I honestly thought the guy was jealous," said Anna, "because Tommy's obviously very good-looking. I thought, 'Oh, you're just being ridiculous.'"

When she mentioned to Tommy that she was attending a small New Year's Eve party at a friend's apartment, she invited him along, not wanting to appear rude. To her surprise, he eagerly accepted.

"I remember thinking, that's so odd on New Year's Eve," she said. She'd assumed Tommy would rather be with friends his own age. "You'd think he'd have all these raging parties to go to, but he wasn't invited to one thing."

On January 14, 2014, Tommy Gilbert had what would be his final session with Dr. Michael Sacks. After six years of psychiatric treatment, Tommy announced that he didn't need his prescribed medication for psychosis and schizophrenia. He told Dr. Sacks he much preferred Dr. Susan Evans's psychological treatment.

"Not taking medication," Dr. Sacks wrote in his notes. "He has no insight into the fact that he actually has an illness . . . and no appreciation that he is psychotic."

When Dr. Evans saw Tommy Gilbert two days later, she was so concerned by this turn of events that she informed Dr. Shapiro, his original psychiatrist.

"Tommy is not currently on any meds," she wrote Dr. Shapiro. "I think he is acting more unstable. Thinking schizo-affective illness is the most likely condition."

During their four months together, Anna Rothschild could never quite work out what was wrong with her new boyfriend.

When they went out, Tommy was always polite but socially awkward and rarely spoke at parties. He told her that he was seeing a psychiatrist, who had him on Xanax for his social anxiety.

"Something was really, really off," she explained. "[I] tried to figure out what was wrong with him. I googled things such as 'autism' or 'on the spectrum.'"

Anna would try to draw him out, asking about his family background for clues. She was surprised to discover he had graduated from Princeton, as she did not consider him particularly intelligent.

"He talked about his dad and seemed really hurt," she recalled. "He said his dad thought he was stupid and nothing he could do was right."

Tommy also claimed that his father refused to allow him to work for him. After Rothschild pressed him about it, Tommy emailed his dad for the first time in months, offering his services.

"I'm free for the next few weeks if you want to do investor meetings," he announced in early January.

Tommy often spoke of his Mameluke hedge fund, boasting to have developed a secret algorithm that would make him rich. He proudly showed Rothschild his PowerPoint presentation, asking for help finding investors. Although she agreed to do so, she never did.

But she did organize a photo shoot for headshots, to launch his prospective acting and modeling career.

"Nothing came of it," said Anna. "I told him acting was not a great idea because he didn't talk."

Their no-strings-attached relationship suited both of them. Several nights a week, Tommy stayed over at Anna's palatial apartment, where they made love and watched movies. She would try to make conversation, but it was always an uphill battle.

"He was a total gentleman," she said. "Wherever we went, he paid for the taxis. Sometimes we'd go to dinner in the neighborhood, like some little sushi thing, or he'd come over and cook. I never took him anywhere expensive, because I knew he was a young guy and he always paid."

On one occasion, Tommy invited her back to his basement apartment on East Eighty-Eighth Street, and she was appalled by its deplorable state.

"He lived in a shithole," she explained. "I couldn't even stay there fifteen minutes because it was so dirty and cluttered."

As she got to know him better, Anna began to realize that Tommy had no friends. During their time together, he never called or texted anyone, only ever receiving a single phone call from his mother.

Most weekends, Tommy drove to the Hamptons to go surfing. He'd invite Anna along, but she felt it would be "too weird" to stay at his parents' house, as they were closer to her age.

On January 19, 2014, Anna organized a charity event for Animal Aid USA for her client Prince Lorenzo Borghese at the Jane Hotel in downtown Manhattan. She brought Tommy as her date, and they were photographed together. A confident-looking Anna has her arm around her bearded boyfriend, who looks very uncomfortable in an open-necked white shirt, a J.Crew sports jacket, and jeans. It was a rare photograph of them together.

"I didn't take pictures with him because he was so much younger," said Anna, "and I didn't want people to know."

By the end of January, Tommy Gilbert was getting more and more paranoid. He was now planning to get a firearm to protect himself and had started googling how to buy a defensive-carry handgun. He was especially interested in the Glock .40 caliber, but because he was on the New York SAFE list, he could not purchase a firearm legally.

In February, he secretly moved into 8 Georgica Association Road, without his parents' knowledge. One night, he accidentally set off the alarm he had had installed, prompting the alarm company to alert East Hampton Town Police. An officer duly checked the house, reporting that all the windows and doors were secure and the alarm had gone off accidentally.

An angry Tom Gilbert then asked for the alarm system password, as the police charged the family every time they had to come out to check the house.

"Tommy," he emailed his son. "Please remotely disarm the ADT system and confirm when done. Also give us the master password and keypad password. We can't go out and have it go off and then pay a $450 fine to the EH police department for a false alarm. Dad."

A couple of weeks later, Tom Gilbert arrived at the house to find the heating thermostat turned on and a stain on a rug in a bedroom upstairs. He called East Hampton Town Police to report a break-in.

"Nothing was stolen or moved otherwise," read the official police report. "No obvious point of entry was visible."

It is unknown whether Tom Gilbert ever challenged his son about staying there without permission, but he was still actively trying to involve him in Wainscott Capital.

On March 21, he invited Tommy to an upcoming luncheon at the Harvard Club, saying there would be potential hedge fund investors there.

"Please stop emailing me," came Tommy's reply. "I'm obviously not responding."

The following day, Tommy became enraged when his father arrived at the River Club while he was playing tennis. He emailed him immediately to leave.

"We were in the middle of a game and you took our court," he snapped. "Please go to your assigned court and do not reply to this email."

Then he threatened to change his email address if his father didn't stop contacting him.

"Again I requested no emails," Tommy told him. "This is a form of harassment."

But a week later, on April 6, Tommy's tone had totally changed, as he needed his father's financial help to get a new apartment. He also felt entitled to ask for a slice of the upcoming lucrative summer rental of the Wainscott house.

> Hi Dad,
> Is there any way we could do the apartment?
> My lease is up and I need to move as quickly
> as possible. It was my idea to rent the East
> Hampton house out for the summer and I found
> a renter. Last year we got $40,000k for the
> month of August but I found someone to pay
> $175,000 for the entire summer. I did not ask for
> any of the profits even though I found the deal.
> The summer rental is generating an additional
> $135,000 and your fund is growing. I think it
> would be appropriate to pay for the apartment
> using some of the money from the summer
> rental. It's also important for me to have a place
> to live and I need to close this deal by Tuesday.
> Please let me know if this is possible.
>
> Tommy

* * *

A week later, Tommy Gilbert's driving license was suspended after he ignored a summons in Sag Harbor Village. He paid no attention and carried on driving anyway.

Then on April 19, he was arrested by East Hampton Police for driving his 2007 Jeep without a valid license or insurance. Once again, he turned to his parents to pay his fines so he could get his license back.

His concerned mother emailed him, telling him to take the proof that Tom had paid his fines to the DMV, so he could get insurance.

"We don't want you driving until then," Shelley told him. "Someone slamming into your car could wipe us out financially if you don't have insurance."

After Tommy had threatened the locker attendant's life at the Maidstone Club, the board had banned him for the rest of the year. Now with summer approaching, he urgently needed a new Hamptons country club to join. In mid-April, he asked his uncle Beck, whom he rarely saw, to use his influence to get him summer membership at Amagansett's exclusive Devon Yacht Club.

> Hi Beck,
> How are you? I was thinking of doing summer membership at Devon and wondering if you could propose me. It's late for this summer but they mentioned they might still be able to do it for this year. Free for a call or email anytime this weekend.
>
> Tommy

Beck Gilbert promised to look into it, but after checking with the manager found Tommy was ineligible.

"Sorry that didn't work out," he told his nephew. "Keep me posted about what you're doing."

Refusing to take no for an answer, Tommy insisted that he was eligible for a summer membership.

"Family members can actually propose to Devon," he emailed back. "Is it alright if you propose me? Will be around today if you want to call."

His uncle apologized, saying there was nothing further he could do.

By that point, Anna Rothschild had decided to break up with Tommy, whom she felt was becoming too dependent on her. They were now seeing each other almost every day, and Anna was afraid the relationship was getting serious.

"I started developing some feelings for him," she explained, "and I decided that wasn't good for me, as I need someone who's age appropriate."

She began distancing herself from Tommy and stopped returning his texts. Finally, Anna told him they were over and to get his stuff out of her apartment.

"He was very upset," she recalled. "I don't think he can take rejection of any kind."

Although they officially split up, they still kept in touch, and within months, Anna would rekindle the relationship.

18

"LIKE A KID WITH
A NEW TOY"

On April 28, 2014, Tommy Gilbert and his father cosigned a one-year lease on apartment 1F at 350 West Eighteenth Street. It was a shabby first-floor apartment across from a methadone clinic and a public school. Tom Gilbert had agreed to act as guarantor for the $2,275-a-month rent, as Tommy's income was too low.

The next day, Tommy started seeing Dr. Jason Kim of Weill Cornell Medical College. He had been referred by Dr. Susan Evans, as he still refused to take his medication and she thought Dr. Kim could help.

Over the next six months, Tommy had seven $450 sessions with Dr. Kim, all paid for by his parents. Dr. Kim would diagnose Tommy as suffering from a host of mental illnesses, including OCD, bipolar disorder, schizophrenia, and delusional disorder.

"I did think schizophrenia was possible," Dr. Kim later testified. "It's a grave diagnosis . . . and would interfere with his ability to work . . . and maintain social relationships."

On April 30, Tommy moved into his new one-bedroom in Chelsea. Later that night, he met Annabelle Summers at the

Bowery Hotel, where she was staying. She brought along her good friend Briana Swanson, who was sharing her hotel room.

Blond and good-looking, Briana resembled Lizzy Fraser and moved in the same social circles. Four years older than Tommy, her main claim to fame was as a contestant on a 2012 episode of *Hell's Kitchen*. She had made it to the third round before being sent home by Gordon Ramsay for her shoddy fish entrée.

"It's a bit like your brain," Ramsay screamed at her, "not only has it shrunk but it's disappeared!"

Originally from Jefferson, Iowa, Briana graduated culinary school in 2005, before moving to New York, where she worked as a trader on Wall Street. After the recession hit, she became a private chef, catering society parties and other high-class events.

"She knew everybody," said Bart Hayes. "She went to nightclubs a lot and would bring along a bunch of cute girls, and clubs would pay them. So she kind of entered an inner network and just became friends with everyone through the nightclub scene."

Briana was immediately attracted to Tommy Gilbert over drinks at the Bowery Bar, although he barely spoke. She ended up spending the night with him in the hotel bedroom, while Annabelle slept outside on the couch.

"I had a feeling that they were going to hook up," said Annabelle.

The next morning, Tommy told Briana all about his new apartment.

"I thought he was gorgeous," said Briana, "and offered to help him move into his new place. It just kind of went from there."

After the move, Briana cleaned the bathroom and kitchen.

To her surprise, Tommy invited her to move in a couple of days after they first met. He told her not to worry about rent.

Initially, Tommy seemed like perfect boyfriend material, except he was painfully shy to the point of stuttering. He explained that he was on antidepressants.

While Briana went to work during the day, Tommy hit the gym, played tennis, and practiced yoga. He told her he was working on his Mameluke Capital hedge fund, but she saw little evidence of it. It was soon obvious that he resented all his peers' success.

"He definitely felt cheated," said Briana. "He's watching all his friends rise in their careers and he's not doing anything. He would tell me he was in finance and I knew he was lying, but I didn't say anything because I didn't want to embarrass him."

A week after Briana Swanson moved into his apartment, Tommy decided to buy a handgun. Over his last several therapy sessions, he had reported being threatened, psychologically harassed, and having his apartment broken into. Nine years after first telling a psychiatrist he wanted to buy a gun, he was finally going through with it.

On Sunday, May 11, he went online to search for a concealed weapon. He soon spotted an ad for a Glock .40-caliber semiautomatic for $575 on a Facebook guns-for-sale forum. The model 22 pistol came in the original packaging with a shoulder holster, laser sight, and 150 rounds of ammunition.

At 10:47 p.m., Tommy fired off an email to the seller, John Jay Bennett, age forty-nine, of Clarksburg, Ohio.

"Hi how are you?" he wrote. "I'm interested in the glock [*sic*] if still available."

Six hours later, at 4:28 a.m. Bennett replied.

Dear Thomas,
Yes, the Glock is still available. Where do you
live?

Your Obedient Servant In Christ,
J. Jay.

On Wednesday afternoon, Tommy requested they communicate through the encrypted email service Hushmail, for an
extra level of security, but Bennett declined.

On Friday, Bennett informed Tommy that it would be illegal to ship the gun to him directly, so he needed to find a
licensed New York State firearm dealer to receive it on his
behalf. After a miscommunication over the shipping fees,
Tommy offered to drive to Ohio and collect the gun himself.

"Hi J. Jay," he wrote. "I might be able to just drive out
there since I will have free time over the next few weeks. The
latter half of next week should work."

Bennett replied that would be "fantastic" and save him
a "huge shipping bill." He apologized that his house was "a
wreck," but looked forward to meeting Tommy in person.

"If you tell me what you like to eat," he wrote. "My Mom
or I can make it. Let me know."

Almost a week later, on May 28, when he hadn't heard
anything further, Bennett emailed Tommy to see if he was
still coming.

"I have a couple of questions first," Tommy replied.
"What's your cell phone?"

Bennett said he didn't own a cell phone but gave his father's phone number instead, offering to do the exchange in
a public place if it made Tommy "more comfortable."

On Friday, May 30, before leaving for Ohio, Tommy officially filed his Mameluke Capital Fund, LP, with the

Securities and Exchange Commission. On the six-page form, he stated that the minimum investment he would accept was $300,000.

After filing it, he celebrated by buying a new set of clothes at J.Crew, running up a $300 charge on his Citibank credit card.

At around 7:30 p.m., he collected his Jeep from his garage and drove to Princeton, New Jersey, for the first stage of his 575-mile trip to collect the gun. He spent the night at a Best Western hotel, checking out early Saturday morning.

He drove straight through Pennsylvania to Columbus, Ohio, before turning south for the forty-mile journey to John Jay Bennett's parents' house in the tiny rural village of Clarksburg.

Around midday, Tommy Gilbert, dressed casually in a white T-shirt and jeans, knocked on the front door. It was opened by the portly Bennett, who immediately assured Tommy that his large barking dog was not a biter.

Then he brought Tommy into the front room, where his mother served refreshments while he went off to get the gun. A few minutes later, Bennett came back proudly holding the .40-caliber Glock and handed it to Tommy, who was visibly excited.

"He seemed like a kid with a new toy," recalled Bennett, "only he was a grown man with a new gun."

As he lovingly cradled the handgun, Tommy kept mumbling about what a great deal he had gotten while Bennett explained how to clean the gun and keep it in good running order. He also showed him all the accessories included in the price.

The genial Ohioan then offered to take him to a nearby shooting range to fire off a couple of rounds, but Tommy said he was in a hurry to leave.

On the way out to his Jeep, Tommy handed Bennett $575

in cash and formally took possession of the Glock, which he placed on the front seat next to him.

Then he drove straight back to his Manhattan apartment, storing the Glock and accessories in a new safe he had recently installed in his bedroom.

At the beginning of June, Tom Gilbert moved Wainscott Capital out of his apartment and into a small office at 800 Third Avenue. He had hired financial analyst Clay LeConey as his marketing chief to raise money and take his hedge fund to the next level. Although it was still a fairly small hedge fund focusing on biotechs, it was already generating a healthy 30 percent return for investors.

Tom Gilbert's new hiring made the *Hedge Fund Alert*'s Grapevine column.

"Biotechnology-stock-shop Wainscott Capital has hired a head of sales and marketing," it reported. "Clay LeConey joined the New York fund manager last month. Wainscott, founded by Tom Gilbert in 2011, runs about $10 million. Its lone fund gained 26.8% in 2012 and 32.2% in 2013, and is up 4% so far this year."

The new duo would both work twelve hours a day, six days a week out of the new office. Tom Gilbert seemed "driven," sleeping only four hours a night and often firing off "frenetic" emails at 4:00 a.m.

"I was his right-hand man," said LeConey, "so he would have time to focus on research and trading."

Although Tommy Gilbert was still prominently listed on the Wainscott website, LeConey was mystified as to what he actually did, as he never came into the office.

"I don't think I ever heard his name once," said LeConey. "Is Tommy actually working here because he's on the website, or is that more of a résumé padder?" he mused.

Tom Gilbert still hoped that his son would finally grow up and start serious work on his newly registered Mameluke fund. He made notes in his computer diary about an upcoming conversation he planned to have with Alex Spiro about Tommy's future.

"Tommy's own franchise," he wrote. "Is he going to work his ass off on the fund. What are the operational details, planning of his time weekly, monthly—does he have a business plan. Can he see it, and will he execute it. If this doesn't work, this is the last train out."

19

"HE WAS KIND OF
FOOLING AROUND"

A few days after returning from Ohio, Tommy Gilbert brought Briana Swanson to the Hamptons for the summer. To supplement the $800 weekly allowance he received from his father, he planned to Airbnb his West Eighteenth Street apartment once he had been approved as a host.

Because his parents' house was being rented for the summer, Tommy ordered a garden storage shed to put on the edge of the property. He told Briana that he had permission from his parents to live in the shed, although they knew nothing about it.

"We were both kind of excited," said Briana. "It was like camping."

During the several days it took to clear off the proposed site, they stayed in a tent on the beach. Finally, the shed arrived and Tommy set it up, even illegally tapping into the main electricity supply.

Everything was fine until his parents' renters arrived and demanded to know what was going on. They weren't expecting squatters.

"Tommy didn't argue with them," said Briana, "and then we left."

When the renters complained to Tom Gilbert about the

shed, he was livid. After all his previous run-ins with the East Hampton planning board, he now feared being sued for not having a building permit, further tarnishing his reputation in Wainscott.

"Tommy building issue," he vented in his computer journal. "Illegal structure. What is driving Tommy. What can we do to stop this. Should this be moved, demolished, retained. Should Tommy be confronted, appeased, bartered with."

Later, when Tommy failed to pay for the storage shed, the company threatened criminal charges against him. Tommy forwarded their bill to his mother.

Tommy and Briana then rented a bedroom in a single-family home in Southampton for $800 a month. Their landlords were a divorced couple, who were living there with their children. They all shared a bathroom and kitchen.

Soon after moving in, Tommy changed the locks on the bedroom door and placed a safe above a closet, ordering Briana never to go anywhere near it or his computer.

Tommy and Briana settled into a routine. After breakfast, they hit Georgica Beach, where Tommy would spend the day surfing while Briana drank beer and read. Then she would cook him a big dinner to satisfy his healthy appetite, before watching movies in bed.

Tommy was often affectionate, putting his arm around Briana as he drove his green Jeep around the Hamptons. Once, he gallantly handed her his ice cream after she'd accidentally dropped hers.

"It was kind of a summer romance," said Briana. "He was considerate."

After a long day at the beach, they occasionally went out to eat at the Indian Wells Tavern in Amagansett and split the bill. Naturally sociable, Briana often talked to people at the bar, which infuriated Tommy.

"He'd get very, very angry," said Briana. "He'd get jealous . . . he thought I was secretly friends with these people."

Briana encouraged him to get a bartending job at one of the local bars, thinking that his good looks would make it easy. But Tommy never bothered to apply for any bar vacancy that came up.

"He did want to have a job," Briana explained. "It wasn't that he was this layabout just living off his parents. He was trying to start a hedge fund, but he's never been a worker."

Once, she arranged for him to work the bar at an event she was catering, but even that was beyond him.

"It was a small house party," she remembered. "And the guy that was throwing it said, 'Is he from money or something?' And I look over and Tommy's sitting in the chair by the bar relaxing. I said, 'You've got to stay behind the bar, even when there's no one around.'"

During the long, hot summer days, Tommy often hung out at the Main Beach Surf & Sport in East Hampton, occasionally giving children surfing lessons.

"He was kind of fooling around," said George "McSurfer" McKee, who worked there. "While he always had plenty of surfboards, he tended to avoid the tough-to-control short boards, preferring a longer, wider 'fishtail' board. He would always find the easiest one to ride."

Most of the local surfers disliked Tommy and thought him arrogant.

"One day, somebody put board wax on his [Jeep] windows," said Briana, "and told him to go home."

* * *

On Father's Day, Briana was surprised that Tommy made no attempt to call his. He often spoke about his dad, making no secret of their tense relationship.

"He was very paranoid about his father," said Briana. "Very paranoid."

Back in the Hamptons and perhaps reminded of his history with Peter Smith, Tommy resumed his campaign of harassment against him. He called the ASPCA's anonymous tip line on three occasions, reporting that Smith was abusing his dog. Finally, an ASPCA inspector arrived at Smith's Williamsburg apartment to investigate.

"She met the dog," said Smith, "and said he was fine, lovely, never been abused."

Peter suspected that Tommy had made the calls, but the inspector refused to confirm or deny it. So he reported it to the police, but there was not enough evidence to arrest Tommy.

Finally, Smith and his attorney went to the Brooklyn district attorney, who ordered a protection order be taken out against Tommy.

On June 18, Tommy was summoned to Kings County Criminal Court in Brooklyn, where Judge Joanne Quinones served him with a restraining order. He was now banned from having any contact whatsoever with Peter Smith, either directly or through third parties.

"Now he couldn't hang out anywhere that Peter could possibly be," said Briana. "That really hindered his social life. He didn't have many friends, and he really did care about being high up in society."

On Friday, July 4, Tommy brought Briana to the Sagg Main Beach in Sagaponack for the Hamptons Music Family Drum Circle festivities and fireworks. They staked out a spot on the beach as the crowds began to gather with their blankets and chairs.

At around 7:00 p.m., a motley group of drummers started pounding out beats on drums, sleigh bells, and tom-toms. Hundreds of people danced around bonfires until the sun set.

"A bunch of pretentious people sitting around in a group just being jackasses," was how Briana later described them. "Credit card hippies being free spirits."

At one point, Tommy spotted Peter Smith, but adhered to the restraining order and avoided him.

The following night, they went to the Stephen Talkhouse in Amagansett to see Tommy's Buckley classmate James Bohannon's band, Mr. Badger, perform. Before the band came onstage, Bohannon spoke briefly to Tommy, who seemed "on edge."

Later, as they drank beers on the outside patio bar with their friends Bosco Diaz and Timmy Briggs, Lizzy Fraser's name came up in conversation.

"[Tommy] had that crazy look in his eyes," said Briana. "He started confronting them about something with Lizzy."

Suddenly, Tommy lost it, threatening to kill them as he lunged at them. He had to be pulled off by astonished onlookers. Fearing for their lives, Diaz and Briggs fled into the main bar to find the club bouncers.

"They said, 'There's a guy in there pushing us around and threatening to kill us,'" said Stephen Talkhouse bouncer Brandon Gabbard. "'That guy's crazy.'"

Gabbard and another bouncer went out to the patio, but as soon as he saw them, Tommy ran into the main club, past Mr. Badger, who were in the middle of their set, and out the front door, taking off down the street.

The next night, he went back to the Stephen Talkhouse, but was barred from entering.

"And he was like, 'Why? What did I do?'" said Gabbard.

* * *

With Tommy's thirtieth birthday approaching, Beck Gilbert worried his nephew was going nowhere. He and his brother often discussed the Tommy situation and how he was wasting his Ivy League education. As Beck had paid all his Princeton tuition fees, he felt that there should be some returns.

"I said he ought to get a job," said Beck. "That is the way we were brought up. We were expected to get a job when we got out of school."

In early July, Beck emailed him a *New York Times* article headlined A MAD SCRAMBLE FOR YOUNG BANKERS to show him what great opportunities there were out there.

The lengthy article said junior bankers with Tommy's background could easily earn up to $300,000 a year after college.

"Hi Tommy," Beck wrote. "Suggest you read [this] article. Call me after you have read it."

Totally ignoring his uncle's advice, Tommy instead urged him to work harder on getting his Devon Yacht Club summer membership. Beck replied that he had spoken to the manager yet again, and Tommy still wasn't eligible.

"Happy 30th Birthday!!!" Beck emailed him on July 13. And then, with a touch of irony, he added, "Best wishes and good luck!"

20

THE COMFORT OF SILENCE

While Briana Swanson traveled back and forth between the Hamptons and Manhattan, working as a private chef, Tommy stayed in the Hamptons and took shooting lessons at the Maidstone Gun Club in East Hampton. It had no affiliation with the Maidstone Club, easily seen by its somewhat sarcastic motto, "A low cost shooting facility for the common man."

"I would go to work in the city," said Briana, "and then come down to the Hamptons and he's spent the money that I made for us."

After being approved by Airbnb, Tommy ordered Briana out of the West Eighteenth Street apartment so his paying guests could move in. He had her leave the key with a bodega around the corner for the renters to collect. He also organized a cleaning service to clean up between guests.

At a mid-July therapy session with Dr. Susan Evans, Tommy said he was trying to decide whether to have a monogamous or open relationship with Briana and which country club in the Hamptons to join. He also felt his mental state had improved with Briana, since she wasn't judgmental.

"He prefers her interpersonal style," noted Dr. Evans. "The comfort of silence."

But he was also regularly cheating on Briana, doing little to hide the evidence. One time, he bought a box of condoms in front of her, even though the couple never used them.

"I knew he was cheating on me," she said. "I would find different strands of long, dark hair in his Jeep, in his bed. Lubed-up handprints all over the mirrors that he didn't bother to clean up. I would say, 'Enough of the other women,' [but] it never ended."

At Tom Gilbert's request, attorney Alex Spiro had been regularly meeting with Tommy to try to persuade him to go back on his medication. Spiro would report back that his son was very sick and it was a dangerous situation. He urged him to do something about it.

"We were using Alex Spiro to try and get through to Tommy," explained Shelley Gilbert. "He was unable to do anything for all the same reasons we were unable to do anything."

Because Tommy was a legal adult, he could not be hospitalized against his will for more than three days. The Gilberts feared his angry reaction to being committed would outweigh any benefit of the short-term treatment.

Tom Gilbert decided he and Shelley should both undergo therapy sessions with Dr. Jason Kim to find what more they could do for Tommy. Tom speculated on whether his son had sustained a traumatic brain injury while playing football and suffered from CTE (chronic traumatic encephalopathy). He tried to arrange for Tommy to have a brain scan at Harvard's McLean Hospital, but that never materialized.

In his computer journal, Tom tried to make sense of his son's constantly mutating fears of contamination.

"Tommy is unbelievably resourceful," he wrote. "You almost need a supercomputer to keep track of all the possibilities in terms of people and places who are or who are not contaminated. However, that is his brain."

At the beginning of August, Tommy pressured Uncle Beck to help him find investors for his Mameluke hedge fund. He artfully cited an old Gilbert family story of how a young Beck had asked his father, Abner Gilbert, to call his tennis partner Walter Wriston to help him get a summer job at Citibank. Papa, as Tommy's grandfather was fondly known, had refused. He told the young Beck to call Mr. Wriston, who was then the executive vice president of Citibank, himself. Beck did and got the job, which started him on his successful career in high finance.

Now Tommy emailed his Uncle Beck, playing the story to his own advantage.

"Hi Beck," he wrote. "When you mentioned the conversation with Papa it sounded like he didn't want to prevent you from talking to his acquaintances but allow you to approach them on your own. Would it be possible to mention some people who could help with the fund and I could approach them independently through mutual contacts?"

He ended the note by asking his uncle to "even up the balance sheet" by securing his summer membership at Devon.

A week later, Beck told him that he would be happy to help with a Devon membership, although he would need a proposer, a seconder, and three letters from senior members in good standing. Even with those credentials, he told him, the earliest he could get in would be the summer of 2016.

He then went on to explain that Papa's conversation bore no relevance to Tommy's situation, and he personally never invested in hedge funds. Once again, he offered to help his nephew find a job.

* * *

Instead of trying to find work, Tommy now decided to take acting lessons. In a recent therapy session, he explained that he felt being an actor would give him "extra charm" and make him more popular.

Two months earlier, he had started emailing New York acting teacher Sabra Jones, who taught a Stanislavski-based Method acting course.

"I will be in the city part-time this summer," he wrote her in June, "and am free for acting classes. Tommy."

In mid-August, he followed up, telling Jones how excited he was to be joining her acting classes in the fall.

"Are there any forms I need to complete?" he asked. "I'm also looking to take additional classes if there's any school you like and recommend?"

Tommy did take some acting lessons but soon lost interest and dropped out.

In late August, Tom Gilbert took his son to lunch, informing him that he was cutting his allowance from $800 to $600 a week. It was the culmination of weeks of discussion between Tom and Shelley about the best way to force Tommy to get the hospital treatment he so desperately needed. Initially, his mother had been reluctant to cut his allowance but had finally agreed.

"I didn't know what else to do," she said. "It was a tough call, quite frankly."

Tommy was furious that his allowance was being cut. Later, back in the Hamptons, he had a raging argument with his mother, overheard by Briana.

"He was upset [and] scared," said Briana. "I could hear him yelling . . . something like, 'It fucking matters.'"

Tommy then broke off all contact with his parents, refusing to answer texts, emails, and phone calls.

After his allowance was cut, Tommy felt desperate and besieged. He started telling people that his parents might be getting a divorce, cutting him off financially. As his paranoia increased to new depths, he told Dr. Kim that Lizzy Fraser was trying to harm him.

He installed a spy camera on his Jeep and changed all his locks, accusing Briana of trying to hack his computer and break into his safe. One morning, she discovered him on her computer reading her texts, demanding to know if she was plotting against him. He accused her of flirting with other men he'd introduced her to. Mostly, he was fixated on his continuing obsession that Peter Smith was messing around with Lizzy Fraser.

A close member of Briana's family suffers from paranoid schizophrenia, and she recognized many of the same symptoms in Tommy.

"I started to see similarities, and he told me he was on anti-depressants," she said. "At first, I thought it was just because he was cheating on me, but then I started to wonder if he was a paranoid schizophrenic."

In late August, Briana invited Annabelle Summers to stay over at Tommy's West Eighteenth Street apartment as she was passing through New York. Briana left her alone in the apartment for a few hours while she caught the jitney to the Hamptons. When Tommy found out, he was furious. Because Summers knew Peter Smith, Tommy thought he had enlisted her as his spy to break into Tommy's safe and steal his secrets. Annabelle was astonished when she found out, as Tommy had given her permission to stay at his apartment.

21

ARSON

The last week of August, Briana Swanson went to Lake Placid for a few days. Tommy stayed in the Hamptons, surfing and taking shooting lessons at the gun club. He also bought a Perfect Point throwing star, like the ninja warriors used in his favorite martial arts movies, and started practicing with it.

While she was away, Briana constantly texted Tommy but received no reply. She became increasingly angry he was ignoring her. Later, she would admit that their relationship came at a low point in her life, which was why she put up with Tommy's odd and often frustrating behavior.

"Hey babe," she texted him on August 28. "Haven't heard from you, haven't been able to relax or have fun because im [*sic*] constantly wondering why i haven't heard from you . . . is everything ok?"

In a stream of texts over the next few hours, Briana told him she was "super confused," asking why he wasn't talking to her.

"If you've changed your mind about wanting to be with me," she told him, "you can just tell me, not sure why your [*sic*] not talking."

Getting no reply, she said that she missed sitting on the beach reading, while he taught her how to read the ocean.

"What's up!" Tommy finally replied. "On long beach [*sic*] as we speak."

Then Briana sent him an explicit nude selfie.

"That pic is incredible," Tommy immediately texted back.

On Monday, September 1, Tommy Gilbert decided to defy the restraining order and confront Peter Smith, whom he knew would be at that night's drum circle in Sagaponack. But first, like a guilty child, he called Lila Chase to tell her he was going to make peace with Smith.

"I got angry at him on the phone," remembered Lila. "I said, 'You cannot do that. They have a restraining order [against you].'"

She told him that he knew it was a bad idea already, or he would have just gone ahead without telling her. Then Tommy lashed out, accusing her of having "anger problems" and that's why they had broken up.

"And I said, 'You're right,'" recalled Lila. "'When people I care about do things that hurt them, I'm angry. I'm very angry.'"

Tommy hung up the phone and headed out to Sagg Main Beach.

Peter Smith was sitting by a bonfire with his younger brother, Chris, and some friends when Tommy Gilbert suddenly appeared. He said he wanted to talk, but Smith said no.

"He approached the fire," Smith would later testify, "and asked if we could bury the hatchet. I told him I couldn't [and] wished him the best of luck . . . that I couldn't be a part of his life anymore."

Then Tommy accused him of trying to put him in jail. He warned that it was his last chance to be friends again and go back to how things were. As Tommy became angrier and more threatening, Smith's friends had to physically restrain him from coming any nearer.

"He was trying to get Peter to leave the crowd," said an eyewitness, "and walk down the dark, desolate beach with him, away from the bonfires and people."

The following day, Peter Smith met with his attorney to discuss reporting Tommy to the police for violating the restraining order. He decided not to. Instead, he called Tom Gilbert, saying his son needed to be institutionalized, as he had become disconnected from reality.

Later that night, Tommy informed Briana, who was in Albany, that he had removed all her stuff from the West Eighteenth Street apartment, but her passport was safe.

"Oh great," she replied. "Where'd you put it? Storage?"

He said he was "psyched" that an Airbnb renter was moving in tomorrow, so he would have some extra cash. Then he asked Briana for more nude pics.

She immediately responded by sending him some selfies, with a smiley-face emoji.

After the drum circle confrontation, Tommy Gilbert was a ticking time bomb, primed to go off at any moment. Publicly humiliated yet again by Peter Smith's rejection, he was now becoming desperate and biding his time until he could carry out his threat.

When Briana returned to the Hamptons, Tommy announced he wanted to spend the winter there and go surfing. It would also allow him to make up for the cut in his allowance by Airbnb-ing his Manhattan apartment, which his father still paid the rent on.

Instead of going back to Manhattan, she offered to stay in the Hamptons with Tommy. "'We can get a little place,'" she told him, "'I'll cook somewhere and get you a job bartending.' And he loved this idea."

On Monday, September 8, they jointly signed a lease on a one-bedroom furnished apartment above a garage on Bay View Avenue, Amagansett. They paid the elderly couple who owned it a $300 deposit toward the $1,700 monthly rent.

The following weekend, Briana arrived back from Manhattan to move into their new place. Tommy was supposed to book her jitney reservation but hadn't bothered to do so.

"He had a really fun habit of making a reservation and not paying for it," she explained.

After she arrived, Tommy wanted to stop off at 8 Georgica Association Road, which was no longer being rented. Briana cooked him breakfast before he left to play tennis. While he was out, Briana cleaned the kitchen for something to do. Suddenly, Tom and Shelley Gilbert walked in, and she introduced herself—they'd never met. Briana apologized for being there, but they were very friendly and left.

Around lunchtime, Tommy returned, and Briana told him that she'd met his parents while he was out.

"Oh, fuck them!" he snarled. "I don't care."

That afternoon, they had planned to move into their new apartment, but Tommy suddenly ordered Briana to go back to Manhattan. He said he needed to be alone for a while.

Briana demanded her passport back, but he refused, driving her to the East Hampton train station. Then he left her and her luggage on the platform before driving off. Tommy, it seemed, wanted Briana out of the way, because he was now ready to even the score with Peter Smith after his recent humiliation.

* * *

At 5:35 a.m. on Monday, September 15, prosecutors believe Tommy Gilbert hurled a gasoline-filled Molotov cocktail device through a ground-floor window of the Smith family's historic house in Sagaponack. It triggered the burglar alarm. Then he crept across Sagg Main Street and into the cemetery to watch the four-hundred-year-old house burn. Peter Smith should have been sleeping in the house alone, but happened to be staying with a friend in New Jersey.

As the first fire engine arrived at 5:42 a.m., Tommy took off in his Jeep, which he had parked at the back of the cemetery.

The Bridgehampton Fire Department arrived to find the ancient house engulfed in flames. They were soon joined by the Southampton, East Hampton, and Sag Harbor Fire Departments, and seventy-five volunteer firefighters.

As an inferno raged inside the huge timber-frame building, firefighters fought it from outside. It took more than three hours to extinguish the flames.

"The fire was well involved when we got there," recalled volunteer firefighter Michael Heller. "All we could do at that point is mitigate and knock it down as fast as we could."

When the smoke finally cleared, the entire south side of the house had been destroyed. The north section, which dated back to the seventeenth century, was still standing but gutted by fire.

Almost immediately, arson was suspected. A neighbor reported seeing a man lurking around the tombstones staring at the fire, and investigators found a gas can wrapped with purple gasoline-drenched rags in the cemetery.

Peter Smith was certain Tommy Gilbert was responsible, telling Southampton police detectives about his threatening approach two weeks earlier.

"He burned down my family's home because he thought I was in it," he said.

On Tuesday, the *New York Post* and *Newsday* both ran stories on the fire in one of the most historic houses in the Hamptons. They reported that Southampton police detectives were treating it as arson and had already identified a person of interest.

Initially, none of his old friends wanted to believe that Tommy could be capable of doing something so horrendous.

"[Everyone] was basically like, 'That's weird that Peter's house burned down,'" said Bart Hayes. "And then they were like, 'Well, who's going to say it? Is this Tommy? Of course it's 100 percent Tommy.'"

For the next couple of days, East Hampton and Southampton police searched for Tommy Gilbert to question him about the Smith fire.

"We were looking for anybody that had a potential conflict with the Smiths," said Detective Sergeant Lisa Costa of Southampton Town Police, "and obviously the order of protection was something we took note of."

Eventually, on September 18, East Hampton police stopped Gilbert's Jeep in Wainscott for driving with a suspended license. He was taken to Southampton Town Police headquarters and charged with criminal contempt for violating the protection order. He was also questioned about the fire but later released, as there was no evidence against him.

Back in Manhattan, Briana had remained in contact with Tommy Gilbert via phone calls and texts. He told her about his arrest for violating the restraining order, saying nothing about the fire, which she still had not heard about.

Soon afterward, they met at his Chelsea apartment for a reconciliation. They had planned to go out to dinner, but Tommy left for a few minutes to run an errand. While he was out, Briana looked at his iPad, discovering an exchange of flirty texts between him and another girl. When he came back, Briana confronted him.

"We got into a big fight," she said, "and I broke up with him."

She packed up all her belongings in a suitcase and turned up at Annabelle Summers's apartment, saying Tommy had kicked her out. Summers reassured her that she could stay as long as she needed to.

A couple of days later, Briana emailed Bart Hayes, announcing that she'd broken up with her "crazy boyfriend." She asked if he wanted to hang out, as she hadn't seen a lot of friends because of Tommy's restraining order and wanted to socialize again.

During their email exchange, Hayes asked her thoughts about Peter Smith's house burning down. He told her everybody thought it was Tommy who had set the fire.

"That was the first I heard of it," said Briana. "I freaked out. They had kept it really quiet and Peter didn't say anything, because they wanted to try and get Tommy [arrested]."

Briana immediately called the police and was interviewed by arson investigators, who showed her a photograph of the gas can with a purple sheet wrapped around it. She recognized it as the same sheets she and Tommy had recently bought for their Hamptons rental, but she was not 100 percent certain because of the poor photo quality. Although partial fingerprints had been found on the can, there was still not enough evidence to charge Tommy with arson.

The Smith house arson, with Tommy Gilbert as the prime suspect, was the talk of the Hamptons. This was highly embarrassing for Tom and Shelley Gilbert. Although Tommy wasn't named, it was an open secret it was him, and Tom Gilbert blamed Peter Smith Jr. for all the swirling gossip. They appeared more concerned about their reputation than their son's highly dangerous mental state.

"Peter Smith's seeding rumors around Maidstone," he wrote in his computer diary. "The fact that I was accosted by a good friend who claimed there was an EH Star article about someone named Gilbert—who was a person of interest. There is nothing in the Star. Should Alex [Spiro] warn Peter Smith of slander—which he probably already has committed."

Tom Gilbert also pondered the state of the Smith family finances, wondering if they had recently increased their house insurance. He carefully laid out all the evidence for and against Tommy setting the fire.

"Evidence of [gas] can very suspicious," he conceded. "Looks more and more like a setup."

On the other hand, he noted that the "sighting of suspect" had been pre-sunrise, so it would be hard to get a definite description.

"Can they convene a trial in the absence of hard evidence?" he pondered. "Can circumstantial evidence be used to convict. IE Tommy had a motive and prior records of potential criminal activity."

He finished by wondering whether his son was a danger to society and should be immediately committed.

Later, Shelley Gilbert would say that both she and her husband were "deeply concerned" about Tommy after the fire but were powerless to have him committed against his will. They could have had him forcibly hospitalized, but after a seventy-two-hour emergency hold at a psychiatric facility, Tommy could discharge himself.

"We were desperate," said his mother. "Can you imagine if he had cancer and we couldn't get him into a hospital? That puts it in stark relief."

* * *

Tom Gilbert's financial analyst, Clay LeConey, moved in the same circles as Peter Smith Jr. and was well aware of the rumors. At first, he discounted them because Tom Gilbert did not seem visibly concerned.

"I found it very hard to believe," said LeConey, "given that I work with Tom twelve hours a day. If his son was on the run from police, I figure that he would be acting very differently."

Soon afterward, LeConey changed his mind after speaking to mutual friends, deciding Tommy was definitely responsible for the fire. He then persuaded Tom to have his son's name removed from the Wainscott Capital website, arguing that it would be bad for business.

22

SPIRALING DOWN

In the weeks after the fire, Tommy Gilbert flew to the Bahamas for several surfing vacations. He passed through JFK International Airport, apparently having overcome his old contamination fears. He sought an escape in the Caribbean waves, where he could forget all the fears that consumed him.

Tommy had now descended into a dark new level of paranoia, knowing he was under an active police investigation for arson. He increased his tech security, taking an online course in how to jailbreak his iPhone and iPad for better encrypted protection.

He went online, researching a private military company called Academi, which offered basic sniper and firearm training courses. And being no stranger to the dark web, he made half a dozen visits to HIRE-A-KILLER.COM, as well as checking out several other murder-for-hire sites.

In late October, he signed up for Muay Thai martial arts training at the Renzo Gracie Academy on West Thirtieth Street, New York. The ancient combat sport of Thailand combined the use of fists, elbows, knees, and shins and could be lethal.

"Tommy seemed to have trouble focusing," recalled his instructor, Brent Bartley. "He was aloof and just kind of had a vague look."

In one particular class, Tommy seemed to be on another planet, and his instructor kept warning him to pay attention so he and his partner would not get hurt. Finally, he was kicked off the mat in front of the whole class for his own safety.

"It was completely humiliating for him," said Bartley. "Tommy just stood there and stared and didn't move. He was just seething."

Then Tommy stormed out of the academy and never came back.

On October 30, Dr. Jason Kim stopped treating Tommy Gilbert, who refused to take his medication. After six months of psychiatric therapy, Dr. Kim told him treatment was useless without any medication.

"It [didn't] make sense to continue working with [him]," Dr. Kim later testified. "It's bad treatment."

The doctor gave him one last chance to restart his medications and continue therapy, but never heard from him again.

Tommy was now running up debts everywhere, constantly having to be bailed out by his father. He owed $4,800 in unpaid rent on the Amagansett apartment he'd rented with Briana Swanson and never spent a night in. Tom Gilbert had to buy him out of the lease to avoid any further embarrassment. He also owed $14,300 in arrears to the River Club, $7,307 in psychiatric fees to Weill Cornell, and hundreds of dollars in unpaid traffic tickets.

On November 7, Tom Gilbert made good on his promise to cut Tommy's allowance down from $800 to $600 a week. He informed his son by email.

"Tommy," he wrote. "This is a heads-up for your planning purposes that I have adjusted the weekly rate back to $600 next Monday, since you don't have time to give me updates. If that changes in the future, I would be happy to go back to $800."

In his computer journal, Tom Gilbert outlined his latest plans to force his son to face up to his responsibilities and start supporting himself.

"Tommy," he wrote. "30 day financial belt tightening—maybe more. Don't sacrifice dream, but find work to make ends meet."

Three days later, Tommy purchased an MSR605 credit card skimmer online for $136, and twenty-one blank credit cards. He had apparently decided to turn to credit card fraud to continue living the good life, to make up for further cuts in his allowance.

On November 17, Shelley Gilbert met her son at the River Club, reporting back to her husband that everything was under control and he just needed distance.

"We should stay out of it," Tom Gilbert noted in his computer jottings. "We should stop stalking him."

Two days later, Tom slashed the allowance a further $100 a week, explaining that he needed to cut back to save on business expenses.

"Are you able to handle it if I take the six hundred down to five hundred?" he asked his son in a voice mail. "Let me know the effective date when you know it. Goodbye."

As he became increasingly desperate, Tommy turned to Lila Chase for validation and emotional support. Toward the end of November, he asked her to go shopping with him for designer clothes in their favorite bargain basement in Yonkers. The first thing he told her when they met was that he was broke.

"He just looked awful," she remembered. "He looked disheveled, and his shoes had holes in them. He was clearly not well."

Lila, who hadn't seen him for months, jokingly said that he only used her as his personal shopper.

"But that was largely our relationship at the end," she said. "He would say, 'Can you help me [go] shopping and we'll go to a movie.'"

That Thanksgiving, Tommy Gilbert languished in his Chelsea apartment, trawling the dark web and checking out the X-rated websites Pornhub and Ashley Madison, a dating site for married people seeking discreet affairs. One night, he went upstairs to his neighbor Catherine Novick to borrow a microwave oven. They had occasionally met in the hallway or getting the mail and made small talk.

The attractive twenty-nine-year-old, who builds large-scale art installations for a living, said she didn't have a microwave. Then Tommy asked for her cell phone number, writing it down on a Post-it.

A few days later, Tommy knocked on her door again, apologizing for not calling. It was late afternoon, and he invited her down to his apartment, 1F, to watch a basketball game. She agreed to come after finishing some chores.

About an hour later, she arrived with a couple of beers. The basketball game had already started, and they sat next to each other on his living room couch. As they watched the game, Novick felt uncomfortable and tried to make conversation, asking Tommy about himself. In his stilted speech pattern, he said that he had gone to Deerfield and Princeton and worked as a day trader.

"He kind of had one-word answers," she remembered. "[He] did not really want to interact or converse with me. He did not ask me anything about myself."

Then suddenly Tommy leaned over and tried to kiss her. She pulled away.

"Things got a bit uncomfortable," she said. "So I left there pretty quickly after [that]."

A month later, just before Christmas, Tommy knocked on her door, asking if she wanted to go out to a bar with him. She made an excuse, and he left.

Meanwhile, in early December, Anna Rothschild rekindled her relationship with Tommy. She was working in Miami on an event for Art Basel and invited him to join her. Then she changed her mind, as the weather was bad, instead arranging a date with him on her return to New York.

Soon they were dating again, and strangely, Anna now found him more outgoing and happier than before. One night, she invited him over for a dinner party, and he got on with everyone.

"He was just talkative," she said. "And I said, 'How's your hedge fund?' and he's just, 'Oh, everything's great.'"

In mid-December, Tom Gilbert pruned Tommy's allowance back a further $100, to $400 a week. Over this period, his mother would secretly wire him money whenever he asked for it to make up the shortfall.

Tom Gilbert was also cutting his own expenses and had applied for a $1.5 million loan from the First Republic Bank. On the application forms, he estimated his net worth at

A lifelong sportsman, Thomas Gilbert (center) was a star of the Princeton squash team. *(Courtesy: Lanny Jones)*

In the early 1990s, Tom and Shelley Gilbert fell in love with the glamorous South Fork in the Hamptons. After renting for several summers, they eventually bought a home in the ultraexclusive Georgica Association where they enjoyed its private beach. *(Courtesy: Shelley Gilbert)*

In the third grade at the Buckley School, the angelic eight-year-old Tommy was a golden boy who seemed to have the world at his feet. *(Courtesy: Shelley Gilbert)*

The Buckley School is one of New York's most prestigious private schools. Alumni include former Manhattan D.A. Cyrus Vance Jr. *(Courtesy: John Glatt)*

After graduating Buckley, Tommy Gilbert enrolled at the Deerfield Academy, where his mental problems began. *(Courtesy: Shelley Gilbert)*

The Gilberts' dream house at 8 Georgica Association Road, where they spent summers.
(Courtesy: John Glatt)

The interior of the Maidstone Clubhouse in East Hampton, where there is still a plaque bearing Thomas Gilbert Jr.'s name as the 2012 mixed-doubles tennis champion.
(Courtesy: John Glatt)

Tom and Shelley Gilbert lived at 20 Beekman Place in Manhattan's fashionable Turtle Bay. In 2015, it became the scene of a shocking crime when Tommy shot his father to death. *(Courtesy: John Glatt)*

CCTV video of Tommy Gilbert on his way to his parents' apartment to kill his father. *(Courtesy: Manhattan District Attorney)*

Thomas Gilbert Sr.'s body in his bedroom, with the murder weapon lying on the bed where the police placed it. *(Courtesy: Manhattan District Attorney)*

Tommy was photographed after he was booked at the NYPD's 17th Precinct.
(Courtesy: Manhattan District Attorney)

Defense attorney Arnold Levine had his hands tied by his uncooperative client, who had to be forcibly removed from the courtroom at one point in the trial.
(Courtesy: John Glatt)

Shelley Gilbert addressing the press after one of her son's hearings.
(Courtesy: John Glatt)

Tommy Gilbert looks a shell of his former self at his verdict hearing, after almost five years of incarceration in Rikers Island.
(Courtesy: John Glatt)

around $20 million, including the Wainscott house and private investments.

A month earlier in an interview with FinalAlternatives .com, Gilbert had boasted that Wainscott Capital Partners now had more than $15 million under management. He talked up Wainscott's success as largely due to his cautious approach to investing.

"We're not cowboys," he explained. "We're not trying to beat all the biotech funds. The performance that we had in September and October really set us apart. People wanted to see how we performed in a bear market, and that worked out brilliantly for us."

On December 17, Shelley Gilbert left three voice mail messages for Tommy on a variety of subjects. In the first, she said his father wanted to discuss how he could help himself and "get further back on track."

In a second, she offered advice on getting his suspended driving license reinstated. She had just heard from the garage that his Jeep had been repaired, but he needed to go to a DMV office and fill out the necessary paperwork before he could drive it.

"But once the sticker's on it," she told him, "then we will pay the bill."

Just over an hour later, she left a third message.

"Hello, it's me," she began cheerily. "I've just sent you the money and give a call. Goodbye."

Tommy Gilbert was now fully immersed in the dark web, searching for how to hire hit men, organized crime networks, and email encryption software. He also looked for blond men's passport photos, presumably to make a fake ID. He disconnected his iPhone and got a new number, as well as buying a cheap prepaid AT&T pay-as-you-go phone.

Several times, he asked the superintendent of his West Eighteenth Street building, Gary Reatz, if he could view footage from the building's four video security cameras.

"He wanted me to search for a certain day," said Reatz, "and I asked him why. He said, 'I just want to see who is coming in and out of my apartment.'"

The week before Christmas, Tommy took Anna Rothschild out to Sushi Yasaka on the Upper West Side. Tommy paid the $150 bill, and they went back to her apartment to spend the night.

The next morning, Anna decided the relationship was not going anywhere and stopped returning Tommy's text messages.

"I felt this is stupid," she explained. "Why am I doing this again? I'm just wasting my time."

Three days before Christmas, Tommy's sister, Bess, received a fraud alert from Citibank that someone had used her account to purchase $200 worth of purchases from Macy's. Shelley immediately suspected Tommy and left him an urgent voice mail.

"We were wondering if somehow you had her information," said his mother. "We would like to press charges if it's not you. But if it is you, we won't press charges, so let me know so you don't have charges pressed against you. So give me a call. Bye."

The Gilberts spent Christmas at their Beekman Place apartment, but as usual, Tommy was a no-show. His mother dutifully left his presents under the Christmas tree in the living room and wired him $200.

"He missed Christmas, which is always a big event in our house," she explained. "He knows the routine [and that] he was always welcome. That was our life together."

As his world collapsed around him, Tommy Gilbert started planning for his future, without having to be dependent on his father's largesse. Over the holidays, he had secretly contacted Hamptons Realtor Laura White of Saunders & Associates, enlisting her to sell 8 Georgica Association Road for $11.5 million. But there would be no way that Tommy could ever hope to benefit from a sale while his father was still alive.

PART 3

23

MY SON SHOT MY HUSBAND

On New Year's Day, Tom Gilbert turned seventy and was full of hope for the future. His brother, Beck, called to wish him a happy birthday. Tom told him he was looking forward to his upcoming trip to San Francisco for the JP Morgan Healthcare Conference and Biotech Showcase. And he spoke enthusiastically about Stephen Hawking's book *The Theory of Everything,* which he'd just finished reading.

"My brother was always positive," said Beck. "He was an optimist [with a] positive viewpoint."

On Friday morning, Clay LeConey spent the day working with Tom Gilbert in the Wainscott Capital office. They were discussing a deal with some of the world's leading institutional investors like Blackstone and Investcorp, who were interested in Wainscott.

"There was a possibility in the range of a hundred million dollars," said LeConey. "We were optimistic."

In his computer journal's birthday entry, Tom Gilbert listed his "January issues" regarding Tommy. He was planning to speak to Alex Spiro about his son's possible involvement in the Smith house fire and whether he had been set up.

"Questions for Alex," he wrote. "Why did he now think the Smiths are a suspect. Why does he now think that Tommy may not have done it. What motivation can he use for Tommy to step up his self care [*sic*]."

He was also contemplating cutting off all payments for his son's "social transport," so he would have "no car access."

"Further reduction in weekly doles?" he asked. "He must take responsibility for his own life, [and] not controlled by other forces—that is a cop out."

On Saturday afternoon, Tommy called Lila Chase for the first time in weeks. He wanted to know where she was, and she told him that she was in Florida for the Winter Equestrian Festival, where she spent every January.

"And he said, 'Oh, I'm just checking,'" she recalled. "Then he hung up. It was not chitchat—it was a confirmation that I was in Florida."

Later, in hindsight, Lila wondered if Tommy had wanted to protect her from what was about to happen.

On Sunday, January 4, Tom Gilbert rose early for a busy morning of doubles tennis at the River Club. Before leaving at 11:00 a.m., he went on the Citibank website and reduced Tommy's weekly allowance from $400 to $300 a week.

Meanwhile, Tommy Gilbert was at his 350 West Eighteenth Street apartment, surfing the internet. At 10:26 a.m., he received an email from the East Hampton Indoor Tennis club, informing him that his credit card had been declined.

Two minutes later, he received another from Hamptons Realtor Laura White, touching base about his plan to sell his parents' Wainscott house.

"I wish you a Happy New Year," it began. "Please could you confirm your open sale price of eleven and a half million dollars, or $11.5 million."

She also told him that she'd recently sold three neighboring houses, all for good prices.

"We are very active in your exclusive neighborhood," she wrote, "and have customers very interested."

At midday, Tommy made four botched attempts to order lunch from the Seamless website, before succeeding with the Hollywood Diner. While he was waiting for his meal to arrive, he accessed the MSR605 credit card skimmer manual online and then went on Twitter and YouTube.

After lunch, he started preparing to free himself from his father, once and for all. He opened the safe in his bedroom and took out the .40-caliber Glock semiautomatic handgun, some hollow-point ammunition, the shoulder holster, and silencer. He inserted a couple of Smith & Wesson cartridges into the magazine before locking it into place.

The hollow-point ammunition was designed for the military and law enforcement, to expand when it hits the target and cause maximum damage.

According to Verizon Wireless records, at 2:29 p.m., Lila Chase called Tommy for thirty seconds. Lila has no recollection of the call, but after receiving it, Tommy turned off his iPhone so his movements couldn't be tracked.

He then put the gun and ammunition into a black gym bag, put on his dark hoodie with a white stripe down the front, and left his apartment.

Tommy Gilbert headed east on Eighteenth Street toward the Fourteenth Street subway station. At 2:30 p.m., he swiped his MetroCard at the turnstile and walked down to the platform, where he caught a Queens-bound E Train at 2:41 p.m.

He stayed on the train for seven stops, getting off at the Lexington Avenue and Fifty-Third Street station. Just after 3:00 p.m., Tommy was photographed by a security camera as he walked east on East Fiftieth Street. Fifteen minutes later, he arrived at 20 Beekman Place with the hoodie down over his head.

Tommy strolled through the lobby and straight past the doorman, Omar Fouad, who didn't recognize him and asked who he had come to see.

"Gilbert," Tommy announced as he stepped into the elevator without looking back. Then, as the door closed behind him, he pressed the button for the eighth floor.

Only Tommy and his father will ever know exactly what happened after Shelley Gilbert left the apartment to get her son a sandwich and a Coke. The forensic evidence shows that Tommy came into the bedroom where his father was lying on the bed watching a football game. After some kind of confrontation, Tommy took out the Glock and pressed the muzzle hard against his father's left temple. He then pulled the trigger, sending the hollow-point bullet tearing into his father's skull before it halted deep in his brain. By the time Tom Gilbert's body hit the floor, he was dead.

Tommy had pressed the muzzle so firmly against his father's head that it had malfunctioned. Although the first round had fired, the second round rendered the gun inoperable, as the bullet casing was still stuck inside the ejection port and had not been ejected.

Then, prosecutors believe, Tommy carefully staged the scene to look like a suicide. He placed the pistol grip of the Glock under his father's left hand, which was clenched tightly into a fist. Then he positioned the gun on top of Tom's chest, the gun barrel facing up toward his right shoulder.

Tommy then rushed out of the bedroom, leaving his father

lying dead on the floor with blood and brain matter oozing out into a puddle below his head.

Less than fifteen minutes after arriving, Tommy Gilbert emerged from the elevator into the lobby, grasping his shoulder bag with his hoodie pulled tight around his head. The doorman wished him a good day, but Tommy ignored him, walking out through the exit doors and disappearing into Beekman Place.

He then calmly retraced his steps back to his apartment and locked the door.

At 3:51 p.m., he powered up his iPhone and called his attorney, Alex Spiro.

When Shelley Gilbert returned to her apartment, there was no sign of Tom, so she called out his name. Then she went into the bedroom and saw him lying on his back, bleeding heavily from a bullet wound to his head. She immediately knew her son had killed him.

"I don't panic," Shelley would later testify. "A million thoughts went through my head."

At 3:31 p.m., she dialed 911 on the house phone.

"What's the emergency today, ma'am?" asked the female 911 dispatcher.

"My husband is, I think, dead," she calmly replied. "Please rush."

The dispatcher called EMS, and another operator soon joined them on the line.

"Is the ambulance for you or for somebody else?" he asked.

"It's for my husband," replied Shelley.

"And he's not breathing?"

"I don't think so," said Shelley. "I can't get a pulse."

After getting her address, the EMS operator confirmed that firefighters, police, and EMS were all on their way. He asked her to do chest compressions until they arrived, instructing her to kneel down and place her left hand on the center of her husband's chest, with her right one on top. He told her to use the weight of her body and do a hundred chest compressions a minute.

Because the Glock .40 caliber still lay across Tom Gilbert's chest, Shelley did compressions around it. She eventually stopped, as it was obvious he was dead but pretended to the EMS operator that she was doing them anyway.

"I think he's dead," she finally told them more than five minutes into the call. "He's been shot."

"He's been *shot*?" asked the EMS operator incredulously.

"Yes," she replied.

Shelley then had to run downstairs to warn the doorman an EMS crew would soon be arriving and to let them upstairs. While she was away from the phone, the 911 dispatcher could be heard asking her colleague if Shelley said "shot" or "shock."

"Shot," replied the EMS operator.

"S-H-O-T?" spelled out the dispatcher.

"Yes, that's what it sounded like to me."

Shelley came back on the line and was told to continue the compressions.

"Can I ask [you] a question?" the dispatcher asked minutes later. "Ma'am, you said your husband was shot. How long ago?"

"Probably ten, fifteen minutes ago," Shelley replied.

"By whom?" asked the dispatcher.

"My son, who's nuts," she replied. "But I didn't know that he was this nuts."

* * *

Shortly after 3:30 p.m., the first NYPD radio call code—
10-54, for cardiac arrest—had gone out to all units. Six minutes later, it was upgraded to 10-34, for a person shot.

Sergeant Zeff Blacer and Officer Philip Guastavino from
Manhattan's Seventeenth Precinct were patrolling midtown
Manhattan when they heard the two dispatch calls. At 3:39
p.m., they arrived at 20 Beekman Place to find Officers Ryan
Wood and Daniel Gross already waiting outside.

They all took the elevator up to the eighth floor and were
let into Apartment 8D by an EMS medic. Shelley Gilbert
came over, and Sergeant Blacer asked if she had made the
911 call. She confirmed that she had.

"I asked about her husband," Sergeant Blacer would later
testify. "She pointed to the bedroom."

Officer Wood went in first, followed by Officer Guastavino and Sergeant Blacer. Tom Gilbert's body was lying on
the floor between the bed and the wall, with a puddle of
blood by the left side of his head. There was blood spatter on
the wall and brain matter by his head.

"There's a gun on his chest!" Guastavino suddenly shouted.
Sergeant Blacer ordered Wood to remove the gun from under Tom Gilbert's left hand and place it on the bed.

The Glock still contained live rounds of ammunition, but
none of the officers thought to take photos of how it had
been positioned over his chest before removing it.

Tom Gilbert Sr. was officially pronounced dead at 3:42 p.m.,
and arrangements were made to transport his body to the Office of Chief Medical Examiner on Twenty-Sixth Street for
autopsy.

More officers from the Seventeenth Precinct Detective and Homicide Squads started arriving at 20 Beekman Place to launch a murder investigation. Detectives Darryl Ng and Edward Hennessy were among the first on the scene.

They were briefed by Officer Guastavino and told that the Glock pistol had been lying on Tom Gilbert's chest before being moved onto the bed for safety reasons. The detectives went into the bedroom to view Tom Gilbert's body while Guastavino secured Apartment 8D as a murder scene until the crime scene investigators could arrive.

Then Detectives Ng and Hennessy interviewed Shelley Gilbert at a table in the dining room. She was visibly upset and occasionally burst into tears, but she managed to hold herself together and answer their questions. At the detectives' urging, she called Tommy's cell phone several times, but there was no answer.

Shelley told the detectives how Tommy had arrived that afternoon without warning to discuss business with his father, whom he hadn't seen in three months. At her son's urging, she had gone out, but changed her mind and quickly turned back.

"She felt that something bad may happen," said Detective Ng. "They had recently cut back his allowance . . . and Tommy wouldn't be happy about that."

Shelley explained that she worried that the discussion might lead to an argument and get physical. She had walked around outside before returning to the apartment to find her husband dead.

"She told me that her son had shot his father," said Detective Ng. "He'd shot her husband."

Shelley told the detectives that Tommy suffered from mental illness and was under psychiatric treatment, although he wasn't taking his medication. Asked about the gun, she said her husband had never owned one and would never have committed suicide.

The detectives asked for a photo of Tommy, and she pointed to his graduation photo, which was hanging on the wall. They said they needed something more recent and asked the precinct to find Tommy's mug shot from his 2013 arrest for assaulting Peter Smith.

When prompted, Shelley gave the detectives her son's 350 West Eighteenth Street address, and the Tenth Precinct police were asked to stake out his apartment building.

Other officers started searching rooftops, landings, elevator shafts in and around 20 Beekman Place, as well as canvassing nearby apartments for any relevant information or sightings.

Just before 4:00 p.m., Detective Joseph Cirigliano of the Seventeenth Precinct Homicide Squad arrived to lead the murder investigation. He walked into Apartment 8D to find Detectives Ng and Hennessy talking to Shelley Gilbert at the dining room table.

Shelley's cell phone began ringing, and detectives urged her to answer it.

"She said it was Tommy," Detective Cirigliano later testified. "She answered the phone and said, 'I'm in the apartment. What happened?'"

As Detective Cirigliano stood beside her, Shelley pretended everything was normal and asked her son if he was hungry. Tommy suggested they meet for lunch, saying he would pick a restaurant and get back to her.

"He wanted to get a bite to eat," Shelley later recalled. "Certainly, the seriousness of it was not apparent to him."

At the detective's prompting, Shelley invited him to come

back to the apartment for lunch instead. Tommy refused, saying he would contact her again as soon as he got to where he was going. Then he hung up.

Back at his apartment, Tommy Gilbert changed clothes and called Alex Spiro, who was abroad on his honeymoon. Getting no reply, he then called the Manhattan office of Spiro's law firm, Brafman & Associates, and was on the phone for almost four minutes.

"I think Tommy put Alex on a pedestal," said Lila Chase, "and he thought, 'Oh, I have my big-shot attorney and I'll call him to make it go away.'"

At 4:54 p.m., the *New York Daily News* website broke the dramatic story of Thomas Gilbert Sr.'s murder.

"Thomas Gilbert, founder of Wainscott Capital Partners Fund, was shot and killed in his lavish East Side, New York apartment," it read. "He was allegedly gunned down by his own son, Thomas Gilbert, Jr., after the two had a disagreement. Now police are looking for Gilbert's son, who is said to be on the run."

Within minutes of the news breaking, reporters descended on 20 Beekman Place. This had all the hallmarks of a classic Manhattan society murder, and everyone wanted the scoop.

At around 5:00 p.m., Detective Cirigliano brought Shelley Gilbert back to the Seventeenth Precinct on East Fifty-First Street for a formal interview. He was also desperately trying to track down Bess Gilbert, who was in church, although Shelley was unable to remember which one.

"Mrs. Gilbert was afraid of Tommy hurting her," said

Detective Cirigliano, "and she didn't want [her] to find out through the media or anyone else that her father was just killed."

Finally, Shelley reached Bess, who was attending Sunday Mass at a downtown church near Tommy's apartment. Detectives Cirigliano and Geneva Eleutice drove her down so she could tell her twenty-five-year-old daughter the terrible news.

During the twenty-minute drive, they devised a game plan to get Bess out of the church before telling her the awful news.

They arrived around 5:30 p.m. and went inside. Sunday Mass was underway, and it was standing room only. An usher asked if he could help them, and Shelley said she had come to see her daughter.

Then suddenly, she spotted Bess at the front of the church and rushed toward her before the two detectives could stop her. When Bess turned around and saw her mother, she immediately knew that something was wrong.

"Dad's dead and Tommy shot him," Shelley burst out.

Bess began screaming, bringing the service to a standstill as the entire congregation turned to see what was happening. Shelley gently put her arm around her daughter, who was sobbing uncontrollably, and led her down the aisle to the back of the church.

The detectives then brought them outside to their unmarked police car, putting Bess in the back seat next to her mother. During the drive back to the Seventeenth Precinct, Bess cried hysterically as Shelley kept reassuring her that everything was going to be okay.

Recalled Detective Cirigliano: "Bess kept saying, 'You said he was getting better . . . and taking his medicine.' And Mrs. Gilbert's response was, 'It's happened. Now we've got to deal with it.'"

24

"TOMMY, OPEN THE DOOR!"

Just after 5:00 p.m., Detectives Geraldo Rivera and Mike Miller of the NYPD Tenth Precinct arrived at 350 West Eighteenth Street. Their orders were to see if Tommy Gilbert was in his apartment and to locate his green Jeep, which was later found at a storage facility in the Hamptons.

They walked to the rear of the building, where through the open blinds they could see into Tommy's ground-floor apartment. The lights were turned off, but the television was on with *The Simpsons* playing.

"I could not see anyone," said Detective Rivera, "nor did I see any movement."

Then they walked around to the front and were let into the lobby by one of the other residents. They entered the vestibule, noting Gilbert's apartment, 1F, was the first door on the right. They looked through the peephole and leaned in closely, listening for any sounds inside. They could see a light coming from the other end of the apartment.

For the next several minutes, Detective Rivera knocked loudly on the door, announcing himself as the police. Receiving no response, the officers concluded he wasn't there.

Detective Rivera reported back to the Seventeenth Precinct

Detectives Squad and was told to remain at the apartment in case Tommy came home.

After Shelley and Bess Gilbert arrived at the Seventeenth Precinct, Detective Cirigliano gave them a few minutes alone. He wanted to interview them individually, but Shelley refused, saying Bess was having a panic attack and could not be alone.

For the next hour and a half, they were questioned together on Tommy's relationship with his father and what could have caused him to turn violent.

Just after 7:00 p.m., detectives escorted Shelley and Bess Gilbert out of the precinct and past reporters, who were shouting questions. They covered their heads to avoid photographs, refusing to say anything.

At 6:10 p.m., NYPD crime scene investigator Anthony D'Amato arrived at 20 Beekman Place and was briefed by Detectives Ng and Hennessy. He was joined by Emily Epstein from the Office of Chief Medical Examiner, who would be in charge of transporting Tom Gilbert's body to the morgue for autopsy.

After an initial walk-through of the two-bedroom apartment, Detective D'Amato began methodically documenting the murder scene. He photographed the body and its fatal gunshot wound to the head from all angles. He then prepared a hand-drawn sketch of the entire crime scene, showing the exact position of the body.

The detective also swabbed blood samples off the bedroom floor for evidence, observing blood on both of the victim's hands. D'Amato removed the Glock semiautomatic pistol from the bed, as well as a live cartridge and a magazine.

Tom Gilbert's remains were then placed into a body bag and brought out of the apartment to a waiting ambulance outside, to be driven to the Office of Chief Medical Examiner for autopsy.

The stunning news that Tommy Gilbert had murdered his father sent shock waves through his old circle of friends. Some went into hiding as reports broke online that he was armed and still on the loose.

"I was frightened, as he knows where I live," said Bart Hayes. "I left my apartment immediately and stayed at a friend's place in case he decided to go on a killing binge."

When Chris Oliver learned about the murder from a mutual friend, he was "deeply alarmed." He, too, lay low until Tommy was caught.

"Everyone in our friend group knew about it pretty quick," he said. "It was sad. His dad was such a sweet guy."

Anna Rothschild received a stream of texts before turning on the television and seeing it all over the news.

"I was really scared that he was going to come here and kill me," she said. "I told my doorman not to let that tall, blond guy come up on any account."

Briana Swanson was in Iowa when New York detectives called to tell her about the murder, asking if she knew Tommy's whereabouts. She suggested they check his apartment.

"Tommy doesn't understand consequences," said Briana. "So that's why I'm not surprised that he shot his dad. Like, he didn't even flee."

In fact, he hadn't fled. Inside apartment 1F, Tommy Gilbert had been busy erasing his computers and iPads, fully aware that detectives were waiting outside his door. Technically proficient, he used the state-of-the-art applications CCleaner and Nuke, which he'd previously downloaded, to wipe his laptops clean. He also disabled his Find My iPhone app so the device could no longer be located.

At 8:56 p.m., he installed WhatsApp on his iPhone 5, a free service for secure calls and messages. Soon afterward, he installed Viber, another app to enable private calls.

He then made several calls on Viber, but after receiving a text from Verizon that he'd used up all his monthly data, he reverted back to his own number.

At 9:12 p.m., Tommy started calling Alex Spiro again. Over the next two hours, he would make a dozen calls to his attorney, the longest being five and a half minutes. He was also in touch with one of Spiro's colleagues at Brafman & Associates.

Later, Spiro refused to discuss their calls, citing attorney-client privilege.

At 9:30 p.m., Tommy typed "Thomas Gilbert" into Google to read media coverage of his father's murder. Over the next twenty-five minutes, he avidly read all the sensational breaking news from *The Wall Street Journal, Daily News, New York Post*, and the MailOnline.

HEDGE FUND HONCHO SHOT DEAD BY OWN SON was the headline of the *New York Post* story. The MailOnline's was 200 MILLION HEDGE FUND FOUNDER, 70, SHOT DEAD IN HIS NEW YORK APARTMENT BY HIS OWN 30-YEAR-OLD SON WHO IS NOW ON THE RUN.

While Tommy Gilbert was busy googling himself, Detectives Rivera and Miller, who were waiting outside in the lobby, realized that he was inside the apartment. Detective Miller had gone for a cigarette, when he noticed that the blinds to Tommy's apartment were now drawn and the television turned off. He immediately returned to tell Detective Rivera.

They looked through the front-door peephole and saw the light inside go off momentarily before going on again, as if someone had been looking out through it. They now knew that the suspected killer was in the apartment, although there was no way of knowing if he was alone or not.

"It was a shock to us," recalled Detective Rivera. "We were investigating a homicide in which a firearm was used, and the entire time we're sitting just a couple of feet from the door and [the suspect] is in the apartment."

The Seventeenth Precinct Homicide Squad was alerted, and Detectives Cirigliano and Ng raced downtown to 350 West Eighteenth Street.

They arrived at around 10:00 p.m. to find officers from the Tenth Precinct already lining the stairwells. Detectives from the Manhattan South Homicide Squad were stationed around the back in an alley underneath a bedroom window— the only means of escape other than the front door.

Fifteen minutes later, three members of the NYPD's elite ESU (Emergency Services Unit) arrived. The highly trained SWAT team had been summoned by Seventeenth Precinct commander Steven Wren, as there was a potentially armed suspect believed to have already committed one murder.

After being briefed by Captain Wren, the ESU officers started putting on their ballistic vests and helmets and collecting reinforced plastic shields, in case they had to breach the front door by force. Although they were still waiting for a judge to sign a search warrant, it was decided that the highly dangerous situation necessitated immediate action.

"We had a homicide, and we believed Tommy to be the perpetrator," explained Captain Wren, "and he may have other firearms. His mental state was . . . highly agitated. We didn't know if he was capable of hurting himself or someone else in that apartment."

ESU officer Sean DeQuatro then took charge of the operation, ordering everyone in the hallway to remove themselves from the line of fire. He began banging on Tommy's front door with a closed fist.

"Police Department Emergency Service!" he shouted. "If there's anybody in there, come to the door!"

After getting no response, Officer DeQuatro took a more aggressive approach. For the next few minutes, he had another ESU officer periodically beat the door with a heavy mallet as DeQuatro yelled, "Tommy, open the door! We're not going anywhere! Open the door!"

Inside the apartment, Tommy Gilbert knew it was all over. After killing his father, he had not even attempted to escape, even though he had a valid passport and could have tried to go abroad. Instead, he had fled back to his apartment, the very first place police would look for him.

With absolutely no endgame, he was helplessly cornered, paralyzed by his mental illness and hoping that his family's wealth and status would protect him as it always had in the past.

As the ESU officers pounded at his door, Tommy made more frenzied calls to Alex Spiro, culminating in a thirteen-and-a-half-minute conversation with Brafman attorney Andrea Zellan.

But the final call to his iPhone came at 10:24 p.m. from Lila Chase in Florida. After learning the shocking news from her father, she had turned on the television and seen Tommy all over the news.

"They were hunting for him," she said. "So I called him to tell him, 'Don't fight.' I didn't want him to be shot or killed."

* * *

After almost ten minutes of pounding on the door without any response, Officer DeQuatro ordered the front-door peephole knocked out to get a better view inside the apartment. After it was removed, he peered inside to see Tommy talking on his iPhone.

"Hello, sir," came a weak voice from the other side of the door. "I'm on the phone with my lawyer."

Officer DeQuatro asked if there was anyone else in there. Tommy replied no and asked who they were.

"NYPD Emergency Service," said DeQuatro. "Can you please approach the door and turn on the lights?"

After a short pause, the lights went on and Tommy unlocked the door. He was ordered to step back a few feet away from the door, which opened inwardly, and lie facedown on the floor. Officer DeQuatro opened the door and entered the living room, holding his ballistic shield for cover. He stepped over Tommy, followed by the rest of the ESU team, who did a protective sweep through the small studio apartment, making sure there was no one else in there injured.

Tommy was still gripping his iPhone when officers took it, bringing him into the kitchen to be searched.

At around 11:00 p.m., seven and a half hours after killing his father, Tommy Gilbert was handcuffed and led out of his apartment.

25

PERP WALK

Outside the apartment, the ESU officers handed Tommy Gilbert over to Seventeenth Precinct detective Joseph Cirigliano, who had been appointed the lead detective on the case. He introduced himself, asking Tommy if he was okay. He replied yes.

Cirigliano told Tommy he was going to go through his pockets, asking if he had anything sharp or any weapons on him.

"No, sir," was his polite answer.

He was then instructed to turn toward the wall and spread his legs to be searched.

"Okay," he told them. "I just want to talk to my lawyer, sir."

Cirigliano said he would be able to do that in good time as he took Tommy's iPhone 5 and wallet into evidence.

The detective noted how "flat and indifferent" Gilbert appeared after killing his father.

"He was very calm," said Detective Cirigliano. "He was very polite [and] didn't say anything really."

Tommy was taken outside and placed in the back seat of an unmarked police vehicle, sitting between Cirigliano and Ng. Then he was driven to the Seventeenth Precinct to be formally arrested for his father's murder.

* * *

Detective Cirigliano brought Tommy upstairs to the Detective Squad's offices and left him in an interview room. He had changed clothes since the murder and was now wearing a trendy pair of pants, a black sweatshirt, and white sneakers.

Tommy was left alone for some time before Detective Cirigliano came back to start the lengthy arrest process. Asked if he wanted to use the restroom, Tommy politely replied, "No, sir," again, requesting to speak to his attorney.

"Tommy didn't appear to need any medical treatment," said Cirigliano. "He appeared normal and in good health."

He kept asking to talk to his lawyer and was told he would be able to later.

Over the next four hours, Detective Cirigliano remained with Tommy in the interview room, at one point ordering him two slices of pizza and a bottle of water.

"He was very polite," Cirigliano recalled. "He didn't answer the questions more than 'yes, sir.' Every time I would ask him something, he would answer right away."

At around 1:00 a.m., Tommy was brought downstairs to a holding cell, where he spent the rest of the night under the eye of a uniformed police officer.

Just after midnight, Judge Abraham Clott signed a search warrant for Tommy Gilbert's apartment. Ninety minutes later, Detective Darryl Ng and three other detectives arrived at 1F, 350 West Eighteenth Street, which had been sealed as an active crime scene.

They walked into a living room area, which had a couch, a desk, and a television. In the bedroom, they found a closet containing clothing, with a pair of handcuffs on a shelf. On top of the closet was a small safe, which used a biometric system to open with a fingerprint. It was opened by an Emergency Services Unit officer.

Inside, they found Tommy's birth certificate, passport, and social security card. There was also a stash of live ammunition, including some hollow-point bullets for a Glock .40-caliber handgun, as well as a tactical laser light and magazines. Next to them was a sealed envelope from the gun manufacturer, containing the Glock's serial number and two test shell casings. The detectives also seized a credit card skimmer with twenty-one blank cards.

They searched the rest of the apartment, seizing an iPhone, iPad mini, two MacBooks, a digital camera, and a video recorder. They also discovered a cache of fireworks in a trash bag.

The apartment was then photographed and everything seized brought back to the Seventeenth Precinct to be vouchered and logged into evidence.

By Monday morning, Thomas Gilbert Sr.'s murder was making headlines from coast to coast. The widely reported motive, from an unnamed police source, was that he'd cut his ne'er-do-well son's allowance.

RICH DAD SHOT DEAD—TYCOON'S SON NABBED IN E. SIDE HORROR, trumpeted the *New York Daily News*. "SLAIN" BY SCION. SON "SHOOTS" HEDGE-FUNDER was the *New York Post*'s headline. PRINCETON GRADUATE, 30, SHOT DEAD HIS $200M HEDGE FUNDER FATHER, roared the MailOnline.

"A wealthy hedge-fund chief was gunned down by his adult son after he threatened to cut his allowance by $100 a week and stop paying his steep rent," reported the *Daily News*. "Spoiled manchild Thomas Gilbert Jr., 30, flew into a murderous rage when he confronted his fed-up dad, Thomas Gilbert Sr., 70, over the downsizing of financial support, police said."

Charlie Suk, the owner of Cleaner de la Mode on First Avenue, was reported as last seeing Tom Gilbert on Saturday morning.

"It's so sad," Suk told the DNAInfo website. "He said, 'Happy New Year!' He brought in two pairs of pants and I still have them."

Gilbert's neighbor Pierre Gazarian told NPR that Tom Gilbert was "incredibly courteous [and] elegant."

"In a building in New York City," he said, "a lot of people barely say hello to each other. That makes the loss for some of us that much more painful."

At 8:00 a.m., Detective Ng checked on Tommy Gilbert in the holding cell to see if he was hungry. He was.

Detective Ng went to a nearby McDonald's and bought him two sausage-and-egg McMuffins and a bottle of water, bringing it back to the holding cell. After Tommy finished breakfast, Ng discreetly took the water bottle with his DNA on it and logged it into evidence.

Soon afterward, Detective Cirigliano came back on duty and went down to Tommy's holding cell. He was sitting on a bench, and the detective asked if he was okay.

"Yes," replied Tommy, "I just want to speak to my lawyer."

At 10:00 a.m., forensic pathologist Dr. Jennifer Hammers conducted an autopsy on Tom Gilbert's body. Before it began, she noted that he was six feet three inches tall and weighed 228 pounds.

There was a gunshot wound to the head and blunt-force

injuries to his body caused by hitting the floor after being shot. Dr. Hammers started by removing the hollow-point bullet—which had mushroomed on impact—deeply embedded.

She also observed a "well-defined muzzle imprint" on his left temple, meaning that Tommy had pressed the gun down hard against his father's head before pulling the trigger. The gunshot wound had caused numerous skull fractures and significant damage to the cerebrum, the left half of the brain.

Tom Gilbert's manner of death was ruled a homicide, caused by a "gunshot wound [to the] head with skull fractures and brain injuries."

Tommy Gilbert spent the day in a holding cell. At 6:00 p.m., Detectives Cirigliano and Ng arrived to take him downtown to Central Booking and his arraignment. Before leaving, they seized Tommy's designer clothes as evidence, giving him an ill-fitting dark gray jacket and white sweatpants from Bellevue Hospital.

At 6:20 p.m., the two detectives, both far shorter than Tommy, handcuffed his wrists behind his back and walked him out of the holding cell area. When they reached the exit door, Tommy saw the small army of TV crews and reporters lined up on either side of two metal barriers that had been set up on East Fifty-First Street. It was a carefully choreographed perp walk for the high-profile murder case and perfectly timed for the evening news shows.

"Wait a second," said Tommy, hesitating. "Is there media out there?"

When Detective Ng said there were, Tommy asked if there was another way out. The detectives told him not to worry, as it would be really quick. Tommy sighed, saying, "Okay," composing himself and taking a deep breath. Then he was marched past the barrage of flashing lights and reporters' questions into a waiting police RV.

As Tommy was being driven to his arraignment, NYPD chief of detectives Robert Boyce held a press conference at police headquarters. Flanked by New York mayor Bill de Blasio and police commissioner William Bratton, he announced that Thomas Gilbert Jr. had been arrested for patricide.

"Yesterday Thomas Gilbert Jr. visited [his] family," Chief Boyce began. "Mr. Gilbert Jr. then asked to speak to Mr. Gilbert Sr. by himself and asked the mother to leave. The mother did leave . . . to get some food for Junior. About fifteen minutes after that, she had a bad feeling and decided to return . . . and found Senior on the floor with a bullet hole in his head."

Chief Boyce said a .40-caliber Glock was found in Thomas Gilbert Sr.'s left hand lying on his chest, and police believed his son had staged it as a suicide. He added that during a search of Gilbert Jr.'s apartment, they had found numerous rounds of live ammunition and a shell casing envelope with the serial number of the gun found at the murder scene.

"It's a substantial amount of evidence to use," he said. "We brought Mr. Gilbert Jr. into the precinct and arrested him at around eleven o'clock this morning for homicide."

At 7:15 p.m., Tommy Gilbert arrived at Manhattan Central Booking at 100 Centre Street with the two detectives. During the thirty-minute drive downtown, Tommy's entire body had started to shake. Detective Ng asked if he was all right and he said he was.

"He did seem nervous," recalled Detective Ng. "I was

sitting next to him at the back of the car, and I could feel him shaking."

On arrival, the detective took him to have his mug shot taken, before walking him over to the EMT for a medical screening. When the examiner asked if he was sick or required medical treatment, Tommy replied, "No." Asked if he was taking any psychiatric or other medication, he said he wasn't.

After the screening, Detective Ng walked him into the Department of Corrections building for processing. While waiting for a corrections officer, the slightly overweight detective attempted to make conversation with his prisoner. He observed what great shape he was in, asking how he did it.

"A lot of it is diet and exercise," Tommy replied.

Detective Ng said he had a problem with carbs and putting on weight, prompting Tommy to describe his personal weight loss regimen.

"Yes, there's a ratio in losing weight," Tommy told him. "There's some calories that you cut back, and this ratio is different for everybody."

The detective then asked if he ran marathons, as he looked so fit.

"I'm not a distance runner," Tommy replied. "How about you?"

Later, prosecutors would point to this conversation to demonstrate that even while being charged with murdering his father, Tommy was mentally stable enough to calmly discuss his fitness regimen.

A few minutes later, Lolita Toro of the Criminal Justice Agency arrived with some pedigree questions. Asked where he lived, Tommy gave the East Eighty-Eighth Street apartment, which he had moved out of almost a year earlier. He also said he worked full-time in finance and earned about $3,000-a-month net pay.

After Tommy was searched and went through an x-ray machine and metal detector, they passed by a luncheon counter. Tommy asked if he could have a couple of sandwiches and an apple, which Detective Ng duly brought to him.

Then a corrections officer arrived to take custody of the prisoner and take him to his arraignment.

Representing Tommy at his arraignment was attorney Andrea Zellan from Brafman & Associates, who had been on the phone with him as he surrendered.

Gilbert was formally charged with murder in the second degree and criminal possession of a weapon in the second degree, unlawful possession of ammunition, and criminal possession of forgery devices. He did not enter a plea.

He was held without bail and ordered back to the court on Friday. If convicted of the charges, he faced twenty-five years behind bars.

Manhattan assistant district attorney Craig Ascher told the judge, "This is a strong case. The defendant brazenly shot his father in the head."

Then Tommy was taken to Rikers to be fully evaluated and to start preparing his defense for the brutal killing of his father.

PART 4

26

RIKERS ISLAND

Strikingly handsome with his refined background and Princeton education, Tommy certainly stood out from the other inmates at the Rikers Island correctional facility. He was also a Caucasian celebrity with a luminous target on his back.

The 414-acre island languishes in the East River between Queens and the Bronx, housing ten jails for inmates awaiting trial. Known by guards as "Gladiator School," it is notoriously dangerous and due to close by 2026.

"Rikers Island is a symbol of brutality and inhumanity," said the New York City Council speaker, Corey Johnson.

After his arraignment, Tommy Gilbert was taken to Rikers and placed on suicide watch. At his initial medical screening on January 6, Tommy told the Rikers clinician, Dr. Harris, that he had no history of mental health or nervous problems. He also denied any mental illness in his family, despite his grandfather Wilton Rae's 1966 suicide.

In his report, Dr. Harris noted that initially the new inmate had seemed composed and relaxed, but soon became anxious and nervous with a "slight shakiness" in his voice.

"He appeared to be either scared or suppressing his anxiety," wrote Dr. Harris. "He might also be in a dissociative phase [and] so overwhelmed by the experience he has not processed yet what's happening to him now. For his level of education and the magnitude of the change in his life . . . his insight was limited."

Dr. Harris also observed that although Gilbert was only complaining of insomnia and mild anxiety, he still might have been a danger to himself.

"Given the nature of the patient's charge and very high profile case," he wrote, "in addition to patient's lack of emotion when discussing the circumstances, he should remain on suicide watch."

Soon after entering Rikers, Tommy called Lila Chase in Florida. He told her it was all a mistake and he would soon be free. The call was being routinely recorded by the Department of Corrections.

"He was totally on another planet," remembered Lila. "He said, 'Oh, this is so wild, I'm in this jail. It will all be over in a couple of days and I'll see you in New York.'"

He also gave Lila his Apple iCloud password, telling her exactly how to access his contacts. Over the next few weeks, he would often request cell phone numbers of people he wanted to call.

On Tuesday, January 6, the *New York Post* revealed that Thomas Gilbert Jr. was currently under investigation for burning down Peter Smith Sr.'s historic Hamptons house. It also featured an exclusive interview with Anna Rothschild.

The double-page spread, with the lurid headline BLOOD MONEY, was written by Page Six editor Emily Smith. It branded Tommy as a "spoiled brat" and the Gilberts as "a family at war."

Rothschild claimed that Tommy constantly complained about his father for being hypercritical and saying he couldn't do anything right.

"He talked a lot about his dad," she said, "and how mean he was to him and how nothing was good enough."

Rothschild described her ex-boyfriend as "troubled" with few friends and no job prospects.

"How could a guy be that gorgeous, that wealthy, that fit, and kill his dad?" she asked. "This is the last thing in a million years that I thought he could do."

The following day, *Hedge Fund Alert* reported that Wainscott Capital had already begun liquidating the fund, as it could no longer continue without its sole stock picker. The fund's Third Avenue office had closed, and marketing chief Clay LeConey was in the process of winding things up.

"Without Tom, there was no trading," LeConey explained. "I'm not a trader, I was more of an operation specialist. So without him there, there was no purpose for the fund to exist at all."

On Thursday, January 8, a grand jury of the County of New York was convened to determine if there was enough evidence to indict Thomas Gilbert Jr. for second-degree murder and criminal possession of forgery devices. Shelley Gilbert testified that morning after going to the Medical Examiner's Office to formally identify her husband's body.

Tommy had indicated that he, too, wished to testify and was scheduled for 10:00 a.m. on Friday, but failed to appear.

On Friday afternoon, the grand jury voted to indict Gilbert on all charges. Soon afterward, he made a brief appearance with his attorney, Alex Spiro, at New York County

Criminal Court. Dressed in a bright orange bulky prison jumpsuit, with a straggly beard and long, dirty, uncombed blond hair, he did not say a word. Spiro did not enter a plea for his client.

Judge Gilbert Hong then ordered him to be held at Rikers Island, without bail, until his next court appearance on February 5.

Outside the courtroom, Spiro briefly addressed reporters, but gave them little information. "No statement in light of the recent tragedy and no comment from the family."

The sensational murder of Thomas Gilbert Sr. by his own son struck a nerve among the upper echelons of New York society. It raised the question of whether it was a good or bad thing for the wealthy to be supporting their children into their thirties.

On Saturday, *New York Times* financial reporter Ron Lieber examined the thorny subject in an editorial entitled GROWING UP ON EASY STREET HAS ITS OWN DANGERS.

"When Thomas Gilbert Jr. was arrested on Monday and charged with killing his wealthy father with a gunshot to the head," he wrote, "the rubbernecking and tut-tutting began almost immediately."

Lieber, who covered Wainscott Capital on his financial beat, noted how Twitter had instantly branded Tommy Gilbert as a "trust fund kid," "spoiled brat," and the whole affair as "morbidly disgusting."

"But at the same time, parents . . . were having a more searching conversation," he continued. "How does it come to pass that a 30-year-old Princeton graduate still gets pocket money from his parents? What, if anything, went wrong in the way his parents raised him?"

Lieber theorized that Tommy's mental health could be

a factor, noting that the children of wealthy parents often have higher rates of depression, anxiety, and substance abuse problems.

On Tuesday, January 13, detectives returned to 350 West Eighteenth Street armed with a second search warrant. They had now viewed CCTV footage showing Gilbert on his way to and from killing his father and were looking for the distinctive hoodie he had been wearing, as well as a dark shoulder bag.

Detective Darryl Ng and his team arrived at Gilbert's apartment at 3:25 p.m., finding a notice on the door that the rent was overdue. They went in and soon found the hoodie and other clothes they were looking for, balled up in a dresser drawer in the living room.

They also saw a plastic bag containing new syringes in the bedroom, as well as boxes of pills and other evidence of drug use. Two weeks later, armed with a third search warrant, they returned to seize them.

The next day, Thomas Gilbert Sr.'s will, signed two years earlier, was filed in Manhattan's Surrogate's Court. Tommy now stood to get a third of his father's estimated $1.6 million estate, with his mother and sister sharing the rest.

Under the terms of the will, which appointed Shelley executor, Tommy would receive quarterly payments from a trust in his name until the age of thirty-five. Then he would get whatever remained in one lump sum.

However, an estimated breakdown of Tom Gilbert's assets revealed he had far less money than previously thought. There was just $50,000 in his bank accounts, $477,000 in hedge funds, $1 million in private equity shares, and

$100,000 in tangible personal property. There was no listing of his real estate holdings.

In the court filing, Shelley requested immediate access to her late husband's bank account to pay household bills. She pointed out that there may be delays in probate, as the "decedent's son" was "currently unavailable" to give his waiver and consent.

By mid-January, Tommy Gilbert had been taken off suicide watch and put in Rikers' general population. Lila Chase regularly visited him and would often be briefed by Alex Spiro, who sought her assistance, as Tommy was not cooperating on his own defense.

"I worked with Alex," she explained, "and he tried to get me to get [Tommy] to do this or agree to that. But after a while, I was just there as a friend."

Tommy was also calling friends with outlandish demands. He asked Annabelle Summers to lend him $100,000 for his defense. When she said she did not have that kind of money, he suggested throwing a benefit on his behalf to raise money instead.

"Who the fuck would come to this benefit?" Summers would later think. "What's it for? Get a gun killer out of jail?"

She told him that she only chaired charity benefits before making an excuse to get off the phone.

He also asked Lila to go to East Hampton Town Hall and get him the deed to his parents' house in Wainscott. He wanted her to bring them to Rikers, so he could use them to finance his defense.

"That does not make logical sense," Lila reflected. "Nobody would hand me a deed that is not in my name. He was very worried about money."

Tommy also tried to contact Anna Rothschild several

times, but she refused to accept his calls and complained to Alex Spiro.

Tommy was regularly seeing the Rikers clinician Dr. Harris, who reported that he appeared dissociated from reality. After a January 13 therapy session, Dr. Harris wrote: "He appears anxious, wide-eyed and well-spoken, but somehow disconnected and distant."

Ten days later, Tommy complained of being harassed by three other inmates. He told Dr. Harris they were deliberately exploiting his OCD, stealing his food, and trying to distract him during phone calls. He was then prescribed the antipsychotic Risperdal, but Tommy refused to take it, saying he needed a clear head to concentrate on his defense.

By the end of January, Tommy was refusing to talk to the Rikers clinicians, claiming his attorney had ordered him not to because of his impending criminal case.

On Thursday, February 5, Thomas Gilbert Jr. was escorted into his arraignment at the New York Supreme Court by armed bailiffs. Dressed in an oversize orange jumpsuit with his hands cuffed behind his back, he appeared in front of Justice Melissa Carow Jackson, who had been assigned his case.

The great-granddaughter of President Theodore Roosevelt and the granddaughter of Supreme Court justice Robert H. Jackson, the former Brooklyn prosecutor came from one of the most distinguished legal families in the United States. In 2011, she made global headlines herself by denying bail to Dominique Strauss-Kahn, the chief of the International Monetary Fund, on a sexual assault charge and sending him to Rikers Island.

With a no-nonsense but fair reputation, the mother of three's patience would be stretched to the limit by Tommy Gilbert over the next four and a half years.

At the start of the hearing, Alex Spiro asked her to ban cameras from the courtroom.

"My client here is wearing an orange jumpsuit," said Spiro, "and has been in unfavorable conditions while incarcerated. His appearance is prejudicial."

Spiro also noted that with no eyewitnesses and a circumstantial case, any inelegant photos of Tommy could "muddy the waters," if any witness were to surface at a later date.

"Counsel, please," chided the judge, "this case has been all over the press for the past month and a half. Your client's photographs have appeared in every single newspaper. I'm denying your application."

Justice Jackson then asked Gilbert to enter a plea to second-degree murder and the other charges. He briefly paused before answering, "Not guilty," in a deep, steady voice. For the rest of the brief hearing, he nervously tapped his feet on the floor.

Manhattan assistant district attorney Craig Ortner opposed bail, arguing that the defendant was a flight risk. He told the judge that there was also a pending criminal charge against Gilbert for breaching the Peter Smith restraining order.

"In addition," Ortner told the judge, "defendant has been suspected—but not arrested or charged—in connection with a September 2014 arson in Suffolk County. In that case, the family home of the person named in the order of protection was burned down."

The prosecutor said that the defendant had friends and family with "considerable resources" who could potentially help him flee. Justice Jackson denied bail.

After the hearing, Manhattan district attorney Cyrus Vance Jr., also a Buckley alumni, issued a press release.

"As alleged in the indictment," it read, "the defendant intentionally shot and killed a member of his own family. He also possessed a private cache of ammunition and firearm attachments that might have enabled him to do even more tragic harm. The presence of deadly weapons can escalate any situation involving domestic or family violence."

27

"MESSING WITH ME"

Tommy Gilbert's only regular visitors at Rikers Island were his mother and Lila Chase. At the beginning, several acquaintances came as "a novelty," but none of his former friends from Buckley, Deerfield, or Princeton wanted anything to do with him.

Lila now became Tommy's link to the outside world, and they were soon closer than they had been in years.

"We still love each other," she explained. "I'm the only person, besides his mom, that Tommy still trusts, as much as he trusts anyone."

They often spoke on the phone, and Lila sent him many books he requested, although she didn't think he ever read them.

"I want to be someone that sticks when it's hard," she said, "unlike some of [his] other so-called friends that can't handle the thought of even writing him a letter, because maybe their name would come out."

Lila also provided emotional support to Shelley Gilbert, accompanying her to many court hearings over the next few months. She even helped Alex Spiro prepare his defense case, advising him on the best way to deal with his often difficult client.

* * *

After being placed in general population, Tommy started picking fights with other inmates whom he did not get on with. He would lash out violently and accuse them of messing with his head. In mid-February, he was brutally attacked by an inmate, who smashed a metal tray over Tommy's head and cut his ear open. From his infirmary bed, he accused two Muslims of attacking him due to anti-American sentiment.

When a prison psychiatrist asked him to elaborate on how he was being provoked, Gilbert said, "Well, I'm watching television and they'll pantomime what's going on to mess with me."

On March 12, he asked to be transferred to the mental observation unit, saying his high-profile case necessitated higher security. He was moved but still got in a series of fights, which he often started.

Alex Spiro enlisted Lila to try to calm Tommy down for his own good.

"I was deputized to go in and talk to him," she said. "And I said, 'How do you think this is going to be perceived? You're getting into fights and this is horrible.'"

She warned him to ignore the taunts and stay out of trouble, or it would only make things worse.

On March 16, detectives arrived at 8 Georgica Association Road armed with another search warrant. Shelley Gilbert let them in and gave them the key to her son's second-floor bedroom, which was still padlocked. Inside, they found a locked safe, which they brought back to the Seventeenth Precinct to be cut open with a power saw.

It contained a cardboard box with 114 loose rounds of

.40-caliber live ammunition and more accessories for the Glock semiautomatic. They also found a throwing star, a handgun manual, a photo of Lizzie Fraser with Tommy, and a love letter he had written her.

That same day, Detective Cirigliano brought Tommy Gilbert's seized iPhones, iPads, and MacBook computers to the forensic laboratory at the BDO accounting company for analysis. The project, which was code-named STYX, would take two years to complete, until technology to process Gilbert's iPhone 5 became available.

Five days later, Tommy Gilbert called his West Eighteenth Street apartment super for a favor. He feared that someone might try to break in and wanted his elaborate alarm system activated.

"Hey, this is Tommy. How's it going?" he announced nonchalantly.

"Tommy who?" replied the super.

"Tommy Gilbert . . . in the building."

"I thought you went to jail," said the super.

"Yeah, I know," replied Tommy. "Actually, I'm still here, unfortunately. I'm just calling from the phone. I can't talk too much. I just had a basic question about the apartment."

He then asked the super to set his alarm system, but the super said that was impossible, as police had changed both locks on the apartment and installed a dead bolt for added security.

Tommy's mind worked fast as to ways of breaking into his apartment. "I was going to say card it," he told the super, "but if it's a dead bolt, then . . ."

The super said that his apartment was still an active crime scene and there were two police stickers on the front door.

"All right . . . no worries," Tommy replied. "If possible, just take the stickers off, so it doesn't look like an eyesore. That should be fine."

Then without saying another word, he hung up.

The April issue of *Vanity Fair* carried an extensive feature on the Thomas Gilbert Jr. case, entitled "A Gilded Rage." The scrupulously researched piece by Benjamin Wallace revealed Gilbert's obsession for socialite Lizzie Fraser, leading to his assault of Peter Smith and the arson attack on his historic family house. It showed a photograph of Fraser as well as one of Tommy with Briana Swanson, taken the summer before he killed his father.

There were interviews from some of Tommy's former social circle, most of whom spoke on the condition of anonymity.

"Nobody thought this handsome, well-educated, privileged Princeton man was capable of violence," said one former friend.

"If Tommy looked like me," said another, "people would have thought he was an insane person fairly quickly."

At the beginning of April, Tommy Gilbert, now temporarily housed at the Manhattan Detention Complex, personally wrote to Manhattan district attorney Cyrus Vance and Justice Jackson requesting bail. In the notarized affidavit of service, Gilbert claimed he was self-employed and had half a million dollars available for his bail. He erroneously listed his residence as 155 East Eighty-Eighth Street, claiming to have lived there since 2009.

* * *

On Thursday, April 30, Tommy Gilbert made his next appearance in Manhattan Supreme Court. Wearing a short-sleeved light tan DOC jumpsuit, he nervously glanced at his mother and Lila Chase in the public gallery as he was brought in in handcuffs.

ADA Craig Ortner told the judge that a search warrant executed on the Gilberts' home in the Hamptons had uncovered more than a hundred rounds of .40-caliber ammunition matching the murder weapon.

The prosecutor also said that his office had now been officially notified by Alex Spiro that he intended to pursue a "psych defense."

"I believe it is insufficient," said Ortner, "as it fails to say what [mental illness] the psychiatric defense relates to."

Spiro disagreed, saying that his client would soon undergo psychiatric evaluation. Justice Jackson denied Gilbert's request for bail and adjourned the case.

At the next hearing a month later, Spiro asked the judge to release his client on bail, arguing that he was not a flight risk and could be easily monitored with an ankle bracelet. Ortner opposed bail because of the seriousness of the charge. He added that prior to the murder, Gilbert had been searching online for "blond men's passport photos."

Justice Jackson denied the application. "He's facing twenty-five years to life if convicted after trial," she said, "which is a significant incentive for anyone to flee."

As he mouthed "Hi" to his mother and Lila Chase, Tommy Gilbert was escorted out of the courtroom and back to jail.

Outside the courtroom, Spiro told reporters that he had fully expected bail to be denied.

"As the case progresses," he said, "it will become clear this is far more complex than the facts appear."

* * *

Alex Spiro hired top forensic psychiatrist Dr. Alexander Sasha Bardey to evaluate his client in preparation for an insanity defense. But on the few occasions Tommy did agree to meet with him, Tommy refused to discuss the case, despite Spiro's pleas to do so.

Tommy had still not made up his mind if he wanted a psych defense, wherein his entire psychiatric history would be aired in a public courtroom.

"I think he would admit to being OCD," said Lila Chase, "but he is not comfortable to say he's a paranoid schizophrenic."

Over the next several months, Gilbert spent a great deal of time in the Rikers law library, researching his legal options and other defense pleas available to him.

"I was nervous about the direction of the case," he would later explain. "I wasn't sure if I wanted to proceed in that direction . . . and wanted to get up to speed."

In the end, Dr. Bardey could only provide the defense with a one-page letter.

"Under a thin veneer of social convention," he wrote, "he's poorly related and appeared internally preoccupied. He was illogical and unable to rationally reflect on his legal situation, including assessing the evidence in this case that has been presented to him. He is currently suffering from a psychotic mental illness with acute symptoms, consistent with what he's been demonstrating throughout the medical records."

However, a June 24, 2015, report from a Rikers clinician found otherwise.

"The patient appeared to be functioning well on the unit," it stated, "socializing with his peers, watching TV. Patient was well-related . . . alert and responsive."

It also noted that Gilbert denied any suicidal, homicidal, and paranoid ideations or visual hallucinations, describing him as "cooperative. Eye-contact strong. Appearance and hygiene good."

Five weeks after Dr. Bardey's report, Justice Melissa Jackson ordered Thomas Gilbert Jr. to undergo a psychiatric examination to see if he was competent to stand trial. The Article 730—as it is known under New York State Criminal Procedure Law—had been requested by Spiro, who claimed his client refused to cooperate with him.

The judge wanted a complete mental diagnosis of the defendant's fitness by the next scheduled hearing on September 10.

"My client has a long history of psychiatric issues," Spiro told reporters outside the courtroom, "and we believe at this time he is not competent."

A few days later, Lila Chase visited Tommy Gilbert in Rikers. He had just celebrated his thirty-first birthday and was studying modern Chinese and learning jujitsu. During her visit, Lila mentioned that she had read somewhere that they had yoga classes at Rikers.

Tommy then tried to sign up for yoga, and someone leaked it to the *New York Daily News*.

DOING A STRETCH—RICH DAD-SLAY SUSP[ECT] AT RIKERS: WHERE'S MY YOGA? was the headline on the ensuing article.

"The spoiled manchild accused of killing his wealthy hedge-fund chief dad," it read, "wanted to know where the yoga classes were being held on Rikers Island, insiders said."

Soon after the article appeared, Gilbert asked to be moved to the Brooklyn House of Detention, complaining that the press were preying on him because he was such "a high pro-file inmate." His request was granted.

On Thursday morning, August 20, Tommy Gilbert was brought to Bellevue Hospital to be examined by two court-ordered psychiatrists, Dr. Daniel Mundy and Dr. Louise Mullan. Alex Spiro arrived early, bearing two large bind-ers of his client's medical records for the psychiatrists. He explained that he used to evaluate psychiatric patients at McLean Hospital, and he believed his client was psychotic.

Tommy arrived for the examination, sitting next to his at-torney across the table from the two doctors.

"He immediately appeared quite anxious," Dr. Mullan would later testify. "He spoke in clipped phrases and seemed somewhat detached . . . and it took much encouragement to get him to talk."

When questioned about his education and family relation-ships, Tommy became evasive and noncommittal about even the most minor details. When asked about the murder, he totally shut down, refusing to discuss any of the evidence.

"He kept referring to a bizarre set of internal guidelines," said Dr. Mullan. "He wouldn't elaborate."

During the two-hour interview, Alex Spiro encouraged his client to cooperate and answer questions, without any suc-cess. The psychiatrists noted that Tommy appeared to pay lip service to his attorney and did not appear to trust him.

Tommy also refused to discuss his extensive psychiatric history, totally distancing himself from it.

"I was very curious and concerned about the disconnect," said Dr. Mundy. "I thought that might be relevant to his fit-ness."

The doctor also observed Gilbert's total indifference to

being incarcerated and charged with murdering his own father, as well as his refusal to assist in his own defense.

In their subsequent joint report, both psychiatrists found Thomas Gilbert Jr. unfit for trial. Dr. Mullan also diagnosed him with unspecified schizophrenia and other psychotic disorders.

On August 29, Tommy Gilbert called Lila Chase from the Brooklyn House of Detention, sounding relaxed and in good spirits.

She told him she had just sent him a package and letter, which he should be receiving shortly. Then she asked how he was doing. He replied that he much preferred the mental observation unit to being in the general population at Rikers.

He said he wanted to read the Russian novelist Ivan Turgenev and was keeping up with sports and politics. When Lila asked if he was taking his medication he said no, because he didn't need it.

28

"THE PRESS PREYS ON
WELL-TO-DO FAMILIES"

On Thursday, September 10, Thomas Gilbert Jr. was found unfit to stand trial by the judge. As his mother and Lila Chase looked on from the public gallery, Justice Jackson told Gilbert that unless the district attorney's office challenged her decision, he would be sent to a state mental facility for treatment until he was deemed competent.

Craig Ortner asked the judge for another week to decide whether to challenge the incompetency findings. Throughout the brief hearing, Tommy, wearing orange regulation DOC garb, sat handcuffed at the defense table without a hint of emotion.

Outside the courtroom, a victorious Alex Spiro said his client would finally get the treatment that he so badly needed.

But just one week later, ADA Ortner challenged the incompetency finding, requesting a third opinion from a psychiatrist of his choosing.

"I want to have him reevaluated by an expert," Ortner told the judge. "We have an expert lined up who can do the examination in the next three weeks."

Justice Jackson then ordered Tommy to undergo another psychiatric examination, setting October 19 for the next hearing when the People's psychiatrist's report would be ready.

After the hearing, a visibly disappointed Spiro told reporters that forensic psychiatric evaluators from Bellevue had "unequivocally" determined that his client was unfit for trial.

"He has a significant history of mental illness for over a decade," he said. "We were hoping the independent state evaluators would convince the DA to let Mr. Gilbert get the treatment he needs."

The next day, Tommy Gilbert handwrote a letter to Justice Jackson, demanding a new defense attorney.

> Hon. Jackson,
> I am writing to request a change of defense attorney and would like to use a public defender.
> I apologize for the handwritten note, but due to the time-sensitive nature, I wanted to put in the request as soon as possible. I will follow with a more formal request to both the ADA and my lawyer. I will begin the application process as soon as I have access to the law library.
> Thomas Gilbert

Two days later, Tommy wrote to Manhattan DA Cyrus Vance, asking him to personally intervene to replace Alex Spiro. He told the former Buckley pupil he needed "a competent, caring, effective and energetic counsel" to prepare his defense. He pointed out that his murder case was now eight months old and complained that Spiro was not visiting him in jail.

"The defendant's concern is that he is facing a large amount of time in the New York State prison system," wrote Tommy, "and does not wish for that period of time to be imposed merely because defense counsel lacks the proper time to gather information necessary for the building of a solid defense and trial preparations."

He followed up with a second letter to the Manhattan district attorney, requesting a new prosecutor and asking for pretrial hearings to begin as soon as possible.

His rambling, often incomprehensible ten-page letter cited numerous legal precedents he had found in the Rikers law library. He claimed his human rights had been abused in "a clear miscarriage of justice."

Then on September 28, Tommy sent a third letter to DA Vance, trying to relate to him as a fellow Buckley alumni from a shared Ivy League background. He appears totally delusional as he desperately plays the privileged class card.

> Dear Mr. Vance,
> I'm writing to you from Manhattan Detention Center where I've been incarcerated for the past 8 months. I'm a graduate of Buckley, Deerfield, and Princeton University. Fortunately, I've had access to the newspaper and have enjoyed reading articles about the DA's offices and the city's various cases. I was impressed by the overall decline in crime this summer, and the success of the all-out program. I've also read your commentary on certain issues and have been following bail reform and the decreases in gun violence.
>
> Currently, I'm approaching trial for indictment #0016 2015, which is a Felony (A). From the beginning of this high-profile case, I've been railroaded through hearings with no access to capital and very little outside contact. Due to publicity received, nearly everyone I've spoken to assumes the case is under control. In fact it is

obviouysly [*sic*] a major person crisis and I still have not made much progress in the case.

In the next few weeks, I will be submitting motions and would ask for objective consideration from the DAs office. First, I will be attempting to hire a new defense attorney. Second, I'm also going to ask for a new prosecutor in this case. The current ADA has denied bail in an unconstitutional fashion and has aggressively prosecuted items that were both obtained without a warrant and unrelated to the case.

Next, I'd like to apply for bail. Bail was initially denied on grounds that were unconstitutional and consistent with the railroading process; furthermore, during incarceration I have encountered many conflicts. These dangerous conditions will continue and/or intensify the longer I remain incarcerated. Additionally, further incarceration will not only be physically dangerous, but also continue to inflict irraparable [*sic*] damage on my personal life and career. There is absolutely no reason for me to remain in jail.

I would also like to include a brief summary of my case. At the time of my arrest, my apartment was illegally incidentally searched. The search warrant later that day was also executed without an arrest warrant. These two searches contaminated all additional searches through the Fruit of Poisonous Tree Doctrine.

Also, immediate and sensationalist news coverage invalidated all witness testimony and discovery. These facts lead approximately 90% of the case vulnerable to suppression.

I will CC you on any motions I send in the next few weeks. Full and objective consideration from the DAs office would be especially appreciated. My optimal goal is to dismiss and seal indictment, which should be possible due to the overwhelming flaws in the case and sensitive personal files which have unfortunately been released to the court.

Sincerely,
Thomas Gilbert

When Lila Chase learned about the letter Tommy wrote to DA Vance demanding a new lawyer, she was furious. She went straight to Rikers and demanded he withdraw his application for a new attorney immediately.

"I went nuts," she recalled. "Alex Spiro is a brilliant lawyer . . . and Tommy thought he was working against him. I said, 'I won't see you again if you don't rescind it,' and he did. That was the only thing I have ever asked him to do."

At 3:00 p.m. on Friday, October 9, Tommy Gilbert arrived at the Manhattan DA's office at One Hogan Place to be evaluated by forensic clinical psychologist Dr. Stuart Kirschner. After refusing to cooperate with the defense's own expert and two court-appointed psychiatrists, Tommy was now "candid and open" with the prosecution's expert. He had decided not to pursue an insanity defense, undermining all of Spiro's hard work over the last ten months.

Before Tommy was brought in, Spiro, who was there as an observer, introduced himself to Dr. Kirschner and mentioned that he had once worked for McLean Hospital. He told the doctor that Tommy was irrational and could not assist in his defense, offering to act as a liaison between them. Kirschner said that would not be necessary. Spiro then joined ADAs Craig Ortner and Craig Ascher in an adjoining room to watch the interview through a two-way mirror.

Dr. Kirschner first told Tommy that the interview would be videotaped and that prosecutors were watching next door. Tommy had no problem with that.

"How are you today?" asked the doctor.

"I'm doing fine," replied Tommy.

"And how's your state of mind now?"

"Stable," he answered.

For the next half an hour, Dr. Kirschner questioned him about his life, his understanding of the charges against him, and the basic court system. Tommy answered every single question articulately and was fully cooperative.

He told the doctor that he'd always gotten good grades in school and had a "diverse" group of friends. He said that he had enjoyed studying at Princeton, graduating with a BA in economics. He had then moved back to New York, working from home as a self-employed stock trader and earning about $30,000 a year.

"Mr. Gilbert stated," wrote Dr. Kirschner in his subsequent report, "that after three years of being self-employed, he decided to explore other vocational opportunities; however, he was never able to cultivate anything that proved to be lucrative."

During the evaluation, Tommy freely discussed his psychiatric history. At the age of twenty-one, he said, he had entered a period of depression, with difficulty focusing and insomnia. Over the years, he had been treated by several psychiatrists and been prescribed Lexapro, Klonopin, and Risperdal.

Tommy downplayed his use of illegal substances, claiming to have only used marijuana, and never to have taken cocaine, hallucinogens, or intravenous drugs.

Dr. Kirschner then asked Tommy several questions related to his competency for trial. According to the so-called Dusky standard, there are two criteria for a defendant to meet in order to be deemed fit for trial. He must be able to understand the charges against him and courtroom procedure, and to participate effectively in his own defense. Tommy aced all of these, saying he felt comfortable having Alex Spiro as his attorney.

"He's my defense," Tommy asserted. "He's coordinating a psychiatric process."

The doctor then asked what the term *not guilty by reason of insanity* meant to him and what would happen to someone found so by a jury.

"That's when the defendant is not guilty because they have a limited capacity at the time of the crime," he replied. "He would receive a reduced sentence compared to a guilty plea and be sent to a psychiatric hospital."

Asked if he thought he could get a fair trial, Tommy replied, "I would hope so; however, I'm always worried about bias that may permeate justice in high-profile cases. The press preys on well-to-do families. A lot of high-profile Manhattan families tend to get more harsh, outlandish judgments."

Toward the end of the evaluation, Dr. Kirschner questioned why he was now cooperating after refusing to do so before.

"You seem pretty candid, pretty open," the doctor observed. "What made you change your mind?"

"I reviewed the law, and I reviewed the records," Tommy replied. "And I learned about different pleading options."

On Monday, October 19, Assistant DA Craig Ortner announced that Dr. Kirschner had found Thomas Gilbert Jr. fit to stand trial. As Gilbert looked on from the defense table,

Ortner handed Dr. Kirschner's report to Justice Jackson, who immediately had it sealed.

"There is not a shred of evidence," wrote the doctor in his diagnostic assessment, "which indicates that he currently has any psychological impairment whatsoever that would vitiate his ability to proceed with trial."

Alex Spiro strongly disputed this, telling the judge that his client's "ten years of psychiatric history" were far more accurate indicators of his mental fitness than Dr. Kirschner's brief interview.

After hearing both arguments, Justice Jackson ordered a full competency hearing with witnesses to begin on November 4, after which she would decide Gilbert's fitness to stand trial for his father's murder.

Outside the courtroom, a distraught Shelley Gilbert finally broke her silence in an impromptu press conference, expressing her anger and frustration.

"My family and I strongly disagree with the findings of the district attorney's independent psychiatrist," she told reporters. "We are extremely upset and very sad that they are delaying Tommy getting the psychiatric treatment he truly needs."

29

IS HE OR ISN'T HE?

At 3:00 p.m. on Wednesday, November 4, Thomas Gilbert Jr. was led into the courtroom for the first day of his competency hearing. Wearing beige DOC regulation scrubs and handcuffed, he was almost unrecognizable; his long, dirty, blond hair was now past his shoulders and he'd grown out a bushy beard. Shelley Gilbert and Lila Chase were back in the public gallery, and half a dozen reporters from news organizations, including *The Wall Street Journal* and *The New York Times,* had their notebooks at the ready.

The hearing began with Craig Ortner calling his expert witness, Dr. Stuart Kirschner. The forensic psychologist told Justice Jackson that the defendant might be "delusional," but that did not prevent him from assisting in his defense.

Ortner then attempted to screen the video of Dr. Kirschner's evaluation with Gilbert but was unable to get his laptop to work. After a few minutes of watching the prosecutor's failed attempts, the computer-savvy defendant whispered in Spiro's ear what was wrong. The solution was relayed to Ortner and the video was played.

The prosecutor asked Dr. Kirschner if it had been a "close call" to find the defendant fit for trial.

"Not in my opinion," replied Dr. Kirschner. "It was very

straightforward. I didn't find any elements that he was not competent. I didn't see any evidence of psychosis [and] he certainly doesn't need any medication to make him competent, which is the ultimate issue."

Ortner asked if Tommy might be "faking" good mental health, but the doctor said that was impossible.

"If a person has that capacity to fake wellness," he said, "then he has the ability to go to trial. He has an editing system."

The assistant DA then followed up by asking why Tommy had not cooperated with all the other psychiatrists in the past.

"When a person's mental instability is brought before the court," the doctor replied, "his whole life can become an open book. So the fact that Mr. Gilbert was very concerned of what the ramification of a psychiatric evaluation might mean shows extremely good judgment and is very prudent. Personally, I think that's an extremely intelligent way of dealing with the situation."

The judge then adjourned the hearing for six days.

The following Tuesday morning, the competency hearing resumed with Dr. Kirschner back on the stand. Despite Alex Spiro's objections, Ortner played one of Tommy Gilbert's many telephone calls from Rikers to Lila Chase, who was in the public gallery.

"Maybe as uncomfortable as that was for me," she said, "I think for him it was the horror of horrors. He stopped making calls after that."

After it played, Ortner asked Dr. Kirschner if he agreed that the books Gilbert told Lila he was reading were "sophisticated."

"Well, he's reading up on literature and history," observed the doctor.

Finally, Ortner asked if the defendant's history of mental illness bore any relevancy to his competency. Dr. Kirschner replied it did not, as he had a "minimal" psychiatric history, compared to "a rather extensive" history of substance abuse.

"Presently, Mr. Gilbert is competent," explained the doctor, "and if he has a diagnosis of mental disorder, which he may very well have, it has no bearing on his present ability to proceed to trial."

In an aggressive cross-examination, Alex Spiro accused Dr. Kirschner of ignoring years of his client's troubling psychiatric history and psychotic episodes. He asked why the doctor thought Tommy had not wanted to appear mentally ill at his evaluation.

"Well, there could be a number of reasons," replied the doctor. "If a person's in a hospital and wants to get out, they might fake symptoms. It's rare that a person may fake being well for incompetency [and] more prominent for people to malinger."

"What if they live in a society where there's a stigma attached to mental illness?" asked Spiro. "Would that be a reason to fake wellness?"

"Yes," agreed Kirschner.

"What if someone's an Ivy League student and doesn't want to be perceived as having issues? Is that a reason to fake wellness?"

"Sure."

"What if somebody's a good-looking guy from a prominent family who doesn't want to be an outcast at their country club? Is that a reason to fake wellness?"

"Yes," replied the doctor.

Under Spiro's questioning, noting that Tommy's paternal grandmother was psychotic and his maternal grandfather had committed suicide, Dr. Kirschner agreed that hereditary mental illness in the Gilbert family could be important.

"I don't know about psychosis," said Dr. Kirschner, "[from] what Tommy told me there's a history of mood disorder in the family."

As the morning session progressed, Tommy became increasingly upset that his psychiatric history was being aired in open court.

"May I interrupt counsel briefly?" asked Tommy as his attorney was detailing the extensive list of antipsychotic drugs he had been prescribed over the years. Spiro went over to speak with him, telling the judge that his client wished to leave the courtroom.

"Mr. Gilbert," said Justice Jackson. "I just want you to understand that you have the right to be present at this hearing, but if you choose not to be here voluntarily, it will proceed in your absence. It's your choice."

The judge then took a lunch break, and Gilbert was escorted back to his holding cell.

When the hearing resumed at 2:30 p.m., Alex Spiro informed the judge that Tommy Gilbert would not be attending the afternoon session. He continued his cross-examination of Dr. Kirschner, focusing on Tommy's obsession that his father was invading his body and stealing his soul. Asked about his various delusions, Dr. Kirschner said he found it "remarkable" that no psychiatrists had ever mentioned the possibility that Gilbert suffered from substance abuse disorder.

"Can we agree that there is a significant delusion history?" asked Spiro.

"Right," agreed the doctor, "but not necessarily that regards attorneys, judges, and trials. His delusions have involved the feelings that people were stealing from him or causing him some distress with no foundation. He has some paranoid beliefs, but also it can't be ruled out that he was using many different substances."

Dr. Kirschner observed that Tommy had not suffered any delusions in Rikers, as he had no access to illegal drugs.

"So do you honestly believe, sir," asked Spiro, "that the psychiatric history that you've been presented with could be explained simply by the use of psychedelic drugs?"

"At least in part," replied Dr. Kirschner.

Spiro then walked the doctor through his client's medical records, including his recurring belief that *Saturday Night Live* was "mocking him," and that his computer was being hacked to sabotage his hedge fund.

"Okay," continued the defense attorney. "'Police at Princeton pushing me toward China.' Does that sound like a delusion?"

"You're just reading things," said Kirschner. "Some things sound like a delusion, and some things don't necessarily have to be, if it's taken out of context."

On Friday, November 13, the competency hearing entered its third day, with Dr. Stuart Kirschner back on the stand for more grueling cross-examination. Once again, the defendant was absent.

Alex Spiro immediately went on the attack, asking Dr. Kirschner if he was aware that Tommy refused to read any of the case discovery and was "unable" to discuss the case with him at all.

"I did not see anything that indicated he was unable," said the doctor.

The defense attorney then accused Dr. Kirschner of merely asking his client yes-or-no questions and not bothering to probe any deeper.

"You have the transcript in front of you," Spiro told him. "Will you please tell us which questions you believe are probing as whether or not my client suffers from delusions?"

Dr. Kirschner stood his ground, explaining that he had asked Tommy why he was cooperating with him after refusing to talk with his own defense psychiatric expert.

"And he said very clearly," said Dr. Kirschner, "that he wanted to research things further. He wanted to see what was discoverable and what was not discoverable. He had concerns about his case, and that after he researched it, he decided that he would speak to me."

Finally, Spiro asked the doctor if he had noticed a flat affect in Gilbert during the evaluation, a sign of mental illness.

"No," he replied. "I saw a sadness in Mr. Gilbert, not a flat affect."

In redirect, ADA Craig Ortner tried to prove that the defendant was functioning in society at the time of his arrest, despite any past mental illness.

"Was he living on his own?" asked Ortner.

"Yes," the doctor replied.

"Was he carrying on relationships with other people . . . women?"

"Yes."

"Was he attempting to build a hedge fund?"

"Yes."

Ortner rested his case, and the judge recessed for lunch, after which, the defense would begin presenting its case that Thomas Gilbert Jr. was unfit for trial.

After lunch, Alex Spiro called his first witness, Dr. Daniel Mundy, one of the two court-ordered Bellevue forensic psychiatrists to find Gilbert unfit for trial. Dr. Mundy testified that over the years, many psychiatrists had treated the defendant without any consistent diagnosis.

"Some diagnoses were a bunch of 'we'll call him nuts' and OCD," explained Dr. Mundy. "Something's going on, but they're never exactly sure of what. You can see their opinions shifting back and forth."

Dr. Mundy said the medical records clearly showed Gilbert's mental deterioration during his teens and early adulthood.

"For someone who's described as having leadership quality in his high school records," Dr. Mundy told the judge, "he's not continuing to demonstrate that. His social skills are deteriorating [and] mental illness is stopping him going out and meeting all these people and socializing. And he has many persecutory themes that people are messing with him and mean to harm him."

The doctor said that during the ninety-minute interview, Tommy had repeatedly referred to his "guidelines," in explaining why he wouldn't discuss his case with his attorney.

"It struck me as really, really odd and concerning," said Dr. Mundy. "Then he started referencing the law library [and] said, 'I want to proceed with [a plea of] not guilty.'"

On Tuesday, November 17, the competency hearing moved into its fourth day. Dr. Mundy was back on the stand; once again, the defendant had excused himself from the day's proceedings.

Under Spiro's direct questioning, Dr. Mundy described Gilbert's refusal to discuss the murder as "notable."

"We don't ask him for a significant recollection of all that was going on at the time of his arrest," Dr. Mundy told the judge. "What we routinely ask is what someone's thinking . . . how they are making decisions. We just want to see how they're thinking. He kept using this phrase, 'I have to refer to my guidelines,' in a way that didn't make sense. There was nothing to suggest a rational reason that he might be refusing to cooperate with his defense or his defense expert."

The doctor said it was "bizarre" and "irrational" how Gilbert had suddenly cooperated with the People's expert.

Toward the end of Spiro's lengthy direct, Justice Jackson asked Dr. Mundy a number of questions about Tommy's drug use and its role in his mental problems. It was an important clue into the judge's thoughts about his fitness.

"It would look like [he was] using cocaine all the time," she noted, "because [he's] going out to party in the Hamptons?"

"It's hard for me to know how much drugs have played overall," answered Dr. Mundy, "but I strongly suspect that there's a primary mental illness there. Have I answered your question?"

"Yes, you did," said the judge.

She then asked about Tommy's string of fights at Rikers Island and whether he was the instigator or not.

"We don't know if the inmates in there are saying, 'Hey, whitey!'" the judge observed. "How do we know he wasn't provoked by something said that was brutal?"

Dr. Mundy said that he had asked about that, and the defendant's only stated reason was being mocked by inmates while watching television.

"How much of the ability to assist," asked the judge, "or the unwillingness to assist, has to do with the defendant's fear of social stigma? His prior psychiatric history [being] laid out for the world to learn about is perhaps his continuing reluctance to not disclose and not face it."

Dr. Mundy agreed that was "understandable," pointing out

that when someone's fitness is questioned, they usually want to explain things.

"He did not make the effort that I would expect from an intelligent, educated person," he told the judge. "He just kind of shut down and had some prepared statement. There's really nothing that could make me entertain that he was just unwilling because he was concerned of [social] stigma."

Then Alex Spiro asked about Tommy's personal letter to Manhattan DA Cyrus Vance and his apparent belief that his fellow Buckley alumni would "magically" make his murder case disappear.

"Would that be impaired rational reasoning?" asked Spiro.

"Yes," replied the doctor. "If he thought that somehow this case will disappear . . . that's a fitness-impairing illusion."

Summing up, Dr. Mundy said he believed Tommy Gilbert was psychotic, and if he were treating him, he would be prescribing antipsychotic medication.

In his cross-examination, ADA Craig Ortner immediately went on the attack. He observed that Alex Spiro worked for one of the most expensive and high-powered law firms in the country, asking if it was usual for defense attorneys to be so cooperative with court-appointed psychiatrists.

"It wasn't just luck," said Ortner, "that Mr. Spiro, or someone that works for him, marshals putting together documents in two binders and then delivers it to you?"

The doctor conceded that it was a first.

Ortner then suggested Spiro had tried to influence the court-ordered evaluation by strongly advocating an insanity defense.

"Do you have an idea what Mr. Spiro is getting paid?" asked Ortner.

"Objection," snapped Spiro.

"Overruled," said the judge.

"I assume he's getting paid well," replied Dr. Mundy.

"A million dollars?" asked the ADA.

"I assume it's a high rate, but I don't know."

"Can we agree," Ortner continued, "he's probably getting paid lots of money for pursuing this case? He works for a fine law firm [and] someone is paying a lot of money to represent the defendant? It's not like a court-appointed lawyer."

"Correct," agreed the doctor.

Ortner then asked if Spiro was "zealous, pushy, and in-your-face."

"No more than many legal aid and common defenders," replied Mundy, standing his ground.

Then Ortner asked the doctor if he was aware that as police were knocking at Tommy's apartment door on the day of the murder, he was calling Alex Spiro for help.

"I was not aware of that," replied Dr. Mundy.

Ortner asked if that was consistent with the defendant's unwillingness to work with his attorney.

"I'm really reluctant to give an opinion on this," said Dr. Mundy. "It demonstrates he's aware of a legal problem and summons the person who solves legal problems."

"Are you aware that since the defendant's arrest in January, Mr. Gilbert has repeatedly urged, exhorted his mother to give her money to Mr. Spiro in support of his defense?"

"That doesn't surprise me," answered Dr. Mundy.

"Are you aware that he has urged his poor widowed mother to dip into his father's estate in order to get the money to pay Mr. Spiro's legal fees?"

"I was not aware of that," replied the doctor. "That doesn't necessarily surprise me either."

On Friday, November 20, the competency hearing entered its fifth day. After a two-hour wait for Tommy Gilbert to be produced from Rikers, he announced that he did not wish to attend the proceedings after all.

Then at 12:55 p.m., as the hearing was about to begin, Gilbert sent word that he now wished to address the court. He was brought in wearing an orange jumpsuit, his wrists cuffed behind his back.

"Good afternoon, Mr. Gilbert," sighed Justice Jackson. "Feel free to speak."

"Your Honor," he began breathlessly, "I have three points that I would like to bring up. First, I'd like to have a bail hearing as soon as possible. I'm in danger from the other inmates in prison . . ."

The judge asked him to slow down and take his time so the court reporter could take everything down.

Gilbert repeated that he wanted an immediate bail hearing and asked for the press to leave the courtroom.

"Since this is a psych hearing, it's essentially a sealed process," he told the judge. "I request that the public not be allowed in this hearing and that it be closed, due to the confidentiality of a health professional."

Justice Jackson said she understood his point of view, with all his personal history being made public.

"I'm very sympathetic to that," she told him. "However, you understand the law prevents me from closing the courtroom under these circumstances. I can't grant that application, sir, as much as I'd like to for your privacy concerns."

She added that any bail application must be made by Alex Spiro after the competency hearing.

"I cannot close the hearing," she told him, "and again, if you choose not to be here, sir, the court will proceed. You understand?"

"Yes, Your Honor," he replied, sounding defeated.

The judge then adjourned for lunch as Tommy Gilbert was led out of the courtroom.

* * *

The hearing resumed at 2:50 p.m., with ADA Ortner's continuing cross-examination of Dr. Mundy. The defendant did not wish to attend the afternoon session.

During his questioning, Ortner homed in on an American Psychiatric Association (APA) diagnostics form that Dr. Mundy had filled out for the defendant. It listed eighteen symptoms of psychiatric illness, each being rated on a scale of zero to six, with zero showing the symptom not present and six extremely present.

"You rated the defendant zero on twelve out of the eighteen categories," stated Ortner as he handed Dr. Mundy the form.

"I see that, yes," he answered.

Ortner listed some of the symptoms that the doctor had marked as zero: attention, mannerisms or posturing, grandiosity, hallucinations, motor retardation, unusual thought content. He had only graded Gilbert one out of six for mild anxiety and emotional withdrawal, and under the category of conceptual disorganization, Dr. Mundy had put a question mark.

Dr. Mundy had graded him two out of six for uncooperativeness, and four out of six for "suspiciousness, delusional or otherwise."

"So out of fifteen of the eighteen categories of symptoms that were on this form," observed Ortner, "is it true that you rated Mr. Gilbert as either not having any symptoms at all or having very mild to mild symptoms?"

"That's correct," replied the doctor.

On the sixth day of the competency hearing, Tuesday, November 24, ADA Ortner resumed his marathon cross-examination of Dr. Mundy. Once again, the defendant absented himself.

Ortner now asked about Tommy Gilbert's psychiatric reports in Rikers and his refusal to take any medication there. The Rikers doctor had agreed to discontinue medication, reporting the defendant's thought process as "spontaneous, organized, and goal orientated."

"It's a common thread," observed Ortner, "that his concentration is good, his behavior is cooperative, and he is generally alert, intelligent, and functioning?"

"Generally, yes," conceded Dr. Mundy.

"Now, after the discontinuation of any psychotic medication," asked Ortner, "there's no indication that the defendant went off the rails?"

"No," said Dr. Mundy. "The medical record doesn't demonstrate their appearance for the first time."

"So according to virtually every metric that they've used to assess mental health, he's acting normally in jail, apart from somebody trying to mess with him?"

"That's correct," answered the doctor.

The People's cross-examination lasted into the late afternoon, when Alex Spiro finally had the chance to mend some fences in redirect. He immediately accused Ortner of cherry-picking his client's mental history, only focusing on his frivolous concerns, like which country club to join.

He had the doctor read out a summary of a report by Dr. Susan Evans, written about six months before the murder, which came under the heading of "Major Conflicts."

"The patient also has some strong paranoid ideation towards his father," it said, "and has avoided contact with his family. The patient is able to reality test [and] states that he found someone to invest in his hedge fund, and seems to continue to think he will be successful at this. In reality the patient is not doing much of anything."

Spiro concluded by asking if his client's request for bail in the middle of a competency hearing so he could go surfing would be delusional and prevent him from assisting in his own defense.

"Asking for bail is never a delusion," said Dr. Mundy. "However, it could certainly represent a break with the reality of the circumstances."

After almost four days of testimony, Dr. Mundy was dismissed and Justice Jackson recessed for two weeks until after the Thanksgiving holiday.

The hearing resumed on Tuesday, December 8, for its seventh day. The defendant made a brief appearance in the courtroom in handcuffs and orange jail jumpsuit. A week earlier, he had written to Justice Jackson, asking to address the court again. But when the judge now gave him the opportunity to do so, he asked to go back to Rikers instead.

Alex Spiro then called his final witness, Dr. Louise Mullan, who, along with her Bellevue colleague Dr. Mundy, had found the defendant unfit for trial. The Northern Irish–born forensic psychiatrist, who has performed more than four hundred competency evaluations, told the judge that it took "much encouragement" to even get the defendant to talk, even though his attorney was present. Dr. Mullan said he even refused to say which schools he attended or the names of the psychiatrists who had treated him, even though Spiro had brought all the records.

"He appeared to be avoiding answering questions," said Dr. Mullan, "which I thought was quite bizarre. There's no reason for him not to tell me that information. It kind of smacked of paranoia."

Under Spiro's direct, the doctor said she diagnosed Gilbert as suffering from delusional disorder with possible unspecified schizophrenia. She said it was not uncommon for people suffering from delusional disorder to be able to function in society.

Then Spiro asked her to describe his client's inability to mentally deal with the hypotheticals of his case.

"Well, in the case of Mr. Gilbert," she explained, "we came up against a brick wall in regards to how he's thinking about the case. So no degree of encouragement would really get him to consider his situation and what his options were. It was almost like his brain can't compute or rationalize his situation."

The doctor said that although Tommy could "eloquently describe" the legal process and the roles of the relevant courtroom personnel, he could not discuss his own case and was extremely guarded about it.

Then Justice Jackson asked if that had anything to do with the lack of confidentiality in the courtroom.

"Yes, I think he was well aware of the lack of confidentiality," said Dr. Mullan. "That's absolutely right."

Spiro followed up by asking if his client had ever cited confidentiality as the reason why he could not discuss his case.

"No, he did not give a rationalization for declining to talk about this," she said. "He just kept referring to some set of 'internal guidelines,' and I was unable to get him to explain them."

"What if the defendant didn't want a psychiatric defense," asked the judge, "and that's why he was unwilling?"

"I would expect him to say so," said Dr. Mullan, "and to provide a reasonable explanation for why he wouldn't consider that. He wouldn't provide a reasonable explanation for anything. We would hit a roadblock, which appeared to reflect the rigidity of thought and paranoia."

"And so there is no evidence that you interpreted," said the judge, "of the defendant not being willing?"

"Yes," replied the doctor.

In the afternoon session, ADA Craig Ortner cross-examined Dr. Mullan, trying to show that she had based her decision on medical records supplied by the defense.

"Are you aware," he asked her, "that within a few weeks of your interview with Mr. Gilbert, he had moved the court to have his attorney replaced?"

"No, I didn't know that," she replied. "It seems even more peculiar."

"So he may have a disagreement with his lawyer about some aspects of this case?"

"Sure," said Dr. Mullan. "It's possible."

"And might that reflect the reason why he may have been reticent to discuss certain matters with counsel either in your presence or out?"

"It's possible," she conceded.

Then Ortner asked if she was aware that the first person Gilbert called after shooting his father in the head was Spiro.

"No, I hadn't heard that," she replied.

"Does that suggest an ability, if not a willingness, to work with Mr. Spiro?"

"I really couldn't say," said Dr. Mullan. "But perhaps a delusional relationship existed before this incident."

The prosecutor then noted how the case had received extensive newspaper coverage around the world, asking if that could explain the defendant's guardedness.

"It's possible," said Dr. Mullan. "In the grand scheme of things, this gentleman has been accused of murdering his father, and the confidentiality issue appears to pale into insignificance in my mind."

30

"DEFENDANT'S APPEARANCE ALONE IS REMARKABLE IN A CRIMINAL COURTROOM"

On the last day of the hearing—Wednesday, December 9—both sides rested their cases to present summations. Thomas Gilbert Jr. did not wish to be present. It was the defense and the People's last opportunity to convince Justice Jackson whether or not Gilbert was fit to stand trial.

Spiro began by telling the judge that his client had faked wellness during his evaluation with Dr. Kirschner, and was well experienced in doing so.

"He's a good-looking fellow," said Spiro. "Ivy League in football, Wall Street, and the Hamptons. It makes sense that he would try to appear better than he is. He's had the experience of faking well for a decade plus, and he has the IQ with which to do it."

Spiro said that his client was incapable of working with him on his defense, a key factor in meeting the Dusky standard for competence. He said that during his visits to Rikers, Tommy refused to look at any discovery or motions.

"He's not fighting with me, Judge," said Spiro. "He's still calling me, and he's telling everybody that he has this great lawyer. If he went to Princeton and he's so smart, why not just say to me, 'Sorry, I don't want to go in this direction [with an insanity defense] in the case'?"

The defense attorney accused Dr. Kirschner of being a professional expert witness who failed to ask any probing questions at his too-brief evaluation.

"All he does is testify," said Spiro. "There's no depth. There's no digging. There's no psychology."

Alex Spiro then appealed to Justice Jackson to allow his client to receive the treatment he needed in a mental hospital and proceed to trial when he was ready.

"So I'm not asking you to acquit, okay," Spiro told her. "I'm asking that he be allowed to be treated . . . and then we can have his trial."

In his summation, ADA Ortner said the competency hearing had nothing to do with whether or not the defendant suffered from mental illness but only whether he was fit for trial. He accused Spiro of turning it into a dry run for a future insanity defense.

"The issue here is simply one of competency," Ortner declared. "Does the defendant possess a rational and factual understanding of the proceedings against him and [is he capable] of assisting his own defense?"

It was clear, he told the judge, that the defendant suffered from some form of mental illness, but there were "far, far sicker people" who stood trial for their crimes.

Ortner then laid out what he termed "objective signs" of the defendant working with his attorney.

"When the police were knocking on his door to arrest him for the murder of his father," he said, "his immediate reaction was to get on the phone and call his trusted lawyer, Mr. Spiro."

Then, after being arrested for murder, he repeatedly asked to call his defense lawyer. As of October 1, Ortner told the judge, the defendant had called Alex Spiro fifty times from jail, many of them for lengthy conversations.

Ortner noted how Gilbert had wanted the judge to close the courtroom to reporters as soon as they started digging into his psychiatric history. When she'd refused, he'd stopped attending hearings, where some very embarrassing personal information had been made public.

"Mr. Gilbert is not the typical defendant," said Ortner. "It's not a typical case. He does come from a prominent family [and] the case has garnered interest in the media. So what you're seeing are the lurid details of this embarrassing and very personal case being publicized, not just in the courtroom but locally, nationally, and internationally."

Justice Jackson then adjourned the hearing for three weeks, so she could review the evidence and decide if Thomas Gilbert Jr. was competent for trial.

In a written decision on Monday, December 21, Justice Jackson found Thomas Gilbert Jr. fit for trial. Her nine-page ruling noted that the defendant's psychiatric history was irrelevant to the competency issue.

"Despite the competing testimony of the experts in this case," she wrote, "the court finds the defendant competent to stand trial."

The judge also observed how prominent the Gilbert family were among Manhattan's wealthy elite, making this case highly unusual.

"Defendant's appearance alone is remarkable in a criminal courtroom," she wrote. "A graduate of the most exclusive schools on the East Coast, with a degree from Princeton University, the defendant stands over six feet tall, blond and blue-eyed."

She wrote that after closely observing Gilbert in the courtroom, he did not appear distracted or agitated.

"[He] responded appropriately to the court," she wrote, "and was able to follow direction. He was articulate when he spoke on the record and in his *pro se* submissions."

She also cited his videotaped interview with Dr. Kirschner and a phone call from Rikers to Lila Chase.

"During that colloquy," she noted, "the defendant requested intellectually advanced reading materials and expressed his desire to stay in the mental observation unit, because he was treated better there. He was laughing, rational, and engaged in a casual, frank conversation."

At a brief hearing after her decision was released, attended by Tommy Gilbert, Justice Jackson emphasized that she did not have to rule on whether or not he was mentally ill.

"This court does find the defendant fit to proceed," she said as Shelley Gilbert glared from the public gallery. "This is the court's decision."

Outside the courtroom, a visibly disappointed Alex Spiro fielded reporters' questions.

"The bar for fitness to stand trial is so low," he said, "that no matter how mentally ill a person is, we too often force them into courtrooms. At some point, we all have to consider whether we need to treat more people in hospitals rather than locking them in prisons."

31

MY CLIENT IS RADIOACTIVE

Over the next two years, the Thomas Gilbert Jr. case crawled along at a snail's pace toward trial. Although his client had been deemed fit to be tried for the murder of his father, Alex Spiro tirelessly battled to have Tommy declared incompetent.

At the next status hearing on February 17, 2016, there was even speculation that Tommy might now decide to represent himself, as he had been spending so much time in the Rikers law library.

"It may be that he becomes counsel and I become co-counsel," Spiro teased reporters before the hearing.

Shelley Gilbert arrived early and sat outside in the hallway playing Bumble Shooter on her smartphone. She told a reporter that she had visited her son the previous week and he looked "excruciatingly thin," and she suspected they weren't feeding him enough.

As the hearing was about to begin, a court officer told Justice Jackson that the defendant was refusing to come out of the holding cell. The judge asked Spiro to go in and try to persuade him to attend.

"To be perfectly candid with the court," said the defense attorney, "I'm not inspired, given my client's psychological issues. In my experience, it's going to be a very quick determination and not a lengthy conversation."

"Okay," said the judge. "I'm hoping that maybe he'll change his mind."

A few minutes later, Spiro reentered the courtroom, shaking his head. He informed the judge that his client refused to attend the hearing and wouldn't say why. Instead, he had asked for the phone number of the president of Cablevision.

"But he would not explain why he needs to speak to the people at Cablevision," said Spiro.

Then Justice Jackson ordered Spiro to turn over additional information about the psychiatric defense he planned to use at trial. Spiro explained that because his client still refused to meet with the defense expert, Dr. Alexander Sasha Bardey, his hands were tied.

"I have nothing further to turn over," he sighed, telling the judge that Tommy remained mentally unfit for trial and still refused to meet psychologists.

"That's the cart that's driving this horse," said Spiro, "and I'm hoping the court can understand that."

Jackson replied that that was "woefully insufficient," ordering Spiro to provide the court with "specific maladies" in support of an insanity plea.

"You have refused to provide enough so the People cannot have the defendant evaluated by their own doctor," the judge chided. "This has led to delays in the case and has prevented the defendant to get his day in court."

ADA Craig Ortner agreed, saying that if the defendant refused to cooperate with his own psychiatric expert, the onus was on the defense.

"That is the defendant's choice," said Ortner. "If he won't comply with the psychiatric examiner, he won't have a psychiatric defense."

The judge ordered Spiro to produce more information or

risk losing the chance for a psychiatric defense, saying she would set a trial date at the next hearing.

"I'm not going to delay this case," she told Spiro. "I am going to set this down for trial sooner rather than later."

After being pronounced fit for trial, Tommy Gilbert had hit rock bottom at Rikers. He became convinced that his life was in danger and started desperately calling Lila Chase for help.

"It was horrible," she remembered. "He was calling almost every day, and they were scary calls. [He said] he wasn't safe or he needed me."

Once he called when she was working in Florida, saying he was very ill and needed her to visit him immediately, as he wasn't safe. Lila explained she was running an equestrian event and could not return to New York.

"I remember calling poor Alex [Spiro]," she said. "And he said that he can't do anything until Tommy says what's wrong."

On March 24, Tommy Gilbert faked a suicide attempt in order to get transferred out of Rikers Island. He told guards that he had swallowed a small battery, which had become lodged in his abdomen.

He was taken to the infirmary to be x-rayed and caught holding a battery over his abdomen during the procedure. The battery was confiscated and he was asked to take another x-ray, but Tommy refused, saying he did not want to be poisoned by radiation.

Several days later, he wrote to Justice Jackson, requesting an emergency bail hearing, as his life was in danger. She immediately called one so he could address her in person.

Tommy Gilbert was brought into the courtroom in handcuffs, his unruly hair and beard noticeably longer. He sat at the defense table with Alex Spiro, who had recently filed a motion for another 730 competency exam. Spiro had only learned about his client's letter to the judge that morning.

"Mr. Gilbert," began Justice Jackson, "I received a letter [where] you requested that you be brought before me in an emergency bail hearing as soon as possible. So I'm granting the application."

"Well, I'm asking for bail, and that's based on multiple parts," Tommy told the judge. "The first of which is the Judiciary Act of 1789, which grants bail as a constitutional right to all defendants."

The Judiciary Act of 1789 established the federal court system in the United States and has nothing to do with bail.

Tommy continued, claiming that all the evidence against him had been illegally obtained, and there was "no reason" to believe he was a flight risk.

"The defendant is also in danger," he told the judge. "I've been attacked a number of times by inmates, and [there are] security risks to my physical safety based on the prior incidents and the violent threats of individuals in prison."

ADA Ortner said that the defendant should have his counsel make bail applications on his behalf and argued that nothing obtained through the search warrants was illegal.

Justice Jackson said she would not be granting bail, but sympathized with the defendant for the fifteen months of his incarceration.

"Of course I am concerned," she told him. "And I'm doing everything I possibly can to expedite this case to trial. We need to move this case forward from here and have a jury decide."

Then, addressing Spiro's request for a second competency examination, the judge told Gilbert that she was giving him "one final chance" to be examined by the defense expert, Dr. Bardey.

"Mr. Spiro has gone to great lengths to arrange that," she said. "He has pleaded with this court to give you another chance to see if you agree to meet with that doctor."

"Yes, Your Honor," mumbled Tommy, acknowledging that he understood.

Two days later, it was revealed that Thomas Gilbert Sr. was far less well off than previously thought. Probate papers filed into Manhattan's Surrogate Court by Shelley Gilbert's attorney showed the hedge funder's estate was only worth $585,555.50—a pittance in his rarified world. He had no life insurance, less than $10,000 in stocks and bonds, and under $20,000 in cash and retirement accounts.

Tommy was a major beneficiary of his father's will, standing to inherit a third of everything.

Shelley had recently sold the Wainscott mansion for $9.75 million, considerably less than the $12.5 million it had originally been put on the market for. The wealthy husband and wife who bought the Gilbert home immediately had it demolished to build a new one.

At a hastily called hearing on April 27, Alex Spiro announced that his client was having a psychological breakdown. As Tommy sat blankly at the defense table, resembling a derelict with his tangled mass of dirty, blond hair and beard, Spiro requested another 730 competency exam and argued that his mental condition had markedly deteriorated.

"My client has been expressing to me two fully alarming concerns," said the defense attorney. "One regarding immediate Cablevision [service in his cell] and secondarily [that] he's suffering from radioactive poisoning."

Spiro explained that Tommy believed he was radioactive,

reaching out to his lawyers and others to help him get treatment in the emergency room.

"This radioactive poisoning that he's suffering from now," said Spiro, "means he isn't able to function and is interfering with his ability to speak to me."

ADA Ortner objected, saying nothing had changed since the defendant had been found fit five months earlier.

"I think a little bit of perspective is in order," he told the judge, "or we will find ourselves in an endless cycle of 730 exams and possibly 730 hearings."

Justice Jackson agreed but nevertheless ordered a second competency exam by two new psychiatrists. She cited Spiro's problems with communicating with his client and a letter from Dr. Bardey saying the defendant was still refusing to meet with him.

"I will remand the defendant," she said, "until we get a report from the examining psychiatrists in about six weeks. Thank you, Mr. Gilbert, we'll see you back then."

Two months later, at the next hearing on June 28, Justice Jackson was informed that the defendant had recently tried to commit suicide by swallowing a battery.

"The defendant did, in fact, swallow a battery," said ADA Ortner as Tommy looked on blankly. "That appears to come on the tail end of a series of gestures that could be interpreted as suicide attempts. It is regrettably sad but not unsurprising that someone in the defendant's unenviable position, incarcerated and facing the prospect of life in prison, would be suicidal."

Ortner told the judge that the Rikers medical staff had x-rayed him several times to ensure he had passed the battery out of his body without complications. Surprisingly, the prosecutor seemed unaware that Gilbert had actually been caught by an emergency room x-ray technician holding a battery over his abdomen.

Alex Spiro then told the judge that the psychiatrists needed more time to complete their competency evaluation, adding that his client now wanted to subpoena the entire Iraqi consulate as a defense witness.

"It suggests acute psychosis," said Spiro. "He can't communicate with me. He's completely unfit [and] telling me he can't think because he's radioactive."

The judge said that the issue at hand was the defendant's competency and not his mental illness, but if the defense insisted it could not communicate with the defendant, her hands were tied.

"The court really is compelled to exercise caution," she said, "and grant an application to have the defendant examined by experts to determine whether or not he is able to proceed. I don't want to have a trial if . . . he's unable to assist his lawyers on the bench. That's not a fair trial, so really I have little choice."

On Wednesday, August 17, Thomas Gilbert Jr. was back at the defense table in handcuffs. He looked dazed and avoided eye contact with his mother, who was sitting right opposite him in the second row of the public gallery. There was much anticipation among the reporters, as the second competency evaluation had been finally completed.

"Good afternoon, Mr. Gilbert," said Justice Jackson. "We have the conclusion of the court's appointed psychiatrists that [you] have been found fit."

Alex Spiro immediately objected to the finding, saying the "inner workings" of his client's mind could not be measured by a normal evaluation.

"We will proceed towards the trial," said the judge. "And

it is my understanding, Mr. Spiro, that you will prepare a psychiatric defense . . . is that correct?"

"Yes, Your Honor."

Four days later, the *New York Post* carried what it billed as an exclusive interview with Tommy Gilbert. Reporter Dana Schuster had bluffed her way into Rikers, claiming to be an old friend from his Princeton days.

The double-page feature carried the headline MURDER, MONEY, MADNESS. HOW A SON OF PRIVILEGE WENT OFF THE RAILS FOR A LIFE OF VIOLENCE, VICE AND ALLEGED PATRICIDE.

The brief interview took place in a visitors' room on Rikers Island, where Schuster described the onetime Ivy Leaguer as "a ghost" of his former self: "His model blond locks now shoulder length and straggly, his nails dirty and cut to the quick."

The feature included interviews with a string of unnamed former friends, with a sole quote from Tommy, saying, "I haven't had many visitors. I understand why."

According to Lila Chase, Tommy had quickly figured out that Schuster was a reporter and ended the interview abruptly. When he read the resulting story, he was very angry and wrote to Justice Jackson to complain.

On November 9, 2016, the day after Donald Trump was elected president of the United States, Shelley Gilbert and Lila Chase sat outside Part 62 of the Manhattan Supreme Court discussing the election. Things were finally moving ahead in the case, and Dr. Bardey had completed his report. Tommy now only had to be evaluated by a psychiatric expert for the prosecution, clearing the way to trial.

When the hearing began at midday, Alex Spiro said his

client did not wish to be present. A month earlier, Tommy had typed a rambling one-page letter to Justice Jackson, again asking her to ban reporters from his case hearings.

"This motion contains a request to limit any unauthorized persons from entering the courtroom," it began. "In July 2016, there were a second round of leaks on television . . . containing portions of personal information from the psych hearings. Additionally, a concurrent NY Post story published information about the case."

The judge asked Spiro if he joined in his client's motion to ban spectators from the courtroom.

"I don't agree that I have the grounds to adopt this motion," he replied.

"That is correct," said the judge, denying what she called his client's "application."

Spiro then confirmed that his psychiatric expert had now completed his report and requested it sealed, until the prosecution expert, Dr. Jason Hershberger, completed his evaluation.

Justice Jackson agreed and adjourned the case until early 2017.

On the second anniversary of Thomas Gilbert Sr.'s death, his son languished behind bars on Rikers Island with no trial date in sight. Now thirty-two years old, Tommy was unmedicated, spending most of his time sitting in his cell staring at the floor. He did not socialize with the other inmates, often refusing to see his mother when she came.

In early 2017, Lila Chase visited Tommy in Rikers and found him barefoot, with a festering open wound under his heel. The other inmates were wearing shoes and socks, and Lila surmised that his contamination fears prevented Tommy from doing so.

"Tommy looked like this weird, ghostly, super-emaciated white guy with long Jesus hair and beard," said Lila. "God, what a dump that place is."

When she asked about his foot injury, Tommy explained that he had cut himself jumping over a table during a fight with another inmate. Lila asked a guard if he could get medical attention. The guard promised to get him help, although Lila had no idea if he ever did.

"I don't know how Tommy copes," she said. "He looks like he's been in a concentration camp . . . he's scary thin. He's lost all his muscle mass."

During the first half of 2017, the Thomas Gilbert Jr. murder case virtually ground to a halt, as the defendant repeatedly refused to see the prosecution's forensic psychiatric expert, Dr. Hershberger. During a series of hearings every six weeks, an increasingly frustrated Craig Ortner complained about the defendant's "willful refusal" to be evaluated by his expert. Again and again, Justice Jackson admonished Tommy as if he were a naughty schoolboy for not meeting Dr. Hershberger, and he would meekly nod his agreement before again refusing to comply.

On March 31, Alex Spiro filed a motion for a third 730 competency examination, citing a sworn affidavit from Lila Chase, remaining anonymous, that Tommy believed all the psychiatrists who wanted to evaluate him were imposters.

Spiro described Tommy's former girlfriend, who was sitting in the public gallery, as a "reliable historian."

"And that is the reason he would not cooperate," explained Spiro. "This friend related to me that Mr. Gilbert doesn't look well. It is my firm belief my client is unfit and remains unfit, unless he is treated and brought back to health."

The judge noted that she had already ordered two competency exams that had found the defendant fit and was refusing a third. She warned Gilbert that he must cooperate with the DA's expert or risk losing his insanity defense.

"Mr. Gilbert, I would like to hear from you," said Justice Jackson. "What is your position?"

When Tommy mumbled something unintelligible, the judge suggested they try another way.

"If you just nod to me, that means yes," she told him, "and a shake of the head means no. So I want you to let me know, do you want to give it another chance?"

Tommy nodded.

"Let the record reflect that Mr. Gilbert nodded yes," said the judge. "This is going to be your final chance to cooperate, and then I'll move the case along."

On Tuesday, June 20, Craig Ortner informed Justice Jackson that the defendant was still refusing to be evaluated by his expert. Once again, Shelley Gilbert and Lila Chase were in the public gallery as Tommy was led out in handcuffs, looking even wilder than he had at previous hearings. He had his head bent down and seemed in another world.

Ortner told the judge that Dr. Hershberger had now attempted to interview the defendant three times without success.

"Our position is that Mr. Gilbert has willfully refused to cooperate with the People's expert," said Ortner.

He said that Dr. Hershberger would need six weeks to complete his report and, if necessary, would do so without the defendant's cooperation.

Alex Spiro maintained that there was nothing willful about his client's noncooperation.

"He remains acutely psychotic," he explained. "He can't participate in his defense."

"We are not going to relitigate this again," snapped the judge. "We had a full and fair hearing, and I ruled on that. What I want now is to get a trial for your client and move this case along. If he doesn't want to cooperate, that is his choice."

"I have wanted a speedy trial from the get-go," said Spiro. "All I want is a fair trial."

"I couldn't agree with you more," said the judge. "And that's why after two and a half years, the time has come to try this case."

32

A PLEA BARGAIN

On Tuesday, October 3, 2017, four long days of pretrial hearings began. Alex Spiro sought to suppress any evidence resulting from the search warrant on the West Eighteenth Street apartment, as well as his client's statements to police after his arrest. He also claimed a lack of probable cause to arrest Gilbert and a rush to judgment in declaring it a homicide.

A nervous-looking Shelley Gilbert arrived early and huddled with Spiro at the back of the courtroom. Lila Chase joined them soon afterward. A large trolley with case discovery was wheeled into the courtroom by ADA Sara Sullivan, Craig Ortner's new second chair string, who would prosecute the case with him.

At around 11:25 a.m., Tommy Gilbert was brought in by a court officer, looking bedraggled with his uncombed dirty hair halfway down his back, and a Santa-size beard. A court officer removed his handcuffs from his loosely fitting orange DOC jumpsuit and sat him down at the defense table.

Over the next few hours, the story of what happened that fateful Sunday in January 2015 would emerge for the first time through the testimony of various detectives who had worked the case.

As the defendant sat stone-faced at the defense table, his

attorney aggressively questioned officer after officer on their actions that day. He zeroed in on the fact that no one had thought to photograph the Glock handgun lying under Tom Gilbert's hand. It was a largely circumstantial case, opening up defense questions of whether the victim had in fact committed suicide.

During questioning of Detective Philip Guastavino, one of the first officers on the scene, several gruesome color photographs of Tom Gilbert's dead body were screened, clearly showing his fatal head injury. His ashen-faced son turned his head away to avoid seeing them, fidgeting and running his fingers through his tangled hair.

"You were the first officer to enter the room in which Mr. Gilbert's body was found?" asked Spiro in cross-examination.

"I believe I was," Detective Guastavino replied.

"Am I correct in the belief that there is no photo of where the gun was positioned on Mr. Gilbert's body when you entered the room?"

"Objection!" shouted Ortner.

"Overruled," said Justice Jackson.

"Am I correct?" said Spiro.

"You are," agreed the detective.

"And that's the reason why you had to describe [to the other detectives who came later] where the gun was?"

After Guastavino admitted it had been the first violent gunshot death he had ever witnessed, Spiro closely questioned him about the exact position of the gun on the body.

"You don't know whether the gun was touching his pinkie, middle finger, his second knuckle, or second finger, right?"

"It was under his hand," replied the detective. "I don't know which part of his hand was touching the gun other than it was under his fist."

The next witness, Sergeant Zeff Blacer, testified that he had ordered the Glock firearm removed from Gilbert Sr.'s body, because he had just returned from a funeral of two NYPD detectives killed in a Brooklyn ambush, so he was on his guard.

"It didn't sit well with me," he explained.

In cross-examination, Spiro homed in on that reasoning like a pit bull.

"Is it your testimony," he asked, "that you ordered your subordinate officer to remove the gun [because] you were thinking about the funeral of the fellow officers?"

"Yes," answered Sergeant Blacer.

"Meaning you have a conscious memory today . . . thinking in your mind the moment you walked into the room and saw the gun, 'Oh my God, I've just been to a funeral.' And that's the thing that triggered you to order the gun removed?"

"Yes," Blacer said resolutely.

"And do you think that was a mistake?"

"Objection," said Ortner, rising to his feet.

"Sustained," ruled the judge, who called a bench conference, where there was an angry exchange between attorneys. Then Justice Jackson asked Sergeant Blacer to leave the courtroom.

"In all due respect to the court," Spiro told the judge, "the purpose of cross-examination is to test the veracity of the witness. I don't believe all these witnesses are telling the truth."

"Mr. Spiro," she replied sternly, "you don't lecture me about cross-examination. I've dealt with you . . ."

The defense attorney refused to back down, telling the judge that he had every right to test the credibility of witnesses, and he believed Sergeant Blacer had invented a nonsensical story to cover his tracks.

"Thank you, Mr. Spiro," the visibly angry judge told him.

"I will decide the credibility of the witness. You made your record, so move on."

"So I can't ask him any more questions about whether or not he thinks he made a mistake by removing the gun?"

"I'm telling you," she replied, "you're not going to ask him whether he believes he made a mistake. I've just given my ruling. Recall the witness."

When Sergeant Blacer returned to the stand, Spiro asked him if it was proper police procedure to remove a gun from a body at a crime scene without photographing it.

"It's not," admitted Blacer, before the judge ordered Spiro to move on to another line of questioning.

The People's next witness was Detective Darryl Ng. In his direct, ADA Ortner asked if he had broached the subject of suicide with Shelley Gilbert. Detective Ng said he had asked Shelley if her husband had any previous history of suicidal ideation, and she said no.

"Did she elaborate as to whether or not she thought her husband had killed himself?" asked Ortner.

"Yes," the detective replied. "She said he wouldn't do this to himself. He didn't kill himself."

"Did you have a belief that the detectives investigating it at the time thought it was suicide or homicide?"

"My belief was that it was murder," said Ng.

"What made you believe that it wasn't a suicide?" asked Ortner.

"Just from [Mrs. Gilbert] saying, 'The worst is coming true.'"

During the next morning's cross-examination, Alex Spiro asked Detective Ng about Shelley Gilbert's decision to return to the apartment after having a bad feeling about leaving Tommy alone with his father.

"She became concerned because her son and husband might get into fisticuffs," said Spiro. "Do you remember that assertion?"

"I can't remember if those were the exact words she used," said Ng, "but she said Tommy would be aggressive and they might fight."

Then Spiro moved on to the morning after Tommy's arrest when Detective Ng had bought him breakfast at McDonald's, asking if he'd given him a bottle of water for the sole purpose of collecting DNA.

"Was that just to be nice?" asked Spiro.

"I often get prisoners food [because] he'd been very cooperative with us," replied Detective Ng. "I asked him if he wanted to eat and with the [Egg McMuffins] I gave him a bottle of water."

"And is that kindness and respect for the person, right?"

"Always," replied the detective, before conceding that several hours later, another detective had impounded the water bottle for DNA analysis.

Later that day, Detective Sean DeQuatro of the NYPD Emergency Service Unit took the stand. Under Ortner's direct questioning, the officer said his team had gone to the defendant's 350 West Eighteenth Street apartment after officers saw lights being turned off inside.

"We knew that a firearm was involved," he said, "and this was possibly an [armed suspect]."

After announcing themselves as the NYPD Emergency Services, they had started banging on the door. Getting no response, they used a regulation mallet to make it louder.

"Why were you trying to make the suspect come to the door?" asked Ortner.

"Basically, just to engage him in conversation," said DeQuatro. "We wanted to speak with him."

He then described how they had donned their ballistic

vests and helmets for protection before Tommy surrendered, saying he was on the phone with his attorney.

"He was very compliant," said Detective DeQuatro. "Eventually, we came to an understanding that he was going to open the door."

In cross-examination, Alex Spiro focused on the lack of a signed search warrant at the time of his client's arrest, rendering anything seized later inadmissible at trial.

"Did you have a search warrant at that time?" he asked the detective.

"No," replied DeQuatro.

"Did you have an arrest warrant?"

"No."

"In becoming an officer," Spiro continued, "are you familiar with the patrol guide that governs the conduct of police officers?"

Ortner objected, and the judge asked the witness to step out so she could discuss with both sides. Spiro then produced a patrol guide, saying it contained five pages about the procedure to be followed when making an arrest without a search warrant. He told the judge that his client's Fourth Amendment rights had been "blatantly violated."

Prosecutor Ortner in turn accused Spiro of going on a "fishing expedition," claiming the Fourth Amendment was irrelevant. Justice Jackson agreed and ordered Spiro to move on.

In redirect, Ortner asked if officers were concerned that the defendant might be armed, as a gun had been found at the murder scene.

"Yes, we were," he replied.

On Friday, October 6, the suppression hearing entered its third day. Craig Ortner called his next witness, Captain

Steven Wren, commanding officer of the Seventeenth Precinct Major Crime Squad. Under Ortner's questioning, Captain Wren said as soon as they had gotten the defendant's address from his mother, he had sent an officer to the DA's office to prepare a search warrant.

A few hours later, he had personally gone to 350 West Eighteenth Street, calling in the Emergency Services Unit, as Gilbert might be armed. He was an eyewitness to everything that had happened prior to the surrender.

"Was there anything that the ESU members did that evening in that apartment that surprised you?" asked the prosecutor.

"No," replied Wren.

"Was there anything that they did that you considered inappropriate?"

"No, sir."

"Were you concerned for the safety of the people outside the apartment," said Ortner, "or anybody else who might be in there with him?"

"Absolutely," said Wren. "There's always an unknown when someone is inside an apartment and he might have other firearms."

Wren said that he was being constantly updated about the progress of the search warrant, but that they had to get a possibly armed suspect out safely as quickly as possible.

In cross-examination, Spiro asked Captain Wren if he thought it appropriate for ESU to enter his client's apartment without a search warrant. Wren said yes, because his officers needed to see if Tommy or somebody else was in there and injured.

"Okay, so let's break this down," said Spiro. "At the time you believed it to have been appropriate to enter the apartment, what objective evidence did you have that anyone was injured in the apartment?"

"None," replied the captain.

"At the time you believed it to be appropriate to enter [Tommy's] apartment, what evidence . . . did you have that there was a second individual in that apartment?"

"I didn't have any information whether there were or not."

"But it's always possible that there's more than one person in the apartment, right?"

"Yes, that's the premise we work under."

"If that's always going to be the premise, that's not a distinguishing factor, correct?" asked the attorney.

"It is when you're dealing with a homicide and the potential offender's inside."

"So according to you," asked Spiro, "based on your investigation, it's a murder, right?"

"I agree with you," said Captain Wren. "It was a murder."

The following Tuesday, October 10—the fourth day of the pretrial hearing—the People rested their case. Summations were about to begin when Alex Spiro dropped a bombshell. He told the court that, the night before, the DA's office had offered his client a plea deal to admit first-degree manslaughter, which, unlike second-degree murder, did not carry a life sentence.

Justice Jackson asked Craig Ortner to confirm it for the record.

"Mr. Spiro had been asked whether his client would consider a plea bargain offer," Ortner told the judge. "We were informed that the defendant is not interested, and it should go without saying that there is no guarantee that a plea offer that was made in the past will be reinstated in the future."

The defense attorney told Justice Jackson that he had explained the DA's plea offer to his client, who had no interest.

"I have explained to him that it doesn't mean a life sentence," said Spiro. "I don't know if my client fully understands it or appreciates it. I suspect, as I have told the court for many, many months, that he doesn't."

Spiro then began his summation, immediately going on the offensive against a faulty police investigation. He accused detectives of "messing up" by moving the "murder weapon" before it could be photographed.

"I'm not going to belabor this," he told the judge. "Their mistake, their lack of probable cause."

The defense attorney said there was nothing voluntary about his client opening his door and being arrested. A heavily armed SWAT unit had surrounded his apartment, removed the peephole, and banged on the door with a mallet, screaming, "Come out! Come out! Don't make us come in here!"

"And so they cross the threshold," he said. "The defendant eventually gives up."

Spiro also told the judge that after his warrantless arrest, Tommy had been denied access to his lawyer.

"This has never been clearer than in this case," he told Justice Jackson, "when you're arrested without a lawyer, without a warrant, in violation of your rights, in your home, while you're on the phone to your lawyer."

Finally, Spiro argued that there was no evidence to support probable cause for his client's arrest before officers seized all his computers and phones.

"I know that this is a very serious case," he told the judge. "But these constitutional mandates were just violated, and the suppression sought by the defense we argue has to be granted."

In the People's summation, Craig Ortner argued that there was probable cause, as the defendant had a previous history of violence and had now added murder and criminal possession of a firearm to his repertoire. Ortner said there were three possibilities after finding Tom Gilbert Sr.'s body: that he killed himself; that a third party had killed him; and that the defendant shot and killed him.

"Through their investigation," said Ortner, "[the investigators] exercised logic and common sense."

He said the evidence of Tommy's guilt had been overwhelming after Mr. Gilbert Sr.'s "estranged son" had suddenly shown up at their apartment and asked his mother to leave.

"And then when she returns, her husband was lying dead," he said. "If [Mr. Gilbert] chose then and there to kill himself, to say nothing of the fact that the Gilberts, to Mrs. Gilbert's knowledge, did not own any guns. But the defendant did.

"So I guess there will be another day when the issue involved in proof beyond a reasonable doubt is litigated, but for today, the question is whether the police had probable cause to arrest the defendant, and it's obvious that they did."

The prosecutor told the judge that the defendant's Fourth Amendment rights had not been violated, as the ESU did not break down the door or even draw their firearms. They just asked him to come out.

"He was perfectly compliant," said Ortner. "He turned the lights on. He unlocked the door for them. He said he was on the phone to his lawyer, who presumably advised him to surrender. Because that's what the defendant proceeded to do."

The prosecutor maintained that the ESU officers had every reason to go into the apartment and arrest the defendant without a signed search warrant.

"Starting with the violent nature of the offense," said the prosecutor, "the police have reason to believe that the defendant had not just committed murder but committed murder by firing a bullet into his father's brain. Suffice it to say crime doesn't get much more grave or more violent than that.

"They also had reason to believe that the defendant had staged a suicide, which I submit suggests a certain cunning, if not intelligence, on his part."

Ortner finished by telling the judge that the ESU had performed in an exemplary manner, as the situation had ended peacefully with no one getting hurt.

"I think the warrants all speak for themselves," he told the judge, "and are all supported by probable cause as set forth."

After a ten-minute recess, Justice Jackson gave her decision, ruling against Alex Spiro on every count. It was a major blow for the defense.

"The court finds the circumstances would justify unlawful entry," she said. "We know that the police were looking for the defendant for a violent crime . . . a murder. The mere fact that a gun, or the murder weapon, had been found at the scene of the crime [would lead] any reasonable person to consider that the suspect could still be armed and capable of hurting himself or others."

She said there was "a strong reason" to believe the suspect suffered from mental illness and could have been a danger to himself or somebody else who might have been in the apartment.

"The court's opinion," she continued, "is that the police acted very reasonably under the circumstances and in a relatively short period of time, [as] the murder to the time of arrest was seven hours."

She also found that any statements Gilbert made to the police were not elicited to try to incriminate him. They were just to make sure he was comfortable and his needs were being attended to.

"Okay," said the judge, "now we can go straight through to the trial date."

Ortner said the only remaining hurdle was his expert Dr. Jason Hershberger's report, which was imminent.

The judge said that would be fine and then addressed the defendant about the DA's plea offer.

"Now, Mr. Gilbert," she asked, "are you at all interested in the plea that's being offered by the district attorney?"

"Ahh, no, Your Honor," he mumbled from the defense table.

Outside the courtroom, a distraught Shelley Gilbert read out a prepared statement to reporters.

"My son, Tommy, is an enormously intelligent young man," she said, "who has always been well respected and well liked by everybody he has known. When he became mentally ill, my family were unable, in spite of having the best doctors, the best lawyers, to get the kind of help he needed.

"The laws and procedures involving mental illness in the State of New York are medieval. The bar for [being] fit for trial is so low that we send our mentally ill into the courtroom, which is unconstitutional. Tommy was declared fit for trial a long time ago, and now he is even sicker than he was then.

"Had our family had access to the kind of care for Tommy that he needed, this horror story would never have happened."

33

"I HAD NO CHOICE"

Two weeks later, Alex Spiro quit Brafman & Associates to join the international law firm Quinn Emanuel Urquhart & Sullivan LLP as a partner. It was a big step up, and Spiro would soon be representing the likes of Mick Jagger, Jay-Z, Elon Musk, and Robert Kraft.

"Alex is a young superstar in the New York Defense Bar," said Quinn cochairman William A. Burck. "His moxie, toughness, and strategic brilliance make him a perfect fit for our firm."

Spiro immediately jettisoned the Thomas Gilbert Jr. case, recruiting his friend Arnold Levine to take his place. The two had first met when Spiro was a young prosecutor for the Manhattan DA's office, finding themselves on opposite sides of the courtroom.

"I beat him at trial when he was a DA," said Levine, "so he loves to tell people that that's the only loss he's ever had."

Immaculately dressed with a prized bow tie collection numbered in the hundreds, Levine is one of Manhattan's leading defense attorneys, with a unique style of his own. Deceptively understated, the seasoned lawyer is a tenacious courtroom warrior who rarely loses a case.

"I think the world of Alex," said Shelley Gilbert at the next hearing on November 6, "but I've hired a new lawyer, Arnold Levine."

Tommy had no known reaction to Spiro's departure, despite his long and at onetime close relationship with the attorney.

Before the hearing, Shelley told reporters that she had recently seen her son in Rikers, and he was very sick and not receiving any treatment.

"He refuses to believe he's as sick as he is," she said. "He wants to present well, and that's the most important thing in the world to him. He needs intense treatment and has needed it for years."

It took all morning for Tommy Gilbert to be produced from Rikers. After spending a couple of minutes with his new attorney in a holding cell, he was brought into the courtroom. His wrists were handcuffed behind his back, and when he moved them back and forth as a signal to uncuff him, the bailiffs ignored him.

"Good afternoon, Mr. Levine," said Justice Jackson. "I understand you were recently retained. Is that correct, sir?"

"That is correct," he replied.

Craig Ortner reported that he was still awaiting Dr. Hershberger's psychiatric report, and the judge adjourned the case until early January 2018—the third anniversary of Thomas Gilbert Sr.'s murder.

Later in the hallway, a reporter wished Justice Jackson a happy holiday as she walked by with a court officer.

"Much ado about nothing," she quipped, referring to the endless proceedings in the Gilbert case.

In early December, Arnold Levine visited Rikers Island to meet his new client and strategize his defense. Tommy Gilbert was guarded and refused to discuss any aspect of the case, saying, "It's confidential." Levine kept assuring him that everything said was protected by attorney-client privilege, but Tommy refused to budge.

"He was clearly paranoid," said Levine. "I've had clients who didn't want to talk to me about cases for one reason or another, but this was different. It was something internal, some psychological thing not to talk about it."

The only person with whom Tommy had ever discussed what happened that fateful day was Lila Chase. During visits, she often asked why he had killed his father. Now, with the trial looming, she told him he needed to start talking to his new attorney and give some explanation at trial for the jury.

"And he said something to the effect of, 'Oh, I had no choice,'" she recalled. "Like it wasn't something he did out of meanness. It was the intonation. The way he said it. Almost incredulous. Like how could the question even be asked, which to me just showed how totally ill he was. And I think that was all anyone needed to hear."

As Arnold Levine began absorbing the thousands of pages of case discovery, he was struck by the similarities between Tommy and John Forbes Nash, a renowned Nobel laureate in economics who also suffered from paranoid schizophrenia. Both were students at Princeton University, where their mental illness had become prevalent. But unlike Tommy Gilbert, Nash overcame his schizophrenia and went onto greatness. His lifelong, triumphant struggle with mental illness was the subject of the 2001 Academy Award–winning movie *A Beautiful Mind,* where he was played by Russell Crowe.

"When I started this case, *A Beautiful Mind* jumped out at me," said Levine. "Tommy being at Princeton and how he could be this brilliant guy with the world at his doorstep, and then become so psychiatrically ill. It just destroys."

On Monday, March 26, 2018, Justice Jackson ordered a third 730 competency test for Thomas Gilbert Jr. The hearing had initially been scheduled to set a trial date, but Arnold Levine said his client was just not communicating with him.

"He won't come down to even see me at Rikers," he told the judge, "so I'm going to ask for another 730 exam."

"You really leave me no choice," lamented the judge, asking Craig Ortner to weigh in. The prosecutor accused the defendant of deliberately manipulating the court to his advantage by feigning symptoms of mental illness.

"The fact of the matter," said Ortner, "is a malingering defendant obviously cannot hold hostage the criminal justice process. This matter needs to move forward to trial; otherwise, we will be in court in an endless cycle of requests for competency exams and possibly having to litigate it."

Justice Jackson agreed, saying she was only too well aware how long it had dragged on.

"This case is getting really old," she said, "and I'm also aware, Mr. Levine, you're relatively new to this case. The benefit of any doubt the court may have as to your client's true mental condition is outweighed by the consideration that you need to be able to really communicate with him."

Then the judge addressed Tommy at the defense table, voicing concerns about him malingering. She warned him that any further refusal to cooperate with examining psychiatrists could lead to another lengthy competency hearing.

"I'll order a 730," she said, adjourning the case until the end of May.

* * *

Once again, Tommy Gilbert went into lockdown, twice refusing to be interviewed by the court-appointed psychiatrists at Bellevue Hospital. Five days before a third interview at the end of July, a frustrated Justice Jackson had him brought in front of her to try to reason with him.

"We really don't want the case to be waiting in limbo," she told him as he stared blankly ahead. "So I implore you, Mr. Gilbert, please, can you comply, so we can at least have something from the psychiatrists and proceed to try and get this case [moving]."

The judge's admonitions had little effect on Tommy Gilbert, who kept refusing to cooperate. In mid-August, the judge signed a force order to make him go to Bellevue and see the psychiatrists, but he still declined to answer any of their questions.

By mid-September, six months after the third 730 competency exam had been ordered, the case was at a standstill. Before a hearing on September 12, Dr. Daniel Mundy, the Bellevue forensic psychiatrist who had found Gilbert unfit almost three years earlier, briefed the judge and all the attorneys in her chambers.

After they finished, the defendant was led into the courtroom, glancing at his mother in the public gallery. He was a pale shadow of his former self, with an orange DOC jumpsuit hanging off his skeletal frame, resembling a vagrant with his long, unbrushed hair and scraggy beard.

The judge told him they were there to discuss the next move in determining his fitness for trial. She noted that because he was still refusing to meet with his lawyer and talk to doctors, the court was considering preparing a 730 report without his cooperation.

"Mr. Gilbert," she said. "The court hopes you will participate in the 730, so we can move this case to trial. So I do exhort you to please speak with your lawyer, who's doing the best he possibly can. And cooperate with these psychologists so that you are not held indefinitely on Rikers Island."

On the eve of Halloween, Tommy Gilbert was back in the courtroom—but the tone had changed. After a year of his case languishing in limbo since the change of defense attorneys, Justice Jackson was now determined to get things moving.

After a lengthy bench conference, the defendant was led into court in handcuffs, ignoring his mother in the second row of the public gallery. The judge began by expressing the court's concern that he was still refusing to meet Arnold Levine.

"So I'm advising you, sir," she told him, "that it is in your best interests to cooperate with your attorney."

Tommy weakly nodded from the defense table.

"Mr. Gilbert, I can see you nodding," she said. "If you prefer not to speak with me orally, on the record, and you would prefer head gestures, I understand it. So I'm glad you understand what I'm doing."

She said he had the right not to talk to Levine, but he was one of the best defense attorneys available.

"I hope you change your mind and speak with him," she said. "I want you to understand that we are proceeding to trial, whatever you decide to do."

ADA Ortner then informed the court that the 730 competency report ordered back in March was still incomplete, because of the defendant's noncooperation.

"This case is nearing four years old," he told the judge. "It's important to note that the vast majority of that period of time has been due to the defense requests for competency evaluation."

Once again, Justice Jackson admonished Gilbert, saying that his trial would begin early next year, regardless of a "final determination" of his competency.

"So do you understand this, Mr. Gilbert?" she asked. "I can see you nod, so I know you understand it."

34

"YOU HAVE THE POTENTIAL
TO BE A GOOD LAWYER"

At the next hearing on Tuesday, December 11, Justice Jackson announced that she had just received Tommy Gilbert's thirty-page competency report, but it was inconclusive. The two court-appointed Bellevue psychiatrists had been unable to decide on the defendant's fitness for trial.

The judge also noted that the defendant had recently written to Judge Jonathan Lippman, under the mistaken impression that he was still the chief judge of the courts, laying out a series of defense motions.

"In that letter," said the judge, "Mr. Gilbert does indicate, to this court's opinion, an understanding of legal process, perhaps not the legal arguments to be made, but the basic foundations of constitutional due process, speedy trial . . . are addressed most cogently, and if I do say articulately, by him."

As the competency report had failed to reach a conclusion, said the judge, it would be up to the court to decide his trial fitness.

Tommy Gilbert said he wished to address the court, requesting his handcuffs to be removed so he could turn the pages of the lengthy letter he had sent Judge Lippman, which he wished to read out to the court. The judge agreed.

"Thank you, Your Honor," he began, "for allowing the defendant to exercise his First Amendment rights to freedom of speech and to petition the government."

Seated next to a poker-faced Arnold Levine at the defense table, Tommy spent the next ten minutes reciting the rambling, mostly incomprehensible list of motions he had prepared.

Citing a string of legal precedents, none of which were applicable, he claimed his civil rights had been violated and all the police evidence was illegal and must be suppressed. He claimed to have suffered "cruel and unusual punishment" for being incarcerated for so long and that all the news stories and courtroom photos of him violated the Grand Jury Secrecy Act of 1789.

He wanted a closed trial within two weeks, a new defense lawyer, and immediate bail, saying he had "solid family ties," a "good reputation," and no criminal record.

"Thank you for allowing the defendant to address the court," he finished.

"Thank you, Mr. Gilbert," said Justice Jackson condescendingly. "That was well spoken. Clearly, you have done your legal research and spent time in the library. You have the potential to be a good lawyer down the road."

"Thank you, Your Honor," replied the defendant smugly.

"It was very well argued," complimented the judge.

She then denied all his applications, finding no merit in any of them.

"Now that I have heard you," she told him, "I have no doubt that you are competent . . . that you know what we are doing here, and you just confirmed it for me today. Your legal arguments may be that of an amateur, because you are not a trained lawyer, but you are no fool."

She said that today's articulate performance had proved that he could speak when he wanted to and was quite fit for trial.

Arnold Levine stood up to argue that his client was anything but competent, as illustrated by his address to the court.

"With all due respect to Your Honor," he said, "you are confusing articulateness, intelligence, and the ability to read, write, and copy with fitness for trial. He is very well educated clearly. He can read and write and he can copy things, but that does not make him fit for trial."

Levine observed that his client spent a great deal of time in the law library, describing his statement as "a mishmash of legal mumbo jumbo, most of which does not even apply here."

The attorney told the judge that his client had even accused the court of being in contempt, which would result in civil charges against her.

"This testimony might impact my defense," interjected Gilbert.

"He can be as articulate as the day is long," Levine continued. "That does not mean what he is saying makes sense. And none of what he said basically makes sense."

Justice Jackson said that although Levine may disagree with her ruling, they were proceeding to trial. She then adjourned for three days, giving the defendant the opportunity to speak to his attorney in private before she set a trial date.

"The bottom line is that Mr. Gilbert wants to move this case to trial," she said, "and I intend to give him that opportunity."

Before the next hearing started, Tommy Gilbert met Arnold Levine in a holding cell outside the courtroom. Once again, he refused to communicate with him.

"He was not responsive to me," Levine told the judge, "aside from the shaking of the head, not verbalizing with me."

Justice Jackson informed the defendant of a potential

conflict of interest, as his mother, who was paying for his defense, was also the prosecution's star witness. It was the first time in the almost four-year-old case that anyone had raised the legal ramifications of Tommy's mother testifying against him.

"There is a high probability," ADA Ortner explained, "that Shelley Gilbert would be called by the People [and] Mr. Levine is being privately retained in this case, and his fee is being paid by Mrs. Gilbert."

"Defense says this testimony is irrelevant," Tommy interrupted, claiming his Eighth Amendment rights were being violated. "[My attorney] is in fact unpaid, he is volunteering services."

The judge corrected him, saying it was in fact the Sixth Amendment, although that was irrelevant anyway. She explained that his mother would definitely be called as a prosecution witness and possibly for the defense too.

"The concern under the law," she told Gilbert, "is that there may be a potential conflict for Mr. Levine, since your mother is paying him, in zealously cross-examining her."

"Yes, Your Honor," agreed Tommy. "Defendant believes there is potential conflict and requests the option to change counsel."

The judge said that if she agreed, his request would delay the trial for many months, as any new attorney would have to get up to speed.

"So you need to think carefully," she told him. "I don't believe there is a conflict . . . but there is an appearance [of one]."

Tommy acquiesced, agreeing to keep his attorney to avoid any further delays. He then addressed the court again, spouting more gibberish about his Fourth and Sixth Amendments being violated and asking for hearings wherein he would represent himself.

"Thank you, Mr. Gilbert," said the judge. "I am denying your application there [as] they are all within the many litigations in pretrial motions. However, I'm going to give you your ultimate quest, which is a date for your trial."

She then set Monday, March 4, 2019, for jury selection to begin.

A few days later, Arnold Levine went to see Tommy Gilbert at Rikers, as he needed his permission to pursue an insanity defense. Finding the defendant not guilty by reason of insanity means the jury would have to believe that he did not know the difference between right and wrong when he shot his father. Now, after being ruled competent under New York State law, Tommy had the right to veto the use of this defense at his trial.

He reluctantly met his attorney but refused to go into a private room with him. Instead, they sat twenty feet apart in a public area with corrections officers milling around.

"I just called loudly over to him," said Levine, "'Tommy, will you let me use an insanity defense?' And he paused for a little bit and nodded."

On January 16, 2019, Shelley Gilbert chatted with reporters in the hallway outside the courtroom, waiting for the next hearing to start. The fourth anniversary of Thomas Gilbert Sr.'s death had just passed, and Shelley had visited her son in Rikers the previous weekend and found him even more delusional.

"My wonderful son is sick," she said. "What kind of country puts sick people into prisons and treats them horribly?"

At the beginning of the hearing, Justice Jackson told Tommy that she wanted to "revisit" the potential conflict of his mother being cross-examined at trial by the attorney she was paying for.

"I want you to understand that there are perceived dangers in this context," she told him. "Do you understand?"

"The defendant is fine with his lawyer," answered Tommy.

Then Levine requested another competency hearing, citing that his client had refused to see him in Rikers the past weekend. He added that he had found three separate cases of trials going ahead with an "inconclusive" competency decision that wound up being appealed.

Levine also apologized for forgetting he had a federal trial scheduled for April, so he would need a later trial date.

"Your Honor," Gilbert interjected, "the defendant would like a January trial."

"I wish," replied the judge. "Today is January 16, and I can't expect the jury to be ready tomorrow."

Then Tommy asked to be transferred out of Rikers to the Manhattan Detention Center, known as the Tombs, directly behind the 100 Centre Street courthouse.

"No, I can't do that," said Justice Jackson, citing security concerns.

Five days later, Tommy claimed a gunman was shooting at him at Rikers. In an alarming letter to Lila Chase, he told her his life was in danger.

"Someone just shot a bullet through my window," he wrote. "I'm trying to change cells, but I think the shooter is still outside."

It was just the latest in a series of disturbing letters he was sending Lila.

"He seemed constantly worried that people are out to get him and the people he cares about," she said. "He had cautioned me about driving into New York City and told me not to reveal my name or location to anyone connected with the courts."

On January 25, ADA Craig Ortner reluctantly agreed to yet another 730 mental competency exam, out of an abundance of caution. At a hastily called hearing, he told the judge that because of the inevitable delays with Levine's federal trial, he had agreed to the defense's request.

"We have decided to consent to a 730 hearing," he explained, "although I think some parameters need to be set forth."

Arnold Levine said that he had arranged for Dr. Alexander Sasha Bardey to conduct the evaluation at Bellevue, although his client had always refused to see him in the past.

Ortner questioned why the defendant would cooperate this time, after not doing so before.

"I don't want to waste anybody's time," said Ortner, "if Mr. Gilbert remains steadfast in the refusal to cooperate with the psychiatric examiner."

Levine said there was no way of knowing whether his client would cooperate until the day of the exam.

"Mr. Gilbert," asked the judge, "do you want to weigh in on this at all, sir, or no?"

"Yes, Your Honor," he replied. "The defendant is willing to cooperate with the interview."

The judge then adjourned the case until mid-February, denying yet another application by the defendant for a new lawyer.

On February 14, Tommy Gilbert met with Dr. Bardey at Bellevue Hospital and underwent a competency evaluation. At a hearing the next day, Arnold Levine told Justice Jackson that Dr. Bardey had found Gilbert fit for trial, although he had just "squeaked by."

"So that is indeed from the court's perspective good news," said the judge. "We can proceed at a pace I would like to with this matter now."

Levine reported that Tommy had communicated with him more than usual before the hearing and expressed a willingness to see him.

"Well, that is good news, Mr. Gilbert," said the judge, "because of course now we are seriously heading towards trial, and it is in your best interest to communicate with your attorney."

Justice Jackson then set jury selection for the week of May 16.

Outside the courtroom, an angry Shelley Gilbert read a statement to reporters, once again condemning the system that found her son competent.

"I think the bar of fitness for trial in New York is so low, that we have people in the courtroom that are not fit for trial," she said. "This is unconstitutional. Certainly, in the history of the law in America, slavery used to be perfectly legal. This process is perfectly legal too, but it is highly, highly wrong."

On May 6, a pretrial Molineux hearing was held to discuss whether Tommy Gilbert's previous criminal acts, such as assaulting Peter Smith and suspected arson of his father's house, could be revealed to the jury at trial. Ortner asked the judge to rule them admissible, as well as the fact that Gilbert's allowance had been cut prior to the killing.

Justice Jackson said she would allow the cut in his allowance, the prosecution's alleged motive.

"The curtailment of financial support," said the judge, "is highly relevant. The court will also permit testimony that several years leading up to the murder, the tension between the deceased and the defendant [increased]. But I will not admit any prior bad acts [that are] alleged in Mr. Ortner's motion."

Toward the end of the hearing, the judge addressed Gilbert, who had recently cut his hair short but kept his ragged beard.

"I'm hoping you'll have some trial clothes that you can wear," said the judge, "which will be seen by the jury."

Then turning to Shelley Gilbert in the public gallery, the judge said, "Please make sure that Mr. Gilbert has clothes that are appropriate."

After more than four years of delays, Thomas Gilbert Jr.'s murder trial was now underway.

PART 5

35

THE TRIAL

On Monday, May 13, 2019, jury selection began, and the *New York Post* carried an exclusive interview with Shelley Gilbert by Rebecca Rosenberg, who had covered the case from the very beginning. The previous Friday, Shelley had finally agreed to a sit-down interview at the *New York Post*'s office on Sixth Avenue.

MOM TO TESTIFY AGAINST IVY LEAGUE SON IN HUSBAND'S MURDER CASE: I DON'T HAVE ANY CHOICE was its headline.

"She loves her husband's killer—as only a mother could," the article began. "She knows her privileged son pulled the trigger, but says it was only under the weight of severe mental illness."

In her first-ever interview, Shelley said she had no other choice but to testify against her son for the prosecution.

"It was obvious he did it," she told Rosenberg. "Most trials you have to prove who did it. That's not true of this one. What's cruel is I have to relive it on the stand."

A few hours after the story ran, more than a hundred prospective jurors gathered in the hallway outside Part 62 on the eleventh floor of the Manhattan Supreme Court.

At around 11:15 a.m., Thomas Gilbert Jr. was brought into the court, looking more like his upper-class self than he had in years. He had smartened up, sporting a stylish Vandyke beard and wearing a starched white shirt and black slacks. After his handcuffs were removed, he sat down at the defense table, where a large legal pad had been placed in front of him.

To the rear of the public gallery sat his old Buckley classmate Nick McDonell and his younger brother, Chris, who were filming a documentary on the case. Next to them was Shelley Gilbert. At Tommy's request, Lila Chase did not attend the trial.

Before jury selection even began, the defendant addressed Justice Jackson, complaining that his right to a speedy trial had been violated and citing double jeopardy.

"Thank you, Mr. Gilbert," the judge replied dismissively. "So we're ready to start. There are about one hundred people standing in the halls outside right now."

She told him to go through Arnold Levine in the future if he wished to put anything on the record.

The first round of prospective jurors was then brought for screening. Around five hundred people had been summoned, so the judge had divided the selection process into two parts. First was a preliminary screening with basic questions from the judge, followed by a more detailed one by the attorneys, to whittle the jury pool down to the final twelve jurors and six alternates.

Over the next several days, Justice Jackson patiently questioned round after round of prospective jurors. For much of the time, Tommy Gilbert looked fully engaged, making notes and occasionally turning around from the defense table with a thin smile on his face.

ADA Craig Ortner told prospective jurors that this was a "terrible tragedy," adding that although they may feel sorry for the defendant, they must be objective.

"Objection," interrupted Gilbert, but the judge immediately overruled him. It would be a harbinger of things to come as the defendant continually inserted himself into the trial, oblivious to his own defense lawyer and basic court rules.

During his questioning, Arnold Levine asked prospective jurors if they had seen *A Beautiful Mind,* noting the similarities to his client. He also probed their attitude toward mental illness, and if they felt the wealthy had better access to psychiatric care than everyone else.

It took five long days to select the twelve jurors and six alternates who would ultimately decide Tommy Gilbert's fate.

On Tuesday, May 28, the Thomas Gilbert Jr. trial began exactly 1,605 days after he had killed his father. Nick McDonell had arrived early and carefully placed two miniature cameras in the courtroom. The Buckley alumni had Justice Jackson's permission to record the opening and closing statements, as well as the verdict and sentencing.

At around 9:30 a.m., two large trolleys bursting with discovery files were wheeled in, followed by ADAs Craig Ortner and Sara Sullivan. Then defense attorney Arnold Levine appeared, wearing an elegant suit and sporting an elaborate red-and-gray-patterned bow tie. As the trial progressed, his choice of bow tie for the day would become a talking point in the press gallery.

Just after 10:00 a.m., Tommy Gilbert was brought in to face half a dozen press photographers, breathlessly waiting by the defense table. It was the first time he had been photographed since his arraignment four and a half years earlier, and he had visibly aged. Now thirty-four, he looked gaunt and deathly pale in his newly pressed white shirt, open at the neck. He stared down at the defense table, attempting to avoid the cameras.

After the photographers finished, Levine told the judge

that his client strenuously objected to having a documentary filmed about him.

"This case is an interesting case," replied Justice Jackson. "I think it is very topical. For that reason I will permit it, over your client's objection."

The twelve jurors and six alternates filed into the courtroom and took their seats in the jury box. For the next twenty-five minutes, the judge lectured them on the law, while the defendant sat at the defense table with his head down and eyes closed.

At 10:55 a.m., Craig Ortner walked over to the lectern in front of the jury to deliver his opening statement.

"Good morning, members of the jury," he began. "Fortunately for most of us, the idea of murdering another human being is so shocking that we cannot understand how a person could do it. Murder is too terrible to contemplate. The idea of someone killing their own parent is absolutely incomprehensible to us. Yet the evidence in this trial will show that the natural bonds between a parent and his child were shattered by two of the oldest and most common reasons for murder in the history of humankind—resentment and greed."

On January 4, 2015, Ortner told the jury, the defendant walked into his father's bedroom and shot him dead because his allowance was being cut.

"Rather than being the impulsive act of a person deranged by mental demons, the evidence will show that this was the planned and calculated act of a self-absorbed and vengeful son," Ortner argued.

The prosecutor told the jury that Thomas Gilbert Sr. had just reached his "milestone" seventieth birthday and had everything to live for. He was in excellent physical health, as energetic and optimistic as a man half his age.

He then outlined Tom Gilbert's self-made success in

running a hedge fund, managing millions of dollars of client assets. It had allowed him to enjoy an affluent lifestyle with a second home in the Hamptons and country club memberships.

Ortner said that in contrast to his hardworking father, despite his Ivy League education, the defendant had not had a full-time job since graduating Princeton. Nevertheless, he still enjoyed a lavish lifestyle thanks to his parents, with a Manhattan apartment, a Jeep, extensive foreign travel, and memberships to several exclusive country clubs. In the two years before the murder, he had received more than $100,000 from his mother and father.

"He regularly smoked marijuana and used other drugs recreationally," Ortner told the jury. "His failure to do anything constructive with his life was a source of tension between his father and himself."

The prosecutor described how the defendant had shown up unexpectedly at his parents' apartment, a few hours after the latest cut in his allowance. He had wanted to discuss business with his father, asking his mother to go out and buy him a sandwich and a Coke.

"The defendant would have known his mother never kept Coke in the house," said Ortner. "She would have to go out for that."

She had returned to find her husband shot dead in their bedroom, with a handgun on top of his chest as if he had killed himself.

"Shelley Gilbert immediately realized what had happened," said the prosecutor. "Her son had done the unthinkable. He had shot his own father in the head."

Moving on to address the insanity plea and Tommy's history of mental illness, Ortner said that although the defendant had seen many private psychiatrists, it had always been on an outpatient basis. Their inconsistent diagnoses had included OCD, anxiety, mood disorders, and Tourette syndrome.

"The evidence will not support that he was legally insane at the time of the murder or ever," said Ortner. "He was never forced to take medication. He was not found to have required long-term intensive care and was never committed to a psychiatric hospital. To the contrary, he was living on his own in New York City and the Hamptons, enjoying some of the finest amenities those places have to offer."

Finishing up, the prosecutor told the jury that the facts would prove beyond a reasonable doubt that the defendant had executed his father in cold blood.

"The evidence will lead you to the unmistakable conclusion," he said, "that the defendant is responsible in every way for the death of his father and for every crime charged."

Then, after forty-eight minutes on his feet, Ortner returned to the prosecution table, and Arnold Levine began his opening statement.

"I will be a little shorter," he announced, "as I'm going to save my summation for the end."

Levine then read out the names of every psychiatrist who had treated Tommy Gilbert over the years, diagnosing a "smorgasbord" of mental illnesses and prescribing a "laundry list" of antipsychotic medications.

"This was a young, good-looking, three-sport school athlete with a five-star education from Buckley, Deerfield, and Princeton University," he told the jury. "He was believing people were trying to steal his soul."

Levine agreed that there was "animosity" toward his father, but this was entirely due to his mental illness.

"Don't be thrown off by motives manufactured after the fact," said Levine. "After you hear all the evidence, you will conclude that Tommy's lengthy and well-documented mental disease and defect rendered him criminally not responsible for his actions that day."

The prosecution's first witness was Lisa Segalas, who had played doubles tennis with Thomas Gilbert Sr. just hours before his death. The longtime River Club member and mother of four described Tom Gilbert as "very well mannered" but reserved. She had also partnered with Tommy in doubles on several occasions.

"Was there anything about the defendant's behavior on the tennis court," asked Ortner, "that stands out in your mind as unusual or inappropriate?"

"He was perfectly kind but hard to read," replied Segalas. "I wasn't sure if he was enjoying himself."

She said that on the morning of his murder, Tom Gilbert had been chatty and played well.

Just before the lunch recess, Shelley Gilbert's harrowing 911 call was played for the jury. Tommy Gilbert lowered his head to the defense table, and jurors listened in rapt attention to Shelley telling the operator that her son had shot her husband in the head.

After lunch, Craig Ortner called Shelley Gilbert to the stand. In an earlier sidebar, the prosecutor had asked Justice Jackson to declare her a hostile witness, citing Shelley's interview with the *New York Post* in which she said her son did not belong in jail. It would allow the prosecutor to ask her leading questions during his direct.

"She has essentially taken a position 100 percent adverse to the People's position in this action," Ortner had claimed.

This dichotomy of Shelley's fervent belief that her son was mentally ill, while being the victim's widow, would dominate the trial. It often placed the prosecution in an untenable position, as she was their star witness and also their biggest threat.

Arnold Levine objected, saying the move was totally premature and pointing out that Mrs. Gilbert had fully cooperated with the DA's office and the grand jury.

"I have a different take on cooperation," countered Ortner. "She actually refused to cooperate with me when I tried to prepare her to testify. I asked her to look at documents . . . and video. She nastily refused to do that. In fact, to be candid, she even threatened me . . . about the idea of bringing up during the trial her son having burned down Peter Smith's house."

He told the judge that although Shelley had been "superficially polite," she had made it passionately clear she sided with the defense.

Justice Jackson then asked Ortner how she had threatened him.

"She acknowledged that her son burned down Peter Smith's house," he explained, "and said she would send the Mafia after me if I repeated that."

"The Mafia?" asked Levine incredulously.

"She said something about razor wire," replied Ortner. "I did not take it seriously. I understood it to be a grieving mother in a very difficult position who is conflicted."

The judge ultimately agreed to have Shelley Gilbert declared a hostile witness, saying she, too, had read the morning's *New York Post* story.

Wearing a light blue shirt and a beaded necklace, Shelley Gilbert was sworn in. For the rest of the afternoon, the seventy-year-old widow showed great dignity as she recounted in excruciating detail the day her husband died. In a steady voice, she answered questions about her own upbringing and family life, referring to her only son as "Tommy."

The prosecutor often became frustrated when Shelley forgot certain details that she had testified to the grand jury four and a half years earlier. When confronted about it, she explained it was all part of her coping mechanism.

"I have been very focused on looking forward," she said, "so it is easy to forget things."

During the afternoon, her son objected more than two dozen times to the prosecutor's questions, citing various amendments. The judge continually overruled him as puzzled jurors looked over at the defense table.

The prosecutor asked Shelley about Tommy's unexpected arrival at their apartment on January 4, 2015.

"I was excited," said Shelley in a wavering voice. "That would be good for both of them, I thought. And then he wanted me to go out and get him a sandwich and a Coke. We never had Coke in the house, so I offered to make him something. He said no, no, he wanted a sandwich and a Coke."

"You said you never kept Coke in the house?" emphasized Ortner.

"I don't ever have Coke in the house," she replied.

The prosecutor then asked what happened when she returned to the apartment to find Tommy gone.

"I went into the bedroom," she said. "My husband was on the floor [and] I was hoping he was just knocked out or knocked down or something. The closer I got the more I thought, 'Oh, Tommy, you are far sicker than we really ever knew.' And then I looked at him and I knew what had happened. I knew he was no longer with us."

When Ortner began asking about the exact positioning of the gun on her husband's dead body, Tommy became increasingly agitated, loudly objecting several times.

"Where was the gun?" asked Ortner.

"On my husband's chest."

"Where were your husband's hands in relation to the gun?"

"I think it was his left hand on his chest next to the gun," she said, placing her own left hand over her chest.

Later, Shelley testified that after graduating Princeton, her son had started a business predicting market trends, using the Elliott wave method.

"He had what I would call a 'shadow fund,'" she said. "It was a pretend fund and he tracked it."

"Objection," Tommy interjected. "This violates the Sixth as well as the Eighth Amendment, Your Honor."

"Overruled," snapped the judge.

Ortner asked if Shelley had invested in his fund.

"Yes," she replied, "I figured it would spur him on and help him establish his business."

When Ortner asked why they had started cutting his allowance, the defendant became visibly upset.

"We for years wanted Tommy to go into the psychiatric hospital," said Shelley, "and were not making any progress. We were at our wit's end [and] we had tried everything we could. I wasn't in favor of cutting back his money . . . but it was the only thing we could do."

"Whose idea was it?" asked Ortner.

"Well, it was my husband's idea. I thought maybe it will help . . . jog him a little, but it wasn't a black-and-white situation. I wanted to get him into a hospital. I wanted him to get better [and] healthy."

As the prosecutor probed deeper on how Tom Gilbert had informed his son that his allowance was being cut, the defendant began objecting to every question. Finally, Justice Jackson called a sidebar, out of the jury's hearing.

"With the outburst that I'm getting," she told the attorneys, "I'm having difficulty distinguishing between Mr. Levine's

THE TRIAL • 281

objections and the defendant's. We're going to have to speak to him afterwards."

Arnold Levine said his warnings to Tommy not to object had fallen on deaf ears. The judge decided she didn't want to dismiss the jury to admonish the defendant, as it would break up Shelley Gilbert's testimony.

After the sidebar, Ortner continued questioning Shelley about cutting their son's allowance in an attempt to rein in his behavior.

"You and your husband came to a decision to use financial support as leverage?" asked the prosecutor.

"Yes," she replied. "I reluctantly came to it. I didn't know what else to do."

Ortner then asked if Tom Gilbert had met his son for lunch in October 2014 to give him the news. After Shelley said she couldn't remember, Ortner produced her grand jury testimony for her to read.

"It says so here," she agreed. "I had since forgotten. This was more than four years ago."

"Your son was clearly displeased?"

"Yes," she replied.

As the proceedings became more heated and the witness more hostile, Justice Jackson recessed for the day.

"I would like to make a statement to the press," Shelley suddenly announced from the witness stand.

"No," said the judge. "You're not going to make a statement to the press, Mrs. Gilbert."

"I just don't want them to call my family. It's too painful."

Then the judge dismissed the jury, warning them not to read any coverage of the case.

After they'd left, the judge addressed the defendant's behavior in the courtroom that day.

"Mr. Gilbert," she told him, "you must refrain from

outbursts, objecting to testimony or rulings that I'm making. It's very disruptive for the jury . . . and it's disruptive for the witness as well. So please try to control yourself [as] I really don't want to have you removed from the courtroom. Do you understand me?"

"Yes, Your Honor," he replied. "Thank you for allowing the defendant to exercise [his] First Amendment right to freedom of speech."

The next morning, the Thomas Gilbert Jr. trial made headlines all over America. The *New York Daily News* devoted its entire front page to Shelley Gilbert's 911 call, with the headline: I DIDN'T KNOW HE WAS THIS NUTS.

The *New York Post* carried a picture of Shelley in obvious distress, leaving the courtroom after her testimony. *The New York Times* ran a slightly soberer story of the proceedings, headlined MOTHER'S VOICE AT SON'S MURDER TRIAL.

On the second day of the trial, Shelley Gilbert retook the stand for Arnold Levine's cross-examination. As he led her through her son's glory days at Buckley and Deerfield, Tommy became agitated again. He began objecting to his own attorney's questions, calling them "belligerent."

When the defense attorney produced a photograph of the annual Buckley father-and-son camping trip, Tommy loudly objected, citing suppression. The judge called a sidebar.

"I'm going to admonish your client and consider whether we have to remove him," she sternly told Levine. "He's getting worse and worse, and the witness can't pay attention."

Justice Jackson then called a restroom break, asking

Shelley Gilbert to leave the courtroom as she reprimanded the defendant.

"We had a conversation yesterday afternoon about your outbursts," the judge told him. "It is very disruptive [and] cannot continue. This is going to be my final warning to you. If you continue to do this . . . I will have you removed. Do you understand?"

"Yes, Your Honor," he replied meekly.

Tommy then asked to address the court. The judge told him to go ahead, reminding him that the press was reporting the proceedings.

"The defendant pleads the First Amendment," he said in a clipped voice. "It guarantees the right to freedom of speech within the courtroom."

For the next few minutes, the defendant spouted a liturgy of complaints to the judge, demanding that most of the evidence against him be suppressed.

"The defendant requests to block any further prosecutorial misconduct or bias during cross-examination," he mumbled, "in terms of lines of questioning that we consider either a misdirection or belligerent."

Justice Jackson said that she had already ruled on the suppression issue, giving him a final warning him to stop his outbursts in the courtroom.

Arnold Levine immediately demanded another competency exam, saying his client's behavior in the courtroom was "undermining" his own defense.

"Objection!" shouted Tommy.

The defense attorney said these illogical outbursts were evidence of his client's unfitness for trial and he must be re-examined.

"He is not assisting his lawyer," Levine told the judge. "He's actually been working against his lawyer at many points during his trial. He's giving me authority to use a psychiatric defense, but won't let me speak to the doctors. That shows you the level of incompetence."

Tommy demanded a new defense attorney immediately.

"Well, I'm denying that application," said the judge. "Now that we are mid-trial, you will have to work with Mr. Levine."

When court resumed, Levine led Shelley Gilbert through her son's deteriorating relationship with his father from the eleventh grade on. She testified that Tommy started becoming easily upset in his junior year at Deerfield and believed his roommate was contaminated.

"We did not quite understand what was going on at the time," she said. "It was difficult for him and the roommate, I am sure."

She said her son's condition had only worsened at Princeton, when he had taken time off in his freshman year to go surfing in Charleston, South Carolina. She had then received a call that he was very sick and was in the hospital. Through the family's medical contacts, they had found Charleston psychiatrist Dr. Kevin Spicer, who said Tommy should be institutionalized.

Over the next few years, she testified, Tommy's mental condition deteriorated as she and her husband watched helplessly.

"It was very painful," she said. "Greater anger, greater distance from us. Long periods of time would go by when he did not want us to email, text, or call. And if we did, he would ignore it."

In redirect, Prosecutor Ortner asked why she felt surfing was so therapeutic for her son.

"It gave him something to do," Shelley replied. "He could not get employment, and he needed a life."

Then Ortner followed up asking whether Tommy had a better relationship with her than his father.

"Historically speaking," said Shelley, "I probably was closer to him, which is not to say that Tom wasn't. They did have a good relationship for years."

36

A CIRCUS

Over the next few days, the prosecution called a string of detectives who had worked on the investigation. Between them, they led the jury through the initial investigation after Shelley Gilbert's 911 call to Tommy's surrender late Sunday night. Their testimony mirrored the pretrial suppression hearing almost two years earlier.

After Justice Jackson's stern reprimand, the defendant appeared calmer, sitting quietly at the defense table taking notes. For a while, it appeared that the judge's school madam warnings had worked.

Then, on the fourth day of the trial, he had a complete meltdown.

Detective Darryl Ng was testifying on direct about Gilbert's arrest at the Seventeenth Precinct and how the police handled emotionally disturbed people. Suddenly, Tommy turned around to address the jury, telling them to disregard the detective's testimony.

"The defendant would like to ask the jury for a directed verdict on all this evidence," he began, "which was illegally obtained under the Fourth Amendment. At the next recess, the defendant would like to address the jury to discuss a directed verdict, which would allow the jury to suppress all search and seizure evidence."

"Thank you," Justice Jackson told him angrily. "Your application is denied, Mr. Gilbert."

The judge then ordered the jury and Detective Ng to leave the courtroom.

"The defendant would request that Detective Ng please remain," said Gilbert.

"Just go through the door there," the judge told the detective.

Once he had left, she addressed the wayward defendant.

"Mr. Gilbert, you and I have had a series of conversations over the past couple of weeks about your outbursts before the jury. Today, you addressed the jury directly, which is absolutely forbidden. Do you understand me?"

"No, Your Honor," he replied defiantly. "The defendant believes this is allowed under the First Amendment."

"I am going to have you removed, Mr. Gilbert," she told him. "I warned you about this. We cannot have this happen during the course of the trial, sir."

As three bailiffs moved in to handcuff him, Tommy objected to the court ruling, babbling on about his constitutional right to address the jury. He told the court officers to uncuff him so he could attend the rest of the hearing.

"I'm not going to allow this," said the judge, visibly annoyed. "Mr. Levine, your client is too disruptive in front of this jury to permit him to continue."

The defense lawyer agreed it was an "aberration," but asked the judge to let him stay if he promised to behave himself.

"He hasn't been continually disruptive," said Levine, "he's not being violent or acting out otherwise. It has to be prejudicial."

Justice Jackson said she was having the defendant removed, but he could come back when he was ready to remain silent and not speak to the jury.

"Mr. Gilbert," she intoned, "I'm going to have you removed from the courtroom. We will proceed."

He resisted when the armed court officers grabbed him by the arms, so they dragged him out through a side door into a holding cell as he railed about "federal and prosecutorial misconduct" and demanded an "unbiased courtroom."

After his client was physically hauled out of the courtroom, Levine immediately requested another competency exam, saying his client's mental condition had clearly deteriorated. He asked for a few minutes alone with Gilbert in a holding cell to try to calm him down.

"Unlike every other time, to my knowledge, in the last four and a half years," he told the judge, "they literally forced him and had to push him against his will as he was trying to resist."

"I am denying your application for a competency exam," said the judge. "Your client is, as I already said repeatedly, fit. The fact that he's interacting now with the court and the jury is no different from the way he's behaved over the last couple of years, frankly."

She called a short recess so Levine could talk to Gilbert in the holding cell, saying she would give him "a second chance" to come back into the courtroom.

A few minutes later, Tommy Gilbert was brought back into the courtroom, looking sheepish.

"I don't want any more outbursts," the judge told him. "Can you assure me you're going to do that?"

Looking defeated and surrounded by seven burly court officers, he weakly nodded.

"I see you nodding your head," said Justice Jackson, "which has been a form of communication between you and me throughout these years. And it shows me that you indeed understand my rules."

For the next couple of hours, Tommy Gilbert sat quietly at the defense table, on his best behavior. But in the afternoon session, during testimony from now retired NYPD Crime Scene Unit officer Anthony D'Amato, Tommy could no longer contain himself. As a series of gory photographs of his father's dead body and the murder weapon were shown to the jury, Tommy began loudly objecting, citing the Fourth Amendment.

Over the next few minutes, he objected a dozen times during his own attorney's cross-examination as the grisly photos were displayed. Justice Jackson ignored him.

He continued objecting during the next witness, a New York City Transit Authority worker who was testifying about Tommy's subway journey to and from his parents' apartment. He became even more agitated during a Verizon Wireless employee's testimony about his iPhone usage on the day of the murder.

As she dismissed the jury and recessed for the day, the judge did not address the defendant's blatant disregard of her instructions.

At the beginning of the fifth day of the trial, Arnold Levine told the judge that his client had declined to appear, but would not say why. Instead, he had asked a court officer to take him back to Rikers.

"He is incapable of assisting his lawyer in his defense," said a frustrated Levine. "So I ask for another competency exam . . . renewing my application for the third time during the trial."

ADA Ortner pointed out that the defendant had often malingered and faked symptoms at Rikers Island to gain an advantage.

"To the extent that Mr. Gilbert is or is not assisting in his defense," said the prosecutor, "that is a volitional choice on his part."

Justice Jackson denied Levine's application, saying she had closely watched the defendant for almost five years and was in no doubt that he was fit for trial. She noted that he obviously wanted to participate in the proceedings, although he didn't follow the court's rules.

"He wants to make his own objections," stated the judge, "as he has throughout this [trial], whether they are based on correct argument or not. He is listening. He knows what's going on, he is choosing whatever course of action he is choosing, which today is not to be here."

She then asked the attorneys how she should explain the defendant's absence to the jury, who might link it to the outburst the day before. After consulting with both sides, she decided to give the jury the standard absent-defendant charge. When the jury was finally brought in after a ninety-minute delay, Justice Jackson addressed the conspicuously empty chair at the defense table.

"I'm sure, as you have noticed," she told them, "that the defendant is not present today in the courtroom. I want to advise you that the defendant has a right to be present in the courtroom and he has the right not to be. So you are not to speculate upon the reason for his absence nor . . . draw any inference."

For the rest of his trial, Tommy Gilbert would appear whenever he felt like it. Each morning, he would be brought from Rikers Island to Manhattan Supreme Court and asked if he wished to attend the day's proceedings. Occasionally, he did, but more often than not, he asked to go back to Rikers.

On day seven of the trial—Friday, June 7—Tommy Gilbert appeared for the first time in several days. Wearing his white starched shirt and slacks, he was led into court as if nothing had happened.

"Good morning, Your Honor," he said brightly. "Defendant wishes to address the court at this time."

Justice Jackson agreed.

Speaking in the third person, Gilbert then objected to all the prosecution's witnesses, referring to them as "character witnesses" with no direct knowledge of the case. He also wanted to bar any testimony from Peter Smith, although it was still uncertain whether his nemesis would be called.

"Many of these witnesses have pending conflicts or legal action against the defendant," he told the judge, "and the defendant wishes to impeach their testimony."

He also asked the judge to block any testimony from psychiatric experts, claiming it was irrelevant.

"All right, thank you, Mr. Gilbert," replied the judge with an almost audible eye roll. "I am denying your application."

"Is it possible to participate in cross-examination of witnesses?" he then asked.

"No, you are not allowed to," she told him sternly. "You have a lawyer who speaks for you, sir."

Lead detective Joseph Cirigliano then retook the stand to continue his testimony about the search of the Gilberts' Wainscott house. From ADA Ortner's very first question, Gilbert began vehemently objecting, citing his Fourth Amendment rights. Again and again, he objected to the prosecutor's questions, becoming particularly incensed when an envelope he'd addressed to Lizzy Fraser was shown to the jury.

"Defendant objects," he babbled. "Believe this is illegal search and seizure [and] asks for a direct verdict on the sentence."

"Overruled," said the judge sternly.

Over the next few minutes, as Detective Cirigliano displayed various accessories and ammunition for the Glock firearm to the jury, Gilbert fired off a barrage of objections.

Finally, Justice Jackson had had enough and called a sidebar. As the attorneys walked over to the judge, all the jurors were watching the defendant, who was rocking back and forth in his chair.

"I have counted almost twenty objections by your client," the judge told Levine. "I cannot take it anymore. I don't think it is right, in front of the jury. It has been intolerable. He even talked to the jury about a directed verdict."

She warned Levine that she would not tolerate any further outbursts, and if his client continued, she would throw him out of the courtroom again.

After the lengthy sidebar, Justice Jackson instructed the jury that the case should be decided on the evidence alone, and the defendant's conduct must not be taken into account.

"You must disregard his conduct, and you may not consider it for any purpose," she told them as Tommy took notes at the defense table.

A few minutes later, Arnold Levine began his cross-examination of Detective Cirigliano. Once again, Gilbert became agitated and started objecting. Visibly angry, the judge then asked the jury to leave for a ten-minute break.

After they'd filed out, the judge told Gilbert that she was having him removed from the courtroom.

"I have warned you repeatedly about your behavior," she told him. "I counted almost twenty-five objections in the last hour despite my warning to you, sir."

She then ordered the court officers to remove the defendant, telling him that he could come back when he decided to obey the rules of the court.

Toward the end of that morning's session, the prosecution called their twenty-eighth witness, John Jay Bennett, who had sold the Glock handgun to Tommy Gilbert. They had flown him from Clarksburg, Ohio, to New York to testify. He nervously walked up to the stand, explaining that it was his first time in New York.

Bennett testified that in May 2014, he had uploaded a photo of a .40-caliber semiautomatic Glock to a Facebook guns-for-sale forum and soon received a response from the defendant.

Three weeks later, Gilbert was in his living room, saying what "a great deal" he was getting.

"He was overwhelmingly pleased . . . with the price of the item," Bennett told the court, "and I can't blame him. It was an expensive gun."

After a lunch break, Justice Jackson asked the court officers to go and see if the defendant wished to attend the afternoon session. He was led into the courtroom to take his place at the defense table.

"I am reminding you, Mr. Gilbert," the judge told him, "refrain from interrupting any witness testimony . . . or I will have you removed."

"Yes, Your Honor," he replied. "Defendant also reserving the right to be absent from trial under CPL 340.52 at any time."

"Of course," answered the judge dismissively.

John Jay Bennett returned to the witness stand as Tommy glared at him and the jury filed in.

"Hope you enjoyed your lunch," the judge told them. "We will now continue with cross-examination of Mr. Bennett by Mr. Levine."

Suddenly, the defendant leaned over to his defense attorney and whispered a few words in his ear. Levine then asked for a sidebar.

"Mr. Gilbert . . . would like to waive his right to be present this afternoon," he told the judge.

"That's fine," she replied.

The somewhat baffled jury were excused, and Justice Jackson told the defendant he could leave.

"Do you want to come back for the rest of the day," she asked him, "or would you like to come back Monday?"

"Defendant declines," was his obtuse response. "However, defendant is available at any time upon request."

On Saturday morning, the *New York Post*'s Page Six gossip column revealed that movie star Jake Gyllenhaal was producing a movie about the Thomas Gilbert Jr. case. It would star Swedish actor Bill Skarsgård, best known for his portrayal of the evil clown Pennywise in the horror movies *It* and *It Chapter Two*.

And according to Page Six, New York's elite were not happy, worrying that the film would "glamorize" Tommy Gilbert.

BLUE BLOOD BOILING OVER JAKE GYLLENHAAL'S 'IVY LEAGUE DAD KILLER' FILM was the headline.

"It's so upsetting," said one unnamed socialite. "Tommy can't be the victim in this film—people need to remember he was a monster—a calculating, rage-filled psychopath."

37

"HE WAS EXTREMELY GOOD-LOOKING"

The following Monday, the eighth day of the trial, the defendant sent word that he did not wish to be present. Maybe it was because his former girlfriend Briana Swanson was testifying that morning. Since they'd split up, Briana had married and now had a sixteen-month-old son.

The private chef told the court how she had first met Tommy in May 2014 through a mutual friend, immediately being attracted to his stunning good looks. They soon started dating, and she moved into his West Eighteenth Street apartment.

Under Ortner's direct questioning, she described their summer fling in the Hamptons, where he mostly worked out in the gym and went surfing.

"Did the defendant ever talk to you about his parents?" asked Ortner.

"Yes," she replied.

"In particular, did the subject of his father come up in conversations you had with him?"

"Yes, he was upset that he wasn't helping him more [financially]."

"Did he say anything about his father's support of him being cut off?" asked the prosecutor.

"Yes," answered Briana, "he was worried that he was going to be cut off. He was scared."

As the summer wore on, Briana testified, she realized that Tommy was a lying cheat, but she continued putting up with it because he was "extremely" good-looking.

"I didn't have the best self-esteem back then," she explained, "and I thought, well, at least he's using protection."

In cross-examination, Levine asked about Tommy's hatred of Peter Smith and his constant fears that Peter was trying to break into his safe and hack into his computer.

"He accused you of actually working with Peter Smith against him, right?" asked the defense attorney.

"Yeah," she replied.

"Were you working with Peter Smith against him?"

"No."

Briana also testified that Tommy was obsessed with Lizzy Fraser and talked about her all the time.

"I think it had been a thing of the past," she said. "He was mad [because] he thought Lizzy was messing around with Peter."

There was much anticipation for the afternoon session; Peter Smith was scheduled to be the prosecution's next witness. His brother, Chris, was already sitting in the second row of the public gallery. Again, Justice Jackson announced that the defendant had declined to attend.

She then called a forty-five-minute sidebar due to an important update from ADA Ortner. The prosecutor explained that he had only just discovered that Smith was writing a book about the defendant. He was still working on the manuscript, and so far, nothing had been submitted to a publisher.

"He told me that the book is about his experiences with the defendant," said Ortner. "Much of it concerns . . . the assault, the fire, and what I would describe as the terror campaign against Peter Smith."

Ortner told the judge that he did not intend to ask Smith about any of these on direct. Arnold Levine said the defense wanted to subpoena Smith's manuscript immediately, as it would be highly relevant to his cross-examination.

"Obviously, that is a treasure trove of information," Levine told the judge. "It's about the very stuff he will be testifying about."

Justice Jackson said she wanted to see a copy of the manuscript before deciding.

"It concerns me," she told the attorneys. "I would like to see it."

Ortner and Sullivan left the courtroom to speak to Peter Smith, returning a few minutes later to resume the sidebar.

"He says he has written about forty or forty-five pages in outline form," Ortner told the judge. "Some of which he says is fictional because he artistically puts himself literally in the mind of the defendant and writes from his perspective."

Smith said his manuscript covered their childhood, their time living together in Williamsburg, the assault, and the fire. He had written it for therapeutic reasons, with a view to having it published one day.

The judge agreed to Smith coming back later in the trial to testify, giving her and the attorneys the opportunity to read his manuscript.

She then called in the jury, who had been waiting more than an hour, apologizing for the delay for "unexpected matters." Dismissing them for the day, she told them not to blame the defendant for their wasted afternoon.

On Tuesday, June 11—the ninth day of the trial—Thomas Gilbert Jr. again declined to attend the proceedings. During the afternoon session, the prosecution called its thirty-sixth witness, George Seymour Beckwith Gilbert—known to the defendant as Uncle Beck—to the stand.

At a pretrial hearing, the stately Gilbert family patriarch had challenged a subpoena to testify, but Justice Jackson had ruled against him.

"And what is your professional background?" asked Ortner.

"I'm in the merchant banker leverage buyout business," replied the defendant's uncle. "Private equity, it's called today."

Beck Gilbert told the court that he was three years older than his late brother, Tom, whom he described as "a good friend." He said he saw his nephew Tommy "very infrequently," usually on the tennis court at the Maidstone Club.

"And how would you describe your nephew, the defendant's demeanor?" asked Ortner.

"He was a good kid," Beck replied. "He handled himself very well, very politely, well spoken."

Beck Gilbert said that Tommy had asked for money for his hedge fund, which he'd declined to give him.

Then the prosecutor displayed a series of emails between Beck and Tommy from the summer of 2014, asking to help him join the Devon Yacht Club after being suspended from the Maidstone Club for threatening a staff member.

Ortner then asked about his brother's concerns that Tommy did not have a job after graduating Princeton, and what advice Beck had given him.

"I said he ought to get a job . . . more than once," said Beck. "That is the way we were brought up. We were expected to get a job when we got out of school."

"Do you recall how recent to Tom's death," asked Ortner, "you told him that you think Tommy ought to get a job?"

"I have a problem with trying to sort the time out on this thing," he replied. "[It's] like a bad dream that I'm trying to forget, only it won't go away."

In his cross-examination, Arnold Levine elicited that Beck Gilbert had paid for his nephew's Princeton tuition, as well as his legal fees in 2013 after the assault on Peter Smith. No explanation was given as to why.

On the tenth day of the trial, Anna Rothschild took the stand. Once again, the defendant declined to attend, and the judge also asked Shelley Gilbert to leave the courtroom, as there was a possibility she might testify again as a defense witness.

The "blonde cougar," as the *New York Post* had labeled her, told the court that her relationship with Tommy was mainly physical.

"He was extremely good looking," explained the fifty-three-year-old socialite.

Under Ortner's direct, she said Tommy had been trying to start a hedge fund, wanting her to help him find investors, which she never did. When Ortner asked how the defendant had explained not working for his father's hedge fund, she was unable to remember.

"I'm nervous," she explained, "so it's hard to remember."

Ortner then showed her notes from their previous interview to refresh her memory.

"He had worked for him for a brief time," she said, "but his father wasn't happy with his performance."

In cross-examination, Levine asked why she had been surprised Tommy had graduated Princeton University.

"He didn't seem to be highly intelligent," she replied, "in my humble opinion."

"What was he like when you were alone with him?" asked the defense attorney.

"Extremely introverted and very quiet. Oddly, oddly quiet."

Anna said that she and a friend had once tried to figure out what was wrong with Tommy, googling "autism" and "on the spectrum."

"Something was really, really off," she explained. "I just didn't know what it was."

For the next several days, Tommy Gilbert remained in a holding cell, returning to Rikers Island at the earliest opportunity. Arnold Levine was growing increasingly frustrated, as he felt that Tommy was deliberately sabotaging his own defense. His bizarre behavior in front of the jury had placed his defense attorney in a weak position.

"His objections were all gibberish and nonsense," Levine said after the trial. "I hope the jury saw that as the real Tommy, because it was. That wasn't a show."

Body language between attorney and client is always an important weapon in the defense arsenal. But on the increasingly rare occasions he did attend the trial, Tommy shunned any physical contact with Levine at the defense table, as if he were contaminated.

"It's a bit uncomfortable when he's sitting there taking notes but won't talk to me," said Levine. "He didn't want any of my stuff on his side of the table, or me to get anywhere close to touching him. I was worried that the jury might think that I was afraid of him."

Tommy Gilbert finally surfaced again at the afternoon session on the following Monday, the twelfth day of the trial. He had now shaved off his beard, and his thinning brown hair was neatly combed. It appeared that the defendant now had an agenda. He was obsessed that Peter Smith would testify against him and was back in the courtroom to try to stop it.

"Good afternoon, Mr. Gilbert," said Justice Jackson. "I am glad to see you wish to attend today's session. I have been informed that you would like to speak to me before I bring the jury out."

"Yes, ma'am," he replicd.

Gilbert then launched into his rant, railing against any witness with "pending civil charges" against him, obviously referring to Peter Smith.

"Defendant believes it creates a conflict of interest," he told the judge, "and defendant again moves to impeach his testimony."

He was also aware that although the prosecution had decided not to call Smith after reading his manuscript, Arnold Levine was now considering doing so.

"The defendant objects to any defense testimony based on the confident interest and potential bias on this examination."

"Is that it?" asked the judge sarcastically. "Nothing more?"

"Also a second point . . . ," he began, going into an incomprehensible diatribe to ban testimony from an investigative analyst presently on the stand, who had prepared detailed PowerPoint presentations of his phone records, emails, and web history. These included searches for contract killers and hit men.

After the judge denied both applications, the defendant asked to leave and was escorted out of the courtroom.

Later that morning, after more than three weeks of testimony and forty-three witnesses, the prosecution rested their case subject to rebuttal. Arnold Levine immediately called for dismissal on all counts.

"The People have failed to make out a prima facie case

of Mr. Gilbert's identity as the person who killed his father," he told the judge, "and that he did so intentionally."

"And, Mr. Ortner, do you wish to respond?" asked Justice Jackson.

"The People oppose the motion and will rely on the record," he said.

The judge denied the defense motion to dismiss the case.

As the defense was about to call their first witness, Tommy Gilbert asked to come back into the courtroom.

"Let the record reflect that Mr. Gilbert is with us this afternoon," the judge wryly noted.

"The defendant would also like to decline to be in the courtroom," he replied.

"I'm sorry?" she asked. "You don't want to be here?"

Gilbert shook his head.

"You changed your mind?" she told him. "We thought you did. We'll take you out."

He was then handcuffed and escorted out of the courtroom before the jury entered.

For his defense case, Arnold Levine called a succession of psychiatrists who had treated Tommy over the years. He was still trying to decide whether to call Peter Smith so he could question him about his book.

Once again, the experienced defense attorney had his hands tied by his client. Although Tommy had approved an insanity defense, he had refused to meet the defense's expert, Dr. Alexander Sasha Bardey. Therefore, Dr. Bardey could not testify about Tommy's state of mind when he shot his father and whether he satisfied the standard of not guilty by reason of insanity.

The defense's first witness was Dr. Michael Sacks of the Weill Cornell Medical College, who had started treating

Tommy in the winter of 2008. After initially diagnosing him with severe OCD and paranoia, Dr. Sacks became convinced Tommy was delusional.

Under Levine's direct, Dr. Sacks testified that Tommy had developed a series of gestures to ward off thoughts that people were trying to steal his soul and personality.

"One was by twisting his neck," he testified. "Another was by giving the finger to someone and . . . a third by spitting."

The next morning, Tuesday, June 18, Dr. Theodore Shapiro took the stand for day thirteen of the trial. Tommy Gilbert was sitting with his yellow legal pad at the defense table when the jury entered. The judge had previously warned him to keep quiet or he would be removed.

Dr. Shapiro testified that back in 2004, he had discussed Tommy's mental condition with his parents after making a preliminary diagnosis of paranoid disorder with possible schizophrenia.

"I'm a child psychiatrist," he explained. "His father saw me because he thought it was an adolescent crisis."

Levine asked if it was unusual for his client to be suffering from schizophrenia and still be able to go surfing and play tennis.

"You can do a lot of things even though you're sick," replied the doctor.

Levine paused questioning to call a sidebar, as he wanted Dr. Shapiro to testify about Tommy's mental condition in Charleston, South Carolina, after his suspension from Princeton. At the time, Dr. Shapiro had referred him to Dr. Kevin Spicer, who had treated him there.

In the middle of the sidebar, a court officer came over, saying the defendant wished to be included to give his input.

"He can't come over to the sidebar," said Justice Jackson angrily.

She asked Levine to speak to Tommy to see if he wanted to leave the courtroom.

"There have been a lot of times he wanted to approach when we were having sidebars," said Levine. "He wanted to be included."

Later in direct, Dr. Shapiro said he had met with Lila Chase after Tommy had asked him to see her.

"She said he was very uncomfortable at home," he said, "although he took advantage of the country club and all of that."

In Ortner's cross-examination, Dr. Shapiro testified that Shelley Gilbert "was in absolute denial" of her son's disturbed behavior.

"[She] was upset about it," he said, "partly, I believe, because she had mental illness in her family and was fearful that it would be seen in her son."

Then Ortner asked the doctor if he thought it inappropriate to refer to the defendant as "Tommy," as he was a thirty-five-year-old man.

"Yes, of course," he replied.

"He is a responsible adult?" asked the prosecutor.

"He should be," said the doctor.

After Dr. Shapiro finished testifying, Justice Jackson excused the jury for a short recess, and the defendant, who had been quiet all morning, let his feelings be known.

"The defendant calls for objection of sidebars," he told the judge.

"I understand your objection," Justice Jackson replied brusquely. "Your objection is overruled, Mr. Gilbert. Thank you."

The defense's third witness was Dr. Jason Kim, who, like

the preceding witnesses, was a psychiatrist at the Weill Cornell Medical College. He had treated Tommy from April to October 2014.

Dr. Kim testified that he had initially diagnosed Tommy with OCD and then several "fluid working" disorders, including schizophrenia.

"What were those psychotic symptoms?" asked Levine.

"Paranoia and potentially some delusions," he replied. "He described harassment from his parents [and] people in a social circle."

The psychiatrist told the court that Tommy was particularly paranoid of his father, whom he felt deliberately did things to "annoy" and "irritate" him. He had prescribed antipsychotic medication, but as far as he knew, Tommy only ever took one pill.

Then Levine asked if paranoid delusions and schizophrenia would interfere with him surfing and playing tennis. Dr. Kim said no.

"Those kind of activities don't require . . . executive functioning," he explained, "which means higher-order thinking. A lot of things are muscle memory."

After the lunch break, Tommy Gilbert was back at the defense table for Dr. Kim's cross-examination. He looked agitated and made copious notes while Ortner probed the doctor about the defendant's heavy drug use.

"He told you that he had abused a variety of drugs," asked Ortner, "including cocaine, mushrooms, and testosterone steroids?"

"Yes," replied the doctor.

Then Ortner asked about Tommy's two-year "romantic relationship" with Lila Chase, when he moved in with her family. He was careful not to mention her by name, as she was not on the witness list, but he wanted the jury to know that the defendant had once had a serious relationship.

"At the time that you first met with the defendant," asked Ortner, "she was an ex-girlfriend?"

"Yes."

"Did he tell you that she came from a wealthy family?"

"No, I don't think so."

"Or that she was the niece of a famous Hollywood actor?"

"No."

After the jury was dismissed for the day, the defendant made a third attempt to prevent Peter Smith from taking the stand. Arnold Levine had now decided to call him the next day, and his client opposed it.

Speaking in the third person, Gilbert appealed to Justice Jackson to stop Smith from testifying, citing a conflict of interest.

"The prosecution has already dismissed this witness," he said, "but the defense . . ."

"I'm sorry," said the judge incredulously, "did you say you wanted to block his testimony?"

"Yes," answered Tommy.

"Your application is denied," she told him. "See you tomorrow morning. We will have a full array of witnesses."

After prosecutors decided not to call Peter Smith Jr. to the stand, Arnold Levine had struggled with whether to do so or not. He had read Smith's manuscript and wanted the jury to hear how Tommy had assaulted him, hurled a flagpole through his window, and then burned down his father's historic house.

He consulted several attorney friends, who had differing

opinions. He finally made up his mind after speaking to Briana Swanson, now Ressner, soon after she testified.

"I told her I was having this struggle," he said, "and she said, 'You should bring it out, as it is such strong evidence of his mental illness and the extremes he went to.'"

38

"IT'S A FREE GAME"

The next morning, Justice Jackson allowed Shelley Gilbert back into the courtroom after Arnold Levine decided not to recall her as a defense witness. Her son was also in attendance, informing the judge that he would stay for the morning session but not for the afternoon, when Peter Smith was due to testify.

"[The defendant] also requests to exercise the right to decline attendance for the defendant's mother for the afternoon hearing," he told the judge.

"I can't preclude your mother from being in the courtroom," replied the judge. "I do understand your request, and unfortunately, I have to deny it. Okay?"

Then Dr. Sacks retook the stand for cross-examination by Ortner. Once again, the prosecutor homed in on Lila Chase, who had met with him in August 2008 at Tommy's request.

"Do you recall the defendant telling you that he felt that [Lila's] family was putting pressure on him to marry her?" asked Ortner.

Initially, Dr. Sacks did not, but after consulting his treatment notes, he said yes.

"Now," Ortner continued, "after the defendant broke up with that young woman, he dated other women, right?"

"Mm-hmm, yes," said Dr. Sacks. "I don't recall much discussion of the other girlfriends."

The prosecutor then steered his questioning toward the poker night incident, when Peter Smith had called Tommy a loser. But first he called a sidebar to check with Justice Jackson before venturing into that thorny territory.

Ortner told the judge that, out of cautiousness, he wanted her permission for the jury to hear about the assault and arson.

"Since it's a defense case, the Molineux ruling no longer applies," said the judge. "It's a free game."

Ortner asked Dr. Sacks if he had reported Tommy under the SAFE Act, to prevent him getting a firearm legally, after Tommy's arrest for assaulting Smith. The psychiatrist confirmed he had, although he had not followed through and had him hospitalized, which he could have done.

Before the afternoon session began, Tommy Gilbert asked the judge again to excuse his mother for Peter Smith's imminent testimony, citing Article 340.50 of New York State Criminal Procedural Law. Justice Jackson explained that she could not make anyone leave a public courtroom.

The next witness was psychologist Dr. Susan Evans, who had last treated Gilbert in July 2014. On direct, she told Arnold Levine that she had diagnosed him with likely schizoaffective illness.

As his defense attorney probed deeper into his psychotic symptoms, Gilbert became agitated, telling a court officer that he wanted to leave. The judge excused him so he could take the bus back to Rikers Island.

* * *

Later that afternoon, Peter Smith Jr. was sworn in on the stand. He had arrived with his brother, Chris, and personal attorney, Kenneth Belkin, who were both in the public gallery. Earlier, Levine had asked the judge to declare Smith a hostile witness, complaining he was ignoring his phone calls. She had refused.

Under Levine's direct, Smith told the jury how he and Tommy had both attended Buckley, only becoming friends in their late twenties after accidentally meeting on a Hamptons beach. When Tommy said he wanted to move out of his parents' home, Smith had offered him a room in his Williamsburg apartment, and Tommy accepted.

Smith testified that he had taken Tommy under his wing, introducing him to his circle of friends and including him in social activities. At first, his new roommate was shy and socially awkward, but he soon came out of his shell.

"And was there a time when the relationship between you and Tommy started to change?" asked Levine.

"Yes," replied Smith.

"How?"

"I couldn't tell you what exactly sparked it," said Smith, "but eventually, Tommy became very aggressive with me. He attacked me on several occasions. He accused me of things [and] eventually he tried to kill me."

"You said he was accusing you of things," asked Levine. "What type of things?"

"He accused me of going into his room and . . . robbing him, hacking his computer and his bank account. Trying to 'mess with him,' is how he usually put it."

Levine then asked about Tommy's assault outside the Williamsburg apartment, a week after hurling a flagpole through the window of the Smiths' Hamptons house.

Smith said he was getting ready to go to their friend Jack Bryan's movie screening when Tommy started ringing his doorbell.

"He said he wanted to talk to me," Smith testified. "I said I didn't have time for that."

Then Smith turned around, and Tommy took a swing at him with a clenched fist.

"He missed," said Smith, "but as I ducked, he grabbed the back of my head with both hands and kneed me in the face about twenty times. My guardian angel was a large Puerto Rican dude. He appeared out of nowhere, grabbed Tommy . . . who immediately jumped up and started pointing at me, saying, 'He attacked me!'"

As Tommy was being restrained, Smith had called the police.

"And you suffered injuries as a result of that?" asked Levine.

"Not really," replied Smith. "Just a bit of a busted nose."

Smith said he had taken out a restraining order against Tommy and hadn't seen him again until the following summer at a drum circle on Sagg Main Beach.

"He approached me around the fire I was sitting at," said Smith. "He said he wanted to talk to me, and I told him that I had a restraining order and I couldn't. He told me it was the last chance to bury the hatchet."

Levine then asked him about a surfing trip to the Dominican Republic the former friends had taken.

"What was he like on that trip?" asked Levine.

"He was quiet," replied Smith. "Aggressive at times. He was also sleeping with a lot of prostitutes."

"In the Dominican Republic, prostitution is legal, right?" asked Levine.

"I believe so," he replied. "I don't know."

In cross-examination, Craig Ortner asked for more details

about Tommy's nocturnal activities during their Dominican vacation.

"The defendant was enjoying the company of prostitutes down there, right?"

"He was, yes," replied Smith.

"Including at least one prostitute who appeared to be underaged?"

"Appeared, yes."

"And that created some friction between you and he on that trip, right?"

"Yes."

"Because, among other reasons," noted Ortner, "it was crimping your style and your ability to socialize with other people?"

"Yes," agreed Smith. "That was really the first time we ever got into a fight."

Then Ortner asked about the poker night when Tommy and Lizzy Fraser had arrived uninvited.

"Now, Lizzy Fraser," asked Ortner, "is the woman who this defendant had this . . . crush on?"

"Yes," said Smith, "he confided in me that he was very interested in Lizzy on multiple occasions."

"Now, I don't want to pry or embarrass you," Ortner continued, "had you at some point in the past had kind of a casual relationship with Lizzy Fraser?"

"Six years earlier," Smith admitted.

Under Ortner's questioning, Smith told the jury how Tommy had accused him of being cruel to his pet dog that night, after he'd picked it up by the scruff of its neck when it knocked over a wineglass. An argument had ensued in front of all the guests in the living room.

"The argument ended when you told him he was a loser?" asked the prosecutor.

"I think so, yeah," he replied. "[It was] the first thing that came into my head."

"You just yelled at him in front of everybody, 'You're a loser!'"

"I think so, yeah."

On Friday, June 21—the fifteenth day of the trial—Peter Smith retook the stand as Ortner continued his cross-examination. Once again, the defendant did not want to be present, asking to go back to Rikers.

As the jury looked on in rapt attention, the prosecutor confirmed that Smith should have been inside his father's historic house when it burned down, soon after he'd berated Tommy at the drum circle.

"I was usually there on Sunday night, alone," Smith said.

"After the fire," Ortner continued, "did you report to police your belief that the defendant had burned down your parents' house . . . and the threat he'd made to you?"

"Yes."

"To your knowledge, was the defendant ever arrested for setting fire to your parents' house?"

"He was never arrested for the fire," answered Smith, "but he was picked up for violation of the order of protection."

In redirect, Levine asked Smith what he had meant when he had testified earlier that his client had tried to kill him twice.

"I figured that the first time he assaulted me that his intention was to kill me," Smith replied. "I think that when he came up to me on the beach and tried to get me to walk away from the group, he was trying to kill me. And I think when he set the fire, he was trying to kill me."

"The assault," noted Levine. "He didn't use a weapon on you, right?"

"Objection," said Ortner.

"He was also six four, 240 pounds on steroids," Smith shot back.

After Peter Smith was excused, the defense rested their case, paving the way for the People's rebuttal by their expert, Dr. Jason Hershberger.

For almost three days, the forensic psychiatrist testified at length about the defendant's mental condition. As Gilbert had twice declined to be interviewed, the doctor's testimony was solely gleaned from therapy notes from psychiatrists who had treated him and his Rikers medical history.

From his research, Dr. Hershberger testified that he had diagnosed the defendant with OCD, cannabis and marijuana use disorder, as well as an unspecified personality disorder. He told the jury he was convinced that the defendant had not been legally insane when he had killed his father.

Under Ortner's direct questioning, he outlined the steps Gilbert had taken to mislead detectives, proving he had the mental capacity to understand his actions.

"In my opinion," said Dr. Hershberger, "when he shot his father in the head, he had both the capacity to appreciate his father would die and that killing his father was wrong."

39

IT WAS REALLY THE
AHA MOMENT

On Wednesday, June 26, the defense and prosecution delivered their closing arguments to the jury. It was the eighteenth day of the trial and both sides' final opportunity to address the six men and six women of the jury before they left to deliberate. Shelley Gilbert had arrived early to take her usual place in the second row of the public gallery. It was standing room only in the courtroom, and many people, including journalists, were unable to get in to hear the closing arguments.

"I looked out, and it was packed," said Arnold Levine. "It was a big deal because it was a Princeton grad . . . who seemed to have it all. The sort of fairy-tale-type family thing that went bad."

The defendant was present at the defense table, but before calling the jury in, Justice Jackson lectured him to keep quiet during the summations.

"I will not tolerate any disruptions or objections," she told him, adding that once the closings began, he could not leave the courtroom. "I want the jury to be able to pay attention to the arguments and not be at all interrupted or distracted."

Tommy nodded.

The jury entered, walking past the defendant, who had his

head down and eyes closed, as they took their places in the jury box. Arnold Levine rose from the defense table and approached the lectern, moving it nearer to the jury box.

"'You said he was getting better,'" he began dramatically. "These are the words Bess Gilbert [said], crying and wailing on hearing the news that her brother killed her father. She didn't say, 'Mom, I told you, you shouldn't have reduced the allowance. Mom, I told you that he hated our dad.' No, she went immediately to Tommy's mental illness."

Levine told the jury that Bess had immediately known why her brother had done it, as had Peter Smith after Tommy's yearlong campaign against him had culminated in arson.

"What did Peter Smith say?" he asked the jury. "His reaction too, like Bess Gilbert's, was, 'He needs to be institutionalized. He needs to be in a psychiatric hospital and not going to prison for years and years and years.'"

He told the jury that both Peter Smith Jr. and Tom Gilbert Sr. had become objects of Tommy's delusional paranoia.

"That's why I put Peter Smith on the witness stand," he said. "I knew these horrible things would come out, but I trust you to judge this case fairly."

Levine said that the cut in Tommy's allowance and hatred of his father did not cause the murder but schizophrenia had.

The attorney then spent a few minutes reading through extracts from Tommy's glowing reports at Buckley and Deerfield. He ran through Tommy's exceptional grades and his SAT score of over 1400 out of 1600.

"Pretty smart guy with the world ahead of him," said Levine as his client took notes. "A bright future and a lot of potential."

He read another extract of one of Tommy's Deerfield reports, describing him as possessing a "dignified, almost courtly manner." It applauded his leadership qualities and razor-sharp debating skills.

"Tommy's work . . . has been a success story I still thrill to witness," his English tutor at Deerfield had written. "Tommy has become my star."

Not only was he an honor roll student, Levine told the jury, but also a star athlete playing varsity football and basketball.

But something bad had happened between Tommy's time at Deerfield and Princeton, and he had been sliding downhill ever since.

"There is a reason for that," argued Levine. "The reason is in his brain. Tommy didn't suddenly become a bad seed who couldn't hold his anger with a bad temper. It didn't just click on and off like that."

At Princeton, he had pretended to be "normal" to fit in, and ever since, he had tried to "fake being well."

Levine asked the jury if they really believed that his client wanted to live off his parents, that he would kill his father over a small reduction in his allowance. He observed that Tommy had had a tremendous earning potential before becoming ill and being unable to work.

"You think Tommy didn't want a job . . . and [to] make a lot more money than his parents were giving him?" he asked the jury, who were listening intently. "You think he was happy with that?"

Levine said mental illness and paranoia also prevented him from having a "real relationship."

"It's all just a sexual relationship," Levine told the jury. "There is no intimate relationship with anybody."

Levine also sharply criticized the People's psychiatric expert, Dr. Hershberger, for concluding that Gilbert was sane when he killed his father. He noted that the doctor had never actually interviewed his client, saying he must be a "mind reader" or "clairvoyant" to reach his conclusion.

"It actually weighs in favor of the insanity defense," reasoned Levine, "because the real prejudice was to the defense . . . because Tommy didn't cooperate with his own expert."

Levine then played the jury Tom Gilbert Sr.'s voice mail message to Tommy on November 19, 2014, saying he was cutting his allowance.

"There is no hostility in that voice mail," said Levine. "None at all. In fact, Tom Sr. is asking permission of Tommy to reduce his allowance: 'Tommy, can you handle it if we do? Let me know.'"

Levine argued that his father had cut his allowance out of necessity, because at the time of his death, he only had $46,000 in his checking account and $38,000 of high-interest credit card debt.

"So there is a reason," said Levine, "at that point in time when Tom Sr. is asking, 'Tommy, can you take less money? We can't afford to keep giving it to you.'"

He told the jury that Tom Sr. was "having a cash flow crisis," forcing his brother, Beck, to pay Tommy's attorney bills after his 2013 arrest for assaulting Peter Smith. Although he may have grown Wainscott from $1 million to $7.4 million, it was just a "tiny dot" in the world of billion-dollar hedge funds. And although the Georgica Association Road house may have been worth $10 million, it was also saddled with a $4 million mortgage.

"The problem is," Levine told the jury, "Tom Sr. had no liquid assets. Cash."

At the end of his arguments, the attorney displayed Tommy's Princeton graduation photograph on the screen in front of the jury.

"It looks like a happy family," Levine observed. "But that's 2009. And Tommy's mental illness, psychotic illness, didn't just stabilize. It got worse."

Levine noted it was no coincidence that the only two

people his client had been violent against were Peter Smith and his father.

"It's driven by his delusions and his paranoia," Levine told the jury. "It robbed him of the ability to substantially appreciate the wrongfulness . . . and the nature and consequences of his actions.

"For that reason, you have to find Tommy not responsible by reason of mental illness or defect. Thank you."

After one hour and forty-three minutes, Arnold Levine sat down, and the judge dismissed the jury for lunch.

That afternoon, ADA Craig Ortner painted a totally different picture of Thomas Gilbert Jr., branding him a spoiled man-child whose free ride was coming to an end.

"Patricide!" declared Ortner. "The act of killing one's own father sounds insane, [but] all murder sounds insane."

As the defendant took notes, Ortner said the only reason Levine was using an insanity defense was because there was no question that his client had killed his father.

"What they are asking you to do," Ortner said, "is relieve the defendant of all criminal responsibility for his crimes because of insanity. This defendant doesn't come close to meeting that standard."

Ortner told the jury that Gilbert had more than one motive to murder his father and that they were all rational.

"Tom Gilbert wanted his son to achieve," said the prosecutor, "and maybe sometimes he pushed his son a little too hard. After all, he sent his son to the best schools money could buy, and he expected some return on his investment."

He told the jury that the defendant "rejected" hard work, preferring an easy life of drugs and partying that was being handed to him on a silver platter.

"Like the defendant, Tom Sr. and Beck were born into circumstances of wealth and privilege. But unlike the defendant, they took advantage of their opportunities, and they worked hard to become successful. The defendant seems to think that he had a right to status and success and wealth."

Ortner pointed out that Tommy Gilbert traveled "in an exclusive social circle" in Manhattan and the Hamptons, attending galas and fundraisers instead of working.

"It was a symptom of entitlement," said the prosecutor. "Enabled by his privileged upbringing, his good looks, his athleticism, and most of all, his parents' money. He enjoyed the life of pleasure and instant gratification."

Ortner said that the defendant's "free ride" was put in jeopardy when his father began cutting his allowance to try to force him to stand on his own two feet.

"He had the audacity to insist that his son finally grow up," said Ortner, "and take some responsibility for himself. It was a form of tough love, but to the defendant, this was his father rubbing his nose in all of his failures."

The prosecutor said that after his weekly allowance was cut, the defendant had gone into debt and had bought a credit card skimmer.

"He was trying to make up for the lost cash flow," Ortner told the jury, "by trying his hand at credit card fraud."

Ortner observed there was no proof that mental illness had robbed Tommy of his capacity to know right from wrong. There was no "psychotic break" to render him legally insane.

Instead, Ortner described the defendant's "violent and scary" conduct against Peter Smith as "premeditated and deliberately calculated," after being called a loser in front of their friends.

"Peter Smith had offended the defendant in the worst possible way," said Ortner, "by tearing down his social standing in front of his love interest, Lizzy Fraser."

After getting away with just a "slap on the wrist" for assaulting Smith and burning down his father's house, said Ortner, the defendant felt emboldened to get away with murder.

"At the end of the day," Ortner said, "what is clear from the evidence is that the defendant's crimes cannot be explained away by mental illness. The defendant had some psychiatric issues. So do many other people in the world. Unlike many of those other people, the defendant actually had the means and the resources to meet these challenges."

Finishing up his eighty-minute summation, the prosecutor told the jury that Thomas Gilbert Jr. "threw the ultimate tantrum" by killing his father. He implored them to apply the same legal standards to him as they would any other defendant.

"The last thing Tom Gilbert ever saw," said Ortner, "was his own son pressing a .40-caliber semiautomatic pistol into his head and pulling the trigger. It's time justice is finally served for Tom. It's been a long time coming, [and] his murderer needs to be held accountable under the law."

Arnold Levine immediately moved for a mistrial, citing the prosecution's assertion that Thomas Gilbert Sr. was entitled to justice.

"Mr. Gilbert Sr. is not entitled to anything," said Levine. "It was inflammatory. It appealed to the sympathy of the jury and is improper argument."

Justice Jackson denied his application.

After a ten-minute recess, Justice Jackson instructed the jury, telling them again to disregard the defendant's behavior during the trial. She reminded them that he had a right to either be in the courtroom or absent, and they must not speculate on his reasons why.

"You must decide this case on the evidence and the evidence alone," she told the jury. "The defendant's conduct in this courtroom is not evidence. Therefore, you must disregard the defendant's conduct, and you must not consider it in any way for any purposes."

Then, after four weeks of testimony, the judge sent the twelve jurors out to deliberate Thomas Gilbert Jr.'s fate.

On Thursday, the jury spent the entire day deliberating. At 11:35 a.m., the foreperson sent out a note requesting all the defendant's school and medical records, as well as a rereading of the forgery charge. They also wanted to see CCTV video of the defendant near his parents' apartment before and after the murder.

Tommy Gilbert was then brought into the courtroom wearing his usual pressed white shirt with several days' growth of beard.

"The defendant objects," he immediately told the judge, "based on the identification evidence under fruit of poisonous tree as well as medical evidence to which I have not signed a waiver."

"Mr. Gilbert," said the judge sternly, "I'm going to remind you again, sir, there are not to be any interruptions or objections during this proceeding. If you continue . . . I'm going to have you removed."

Gilbert then asked to leave the courtroom, and the judge agreed, telling him to take the bus back to Rikers if he preferred.

"The defendant would like to return if possible," he replied.

The judge then reminded him that there could be a verdict

at any time, asking if he still wished to leave the building. Tommy looked confused as the judge explained that it was possible there would be a verdict today.

"Do you want to be present for that verdict?" she asked him. "You are shaking your head. You have absolutely every right to."

Then he was handcuffed and led out of the courtroom. The judge said she would check in with him tomorrow and see if he wished to be present.

Early on in their deliberations, the jury had taken a vote and were split fifty-fifty as to his guilt. They all agreed he suffered from mental illness but differed as to whether he was criminally responsible for murdering his father.

As the deliberations stretched on, things began to get more heated.

"There was a lot of emotion," said juror #11, Steven David Torres. "We had one side that were just yelling, 'He's guilty.' And others going, 'He's not guilty! He's sick.'"

Later that day, they asked for the prosecutor's opening and closing arguments, Shelley Gilbert's 911 call, and all the defendant's phone records and online activity for the day of the murder. They also requested the judge reread them the definition of the affirmative defense of insanity.

"Under our law," Justice Jackson told them, "it is an affirmative defense to a crime charged that when the defendant engaged in prohibited conduct, he lacked criminal responsibility by reason of mental disease or defect. That person lacked substantial capacity to know or appreciate either the nature and consequences of such conduct or that such conduct was wrong."

Back in the jury room, they took another vote. After

studying the definition of the insanity defense, there were still a couple of holdouts.

"We were arguing about, was this calculated?" said Torres. "But I'm like, 'Well, he didn't plan his escape and went straight back to his apartment.'"

Throughout the afternoon, there was a steady flow of jury notes, making the judge quip, "They're fast and furious."

Finally, at 4:25 p.m., the jury sent out a note. "We need a mental break for the evening—request fresh start at 9:30 tomorrow."

The defendant was back on Friday for the second day of deliberations. At 10:00 a.m., the jury sent in a note asking for a copy of the *Diagnostic and Statistical Manual of Mental Disorders* (*DSM-5*). They also asked for the PowerPoint presentation showing all phone calls, texts, and messages between Tommy and his mother. Over the next few hours, they asked to hear the legal definition of the insanity defense several more times.

"We kept asking for it to be read," said Juror Torres. "We wanted to make sure."

A couple of holdouts remained until one of the jurors zeroed in on the fact that Tommy had asked his mother to go out for a Coke, well aware that she never kept any in the apartment.

"The Coke was the aha moment for a lot of us," said Torres. "It was the conversation when he asked his mom to go out and get him a Coca-Cola and come back in an hour. He knew that they didn't have it in the apartment, and that's when it clicked that he knew what he was doing."

Juror #8, Julie Thiry-Couvillion, said they had spent the morning closely examining whether the defense's argument had met the insanity defense.

"Did he know what he was doing was morally wrong?" she asked. "The can of Coke answers this, because he knew he had to get his mother out of the apartment and that's the reason. No, he didn't want her to make a sandwich there . . . he wanted her to go."

At 3:45 p.m., the jury sent its twenty-first note to Justice Jackson, announcing a verdict after two grueling days of deliberation. A few minutes later, the courtroom was abuzz as word spread through the building that there was a verdict.

The attorneys came in, and about a dozen reporters crammed into the first two rows of the public gallery. A nervous-looking Shelley Gilbert sat alone, looking pensive.

The judge allowed half a dozen press photographers in front of the defense table as Tommy Gilbert was brought in handcuffed. He stood with his eyes tightly closed next to Arnold Levine while photographs were taken. A couple of minutes later, the judge dismissed the photographers out of a door at the back of the court.

"So good afternoon, Mr. Gilbert," said Justice Jackson as his handcuffs were removed. "We will bring the jury in."

As the six men and six women took their places in the jury box, Tommy Gilbert looked straight across the courtroom at them.

The clerk of the court then asked the foreperson if they had agreed on a verdict, and he said they had.

"How say you to the first count of the indictment charging the defendant, Thomas Gilbert Jr., with the crime of murder in the second degree, guilty or not guilty?"

"Guilty," he replied.

"Did you find that the defendant is not responsible by mental disease or defect?"

"No, we did not," he answered.

The foreman said the jury had found the defendant guilty of two charges of criminal possession of a weapon in the second degree, but not guilty of possessing forgery devices.

The members of the jury were then polled one by one to affirm the verdict.

Justice Jackson dismissed the jury, telling them she had been watching them throughout the twenty-day trial and been impressed by the "very careful" attention they had given the testimony.

She set a sentencing date of August 9, as the stone-faced defendant was handcuffed and led out of the courtroom.

Arnold Levine expressed disappointment at the result, but said there would definitely be an appeal. It would also be his last trial as a private lawyer, as he was joining the Legal Aid Society's newly formed Homicide Defense Task Force.

Later that day, the Manhattan district attorney Cyrus Vance Jr., who had personally attended several sessions of the trial, issued a press release.

"A brilliant businessman, passionate tennis player, and beloved family man," it read, "Thomas Gilbert, Sr. meant a great deal to all who knew him. But in spite of his love and generosity, this defendant shot his father at close range in his own apartment in an unconscionable and brutal crime. I thank my office's prosecutors for their years of dedication to this case and for ensuring a just outcome."

40

"THE ULTIMATE TANTRUM"

A few weeks after the verdict, Lila Chase visited Tommy Gilbert in Rikers. To her horror, he did not seem to understand that he had been found guilty of second-degree murder. Although he now faced twenty-five years to life in prison, he assured Lila he would soon be free on bail.

"He thought the trial was still going on," said Lila. "Like most schizophrenics, he oscillates wildly between being in some sense of reality and being very far from it."

His sentencing had been delayed for six weeks to allow Arnold Levine enough time to make a written submission to the judge for leniency.

During her visits, Lila urged Tommy to publicly express remorse for killing his father, as it was his only chance of getting a lighter sentence.

"I told him, 'I don't care if you feel it or you don't,'" she recalled. "'You've got to express it like crazy. That's your best chance.'"

At 3:15 p.m. on Friday, September 27, Thomas Gilbert Jr. was led into Justice Jackson's courtroom for the last time. He was back in a bright orange DOC jumpsuit and remained in handcuffs throughout the sentencing.

Shelley Gilbert, who would be reading a victim's impact statement, took her place in the public gallery next to a barrage of reporters. Across the aisle sat Detectives Joseph Cirigliano and Darryl Ng, and farther back was Peter Smith Jr., there to witness the final act of the drama.

Before sentencing began, ADA Ortner addressed the paradox of Shelley Gilbert being both the victim's wife and his killer's mother. He told the judge that, by statute, the statement is delivered on behalf of the victim, noting that Shelley had written to the court begging for the minimum sentence.

"She does not mention in the letter," said Ortner, "the victim in this case [is] Thomas Gilbert Sr., so I'm not sure if she can address the court . . . on behalf of the victim."

He added that he also didn't want to deprive her of being heard by the court.

"This is a really unusual case," said Justice Jackson as she consulted the statute. She asked Arnold Levine for his input.

"Just because she's not asking for the maximum punishment and wants leniency for her son," he said, "that doesn't mean she can't speak on behalf of the victim, who she knows better than anyone else."

Levine pointed out that they had been married for more than thirty years, often discussing their son's mental illness. She would now be speaking on behalf of her late husband, saying exactly what he would have wanted her to.

"Okay, that's enough," said the judge. "I thought this trial was over. I will listen to Mrs. Gilbert. If you want to make a statement before the court," she told Shelley, "[please] step up to the podium and you may speak."

Shelley Gilbert walked up to the podium, reading from a handwritten statement she had prepared the night before.

"I can assure the court," she began, "that I know everything that I say here today [Tom] would agree with. He is gone. I can no longer do anything for him."

She said she wished the judge could have known her son before he was struck down by schizophrenia and that he had been much loved and respected by everyone.

"Our hearts have been shattered," she said, "by the loss of a husband and a son; a father and a brother."

She then reminisced on Tommy's proudest accomplishments at Buckley and Deerfield, like his mentoring of an eight-year-old boy for the Big Brothers Big Sisters program.

"We were once a very happy family," she told the judge, "and are determined to be happy again. In order for this to happen, we need Tommy to be given as light a sentence as possible."

She asked Justice Jackson to give him a chance and some hope for the future, instead of spending the rest of his life behind bars.

"I know that if my husband could speak from heaven, he would be saying the same thing. If we had been able to get Tommy into a psychiatric hospital fifteen years ago, my husband would still be alive today."

Next, Craig Ortner addressed the court.

"Judge," he began, "the defendant today is being sentenced for murdering his seventy-year-old father, using a loaded handgun that he obtained illegally."

The prosecutor said that some defendants make rash decisions without thinking through the consequences of their actions.

"Not so this defendant," he told the judge. "He wanted his father dead, and so he devised a plan to murder him. In order to do that, he disguised himself. He armed himself with a loaded pistol, which he concealed in a bag, while he rode the subway across town."

Ortner called it "cruel" how the defendant had gone into his father's bedroom, where he was relaxing with his guard down in the safety of his sanctuary.

"But he was wrong," said Ortner, "because the defendant pressed his pistol directly against his father's head and fired a bullet. And he left the mess for his mother to deal with.

"I don't think we'll ever know whether he gave Tom Sr. a chance to beg for his life. I don't know that there were any words exchanged between the two men [or] how long he spent in that room before he pulled the trigger."

Describing it as a "calculated, cruel, and brutal premeditated murder," Ortner said the defendant bore the full weight of responsibility for killing his father. He pointed out how fortunate it was that Mrs. Gilbert hadn't returned home earlier while her son was still there.

"I sympathize deeply with Mrs. Gilbert and the surviving members of the Gilbert family," he said. "She has endured an unimaginable tragedy, and [no one can blame her] for coming to her strategies for her son's defense. That's her prerogative."

He then asked the judge to hand out a sentence of thirty years to life so that Gilbert would not harm any more innocent people.

"This defendant will resort to extreme acts of violence to settle the score if he thinks someone has disrespected him," he argued. "We saw in evidence his narcissism, [and] he believes himself entitled to a respect from others that he had not earned, and believes the rules do not apply to him."

Ortner alleged that the defendant was a sociopath and a

real threat to public safety and must suffer the consequences of his actions.

"This was a cold, calculated murder committed by a thirty-year-old man," he said. "The defendant didn't want to grow up and be an adult. When his father tried to push him along in that direction and cut his allowance, he threw the ultimate tantrum."

Then Arnold Levine stood up, asking the judge for the minimum sentence of fifteen years to life, which he said would be sufficient. He took issue with the probation report, which said that Tommy had frequently called his mother from Rikers Island but never once expressed remorse. Levine said the very first thing any good defense lawyer tells his client is never to discuss the case on the phone, as all calls are recorded.

"That doesn't mean he doesn't have any remorse," said Levine, "it means that he listened to his lawyers for a change."

He told the judge to consider what his client had been like before mental illness had derailed his life and that he had never displayed any violent tendencies before his schizophrenia took hold.

"He targeted his father because of his delusions [and] mental illness," said Levine. "It wouldn't rise to the insanity defense, but mental illness is the cause of the conduct. Because if Tommy does agree to take medication, and remains on medication and is compliant, then there's no reason to think he's ever going to do violence to anybody again . . . just like he was before his illness."

Justice Jackson then asked the defendant if he wished to address the court before she passed sentence on him.

"Yes, Your Honor," he replied. "First, the defendant requests the judge delays sentence and declare a mistrial because of illegal press coverage."

"I'm going to deny that application," answered the judge coldly, "so go ahead."

Then, referring to notes he had written on a legal pad, Tommy launched into a rambling ten-minute diatribe. He cited a string of unrelated court statutes and aired grievances, calling himself "the sole voice of the defense."

"The court should also declare a mistrial," he railed, "because the defense lawyer stated that the defendant committed a crime. The defendant requests the dismissal of all charges because of a lack of evidence."

He told the judge that because his case was so high profile, his life would be in danger in prison.

"In this sense, it has the potential to be a death sentence," he said, "and is cruel and unusual punishment."

Finally, he asked the judge for the minimum fifteen-year sentence, as he had no criminal record and strong family ties.

"Defendant expresses remorse," were his final words to the court.

Justice Jackson told him that she had now sat on this case for almost five years and there would be no new trial.

"Now, there is no doubt," she said, "that what occurred in January 2015 is a tragedy on many, many levels. However, the jury got it right and found you guilty of murder in the second degree, because you were not insane at the time that you committed the crime and killed your father. You were very mentally stable and the jury found so, and I agree with that verdict.

"There's no doubt . . . that you planned to kill your father and you had a ruse all set up to get your mother out of the apartment. And you went into his bedroom. You shot him dead and you placed the gun on his chest. You knew exactly what you were doing. You were not insane then, and you're not insane now."

She said that whatever the motive he had for murdering his father in cold blood, he had done it in a "deliberate and calculating" manner.

Justice Jackson then sentenced Thomas Gilbert Jr. to the maximum under the law of thirty years to life in prison on the second-degree murder and two weapons charges. He would be eligible for parole when he was sixty-five.

"My hope is that in prison you will take your medication," she told him as he stared blankly ahead, "and when you are released on parole you continue with that medication. Because I have no doubt that there are mental issues involved, and if you had taken your medication, perhaps you wouldn't even be here today."

As Tommy Gilbert was escorted from the courtroom, he looked over at his mother and gave her a thin smile.

After the sentencing, Manhattan district attorney Cyrus Vance Jr. released a statement marking the completion of the case.

"While nothing can undo the tragedy of Mr. Gilbert's death," it read, "I hope that the resolution of this case helps his loved ones as they continue to heal from this devastating loss."

When Shelley Gilbert read this, she was furious and felt terribly hurt by the glib statement.

"It was so 180 degrees off the mark," she said. "I don't usually complain about life being tough, you just marshal forward. But I told them the impact this was having on my family in detail."

Shelley said the district attorney had no appreciation of mental illness or that the harsh sentence would not heal the Gilbert family.

"The State of New York and its lack of adequate treatment

for the very mentally ill," she said, "has caused the agony we have had to endure for a very long time. If my schizophrenic son ends up in a hospital in upstate New York, where we would not be able to visit him often, that would add to the trauma my daughter and I have to endure."

EPILOGUE

Several months later, Tommy Gilbert was placed in the Clinton Correctional Facility in Dannemora, New York, just south of the Canadian border. Known as "Little Siberia," it is 320 miles from Manhattan.

As of October 2020, one year after sentencing, he has still not received any visitors, as it is too far for his mother to travel. Due to the COVID-19 pandemic, no visitors are allowed for the foreseeable future.

Lila Chase writes to Tommy regularly and sends him cards on his birthday and Christmas.

"Tommy wrote that he was adjusting and he felt 'pretty safe,'" she said. "But who knows, as he's not a good reporter."

Dannemora has a psychiatric unit, where Tommy has been treated since he arrived. But he refused to sign a HIPAA release form, so doctors cannot access his previous medical records.

"Finally, after fifteen years, we finally have him getting psychiatric help," said Shelley Gilbert in February 2020. "But they can't tell me anything because he hasn't signed the HIPAA.

"It's about six hours to get up there, and sometimes when I went to visit him [in Rikers], he wouldn't see me and sometimes he would. If I go all the way up there and he doesn't see me . . . I will try to do that at some point, but it's not easy."

Lila vowed to stand by Tommy and do everything she could for him until his eventual release. He is not eligible for parole until 2049.

"Of course his mother will stand by him, too," she said. "He has a very long sentence, and I will always be there for him."

The celebrated case, which was closely followed in the press, raised many questions of mental illness and the law, especially Thomas Gilbert Jr.'s fitness for trial. His original attorney, Alex Spiro, describes it as a very sad human tragedy and a complete failure of the legal system.

"It's really a shame that when . . . he wasn't in the system, there was no way to help him," he explained after the verdict. "Because you can't force an adult, absent extraordinary circumstances, to get treatment. So everybody was helpless before he was in the system."

Spiro maintains that if Tommy had only received the treatment he needed when he was first incarcerated, everything might have been different.

"At least it would have been humane," he said. "He could have helped his lawyers, and we could have had an honest verdict. It was so clear that he needed help and the system failed him. To me, it's inhumane and unconscionable, and it led to a tragic result that didn't help anybody. We never gave him a chance."

As of November 2020, an appeal has still not officially been filed.

ACKNOWLEDGMENTS

Golden Boy is without a doubt my most challenging true crime book. I began work in early 2015 and for the next five years followed its labyrinthine path through scores of court hearings, eventually leading to Thomas Gilbert Jr.'s murder trial in May 2019. Although no one doubted that he had murdered his father in cold blood, the question was whether or not he knew what he was doing when he pulled the trigger.

The inexplicable patricide made lurid front-page headlines for weeks, bewildering New York high society, where the Gilbert family had been fixtures for years. It soon emerged that the handsome thirty-year-old socialite, known to everyone as Tommy, was under investigation by Southampton police for arson. He was the prime suspect for burning down a historic seventeenth-century house in Sagaponack belonging to the family of his estranged best friend, Peter Smith Jr., who had recently taken out a restraining order against him.

The complicated question of Tommy's competency consumed many days of cut-and-thrust legal arguments in Manhattan Supreme Court with his attorneys maintaining he was totally unfit for trial. But after four years of bitter wrangling, New York Supreme Court justice Melissa Jackson, a great-granddaughter of Theodore Roosevelt, ruled him fit.

She even complimented him on having the makings of a good lawyer.

Ultimately, after a monthlong trial, a jury decided that Tommy knew the difference between right and wrong at the time of the murder, although no one doubted that he had suffered from crippling mental illness since childhood. After sitting through scores of hearings and finally the trial, I watched Tommy's mental and physical decline. It was horrible to witness him sabotaging his own defense and refusing to even acknowledge his attorney Arnold Levine.

Over the years, I got to know his mother, Shelley, who stood by her beloved son every inch of the way. Her courage and dignity are amazing, and I cannot begin to fathom how difficult it must have been to lose a husband and then a son to this terrible disease, and then become the prosecution's star witness.

I would like to thank Shelley for trusting me with her story and overcoming her many fears to participate in this book. Her objective was to shine the light on mental illness and the total failure of the system to deal with it humanely. As she said many times, if her son had suffered from cancer, he would have received the treatment he needed.

I also owe a huge debt of gratitude to Lila Chase, who has spoken publicly for the first time about her two-year relationship with Tommy to reveal how she tried to help him through his escalating mental illness. Lila knows the real Tommy Gilbert better than anyone and remains in close touch with him as he languishes in prison. I also want to thank Arnold Levine for all his help and encouragement with the book. Although he came on board late, he really stepped up to the plate, giving Tommy the best legal defense possible under some very trying circumstances.

There are so many people who helped me with this book. Many of Tommy's closest friends spoke to me but wished to remain anonymous, as did several others who knew him casually.

I also want to thank Alex Spiro, Briana Swanson, Anna Rothschild, Jack Bryan, David Patrick Columbia, Berit Edelson, Michael Heller, Lanny Jones, Max Honerkamp, Arianna Lee, Tim Loh, George "McSurfer" McKee, Jim Mettler, Martin Mumford, T. E. McMorrow, Alex McCabe, Caleb Smilgin, Brent Bartley, Thomas MacMillan, Benjamin Wallace, Rebecca Rosenberg, Shayna Jacobs, Edgar Sandoval, and Daniel Carfi.

Much gratitude to Charles Spicer and Sarah Grill of St. Martin's Press for their patience and guidance throughout the years it took to deliver the manuscript. As always, my agent, Jane Dystel, of Dystel, Goderich & Bourret Literary Management, was there for me, even when I couldn't see the light at the end of the tunnel.

In August 2016, I left Manhattan for the Catskill Mountains, so I owe a huge debt of gratitude to Annette Witheridge for her generosity and use of her couch when I visited for hearings. I am also indebted to Danny, Cari, and Allie Trachtenberg, whom I lived with for the duration of the trial. Their hospitality went well beyond the call of duty.

Thanks also to Gail Freund, Dr. Michael Stone, Elisa Rivlin, Jo Greenspan, Berns Rothschild, David Bunde, Patty Disken-Cahill, Virginia Randall, Martin Gould, Wensley Clarkson, Debbie, Douglas, and Taylor Baldwin, Emily Freund, Lenny Millen, and Galli Curci.